EUROPEANS ON EUROPE

Also by Mairi Maclean

WATER WITHOUT FRONTIERS: France and Britain's Water

Also by Jolyon Howorth

EDOUARD VAILLANT. DÉLÉGUÉ AU BUREAU SOCIALISTE INTERNATIONAL: Correspondence avec le secrétariat international, 1900–1915 (*with Georges Haupt*)
ELITES IN FRANCE: Origins, reproduction and power (*editor with Philip Cerny*)
EDOUARD VAILLANT ET LA CRÉATION DE L'UNITÉ SOCIALISTE EN FRANCE
DEFENCE AND DISSENT IN CONTEMPORARY FRANCE (*editor with Patricia Chilton*)
FRANCE: THE POLITICS OF PEACE
CONTEMPORARY FRANCE: A Review of Interdisciplinary Studies, three volumes (*editor with George Ross*)

Europeans on Europe

Transnational Visions of a New Continent

Edited by

Mairi Maclean
Lecturer in French
Royal Holloway and Bedford New College
University of London

and

Jolyon Howorth
Professor of French Civilisation
University of Bath

Foreword by

Edgard Pisani
Foreign Policy Adviser to François Mitterrand
President of the Institut de Monde Arabe, Paris

St. Martin's Press New York

First published in the United States of America in 1992

Printed in Hong Kong

ISBN 0–312–06834–4

Library of Congress Cataloging-in-Publication Data
Europeans on Europe : transnational visions of a new continent / edited by Mairi Maclean and Jolyon Howorth; foreword by Edgard Pisani.
p. cm.
Includes bibliographical references and index.
ISBN 0–312–06834–4
1. Economic forecasting—European Economic Community countries. 2. European Economic Community countries—Economic conditions. 3. Europe 1992. 4. European Economic Community countries—Politics and government. 5. European Economic Community countries—Forecasting. I. Maclean, Mairi, 1959– . II. Howorth, Jolyon.
HC241.2.E8653 1992
330.94—dc20 91–24048
CIP

To Alexander, Emily and Stephanie

'We have not inherited the earth from our parents. We have borrowed it from our children'

(Greek proverb)

Contents

List of Tables

Foreword: Being and Doing in Concert

Edgard Pisani

When the British say 'Nation-State' and the French 'Etat-Nation', are they talking about the same thing? I believe they are giving expression to rather different concepts and that the problem goes beyond a mere geometrical inversion of words.

For the French, the State is more than it is for the British. Indeed, it is more than it should be. It is almost more than the Nation itself, and yet the French are seemingly ready to sacrifice its essential attributes on the altar of Europe. It is as if, after having assisted in the birth of the Nation, the statist concept were destined, no doubt in a different guise, to lend a hand in the delivery of what is not – and for the foreseeable future will not be – the European nation. In this, the French are not altogether wrong for it is reasonable to assume that France-as-State will not find salvation on its own. But at the same time they are clearly being reckless because they are heading blindfold into uncharted territory.

Let us therefore try a fresh type of analysis, a fresh approach.

Humans come together to create, say, an association, a society, an institution, a club, for one of two reasons: to *be* together or to *do* together. This distinction is probably too categoric, but it is illuminating. An association is for *being* together, society is for *doing* together.

In the French model of public institutions, the traditional commune has become a place for being; the *syndicat de communes* a place for *doing*; the department is now a place for *being* (*we come* from the Var; *they live* in the Dordogne); the region is for *doing*. But at the level of the 'Hexagon' (as the French call their national territory), *being* and *doing* come back together in the *Etat-Nation-Patrie*.

But now we have the twin intervention of Europe and decentralisation. And Jacobinism, which has left such a profound mark on French political culture and practice, is torn in two conflicting directions, doubly called into question. What will remain of the *Etat-Nation-Patrie*?

Let us therefore pursue our train of thought. *Being* and *doing* – with as many nuances as one might wish to inject – remain and demand different modes of democracy. The rule of *being* is consensus, that of *doing* is the majority.

Thus Europe finds herself both giving rise to and having to resolve two essential problems: where, today, is her *being*; or is she destined simply to remain at the level of *doing*? Will she ever go as far as to become a place of *being*? In other words, are we heading towards a European State, something less than a State (if so, what?) or towards a new Nation-State? And, depending on which of these it is to be, what democratic attributes, what system of political democracy (power by the people for the people) will she bestow upon herself?

The construction of Europe, driven forward by economic dynamics, by political circumstances which often emanate from without and by the will of a small number of inspired individuals, is proceeding at a dizzy pace. Is it not now time for some more serious forward thinking about the possible and desirable political essence and existence of what it is we are constructing together?

The present volume is an invitation to engage in such reflection. But the road will be long because we are not only dealing with texts and politics. We are dealing with symbols and sensitivities. We are involved in chipping away, in many different ways, at a certain sacred heritage.

EDGARD PISANI

Acknowledgments

Various people have helped the editors, directly and indirectly, in the compilation of this book. Our first thanks go to the contributors, who, with few exceptions, had planned, if not actually written their chapters as the bricks and barbed wire of the Old Europe passed into history on 9 November 1989. Thereafter, in reworking their drafts, they found themselves repeatedly rethinking sentences referring not only to bricks and mortar but also to ministers and prime ministers (and even one entire country) which had suddenly spun off the map. Those in many countries with whom the present and future of Europe have been exhaustively discussed are too numerous to mention, but special thanks go to Dominique David, Jacques Maisonrouge, Edgard Pisani, Michel Pauwels, Gisela Weber. Thanks, too, are due to Vincent Wright, John Roper and the late and much missed Georges Lavau, with whom we discussed an early plan of this book. Our respective academic departments – French and Management Studies at Royal Holloway and Bedford New College and Modern Languages and International Studies at the University of Bath – provided much needed support in the form of research time. Most of all, a special word of gratitude is due to Jill O'Brien for deploying such unfailing good humour in the endless task of transferring successive drafts to floppy electronic memory.

MAIRI MACLEAN
JOLYON HOWORTH

List of Abbreviations

ABM	Anti-Ballistic Missile
BAOR	British Army of the Rhine
BMD	Ballistic Missile Defence
CAP	Common Agricultural Policy
CDS	Centre des Démocrates Sociaux
CDU	Christian Democratic Union
CERES	Centre d'Etudes, de Recherches et d'Education Socialistes
CFDT	Confédération Française Démocratique du Travail
CFE	Conventional Forces in Europe
CSCE	Conference on Security and Cooperation in Europe
CSU	Christian Social Union (Bavarian ally of CDU)
DTI	Department of Trade and Industry
EC	European Community
ECJ	European Court of Justice
ECSC	European Coal and Steel Community
ECU	European Currency Unit
EDC	European Defence Community
EEC	European Economic Community
EFTA	European Free Trade Association
EMS	European Monetary System
EMU	Economic and Monetary Union
ERDF	European Regional Development Fund
ERM	Exchange Rate Mechanism (of EMS)
FAR	Force d'Action Rapide
FCO	Foreign and Commonwealth Office
FN	Front National
FRG	Federal Republic of Germany
GDP	Gross Domestic Product
GDR	German Democratic Republic
ICBM	InterContinental Ballistic Missile
INF	Intermediate Nuclear Forces
MAFF	Ministry of Agriculture, Fisheries and Food
MEP	Member of the European Parliament
MRP	Mouvement Républicain Populaire
NATO	North Atlantic Treaty Organisation

NIESR	National Institute for Economic and Social Research
OECD	Organisation for Economic Cooperation and Development
OEEC	Organisation for European Economic Cooperation
OFCE	Observatoire Français des Conjonctures
PCF	Parti Communiste Français
PS	Parti Socialiste
PTB	Partial Test Ban (Treaty)
RPR	Rassemblement pour la République
SACEUR	Supreme Commander of Allied Forces in Europe
SDI	Strategic Defence Initiative
SEA	Single European Act
SLBM	Submarine Launched Ballistic Missiles
SMIC	Salaire Minimum Interprofessionnel de Croissance
SNF	Short-range Nuclear Forces
SNP	Scottish National Party
SPD	Social Democratic Party
START	Strategic Arms Reduction Talks
TASM	Tactical Air-to-Surface Missile
TGV	Train à Grande Vitesse
TUC	Trades Union Congress
UDF	Union pour la Démocratie Française
WEU	Western European Union
WTO	Warsaw Treaty Organisation
YTS	Youth Training Scheme

Notes on the Contributors

Maurice Baslé is Professor of Economics in the Faculté de Sciences Economiques, Université de Rennes. He has published eight books and fifty articles of economic research. His areas of research have included public finance and taxation applied to macro-economics, and, more recently, the history of economic analysis and also industrial policy with a historical approach (the concept of 'progress'). Recent publications include *Histoire des pensées économiques* (2 volumes; Paris: Edition Sirey, 1988 and 1989) and *Systèmes fiscaux* (Paris: Editions Dalloy, 1990).

Christoph Bluth is Research Fellow at the Department of War Studies, King's College. His current areas of research are 'Conventional Arms Control' and 'Soviet Military Policy'. Previous research topics included 'The Role of Nuclear Weapeons in British-German Relations' and 'Just War Theory and the Falklands/Malvinas Conflict'. He studied at Trinity College Dublin (BA, M.Phil.) and King's College London (PhD). He was previously a Research Associate at the Royal Insitute of International Affairs. He is the author of *New Thinking in Soviet Military Policy* (London: Pinter, 1990) and *Soviet Strategic Arms Policy Before SALT* (Cambridge: Cambridge University Press, forthcoming), as well as numerous articles on strategic studies.

André Brigot is Lecturer in Economics and Social Sciences and currently Research Director at the Fondation pour les Etudes de Défense Nationale in Paris. A specialist in the study of defence and security in Europe, his recent publications include chapters in: *French Security Policy in a Disarming World* (edited by Philippe G. Le Prestre, Boulder and London: Lynne Rienner, 1988); *Sicherheits und Ostpolitik: Deutsch-französisch Perspektiven* (edited by Brigot, Schmidt and Schültze (HRSG), Baden-Baden: Nososverlag, 1989); and *Le Système régionale européen après 1989: La fin de la guerre froide* (Quebec: CQRI/FEDNO, 1990)

Alan Butt Philip is Senior Lecturer in the politics of the European Community at the Centre for European Industrial Studies, School of Management, University of Bath. Holder of the Jean Monnet 'chair' in European Integration for Business Studies, he has written and researched widely on subjects connected with the European Community, in particular with regard to the implementation of the single market programme, and the role of pressure groups in EC decision-making. Winner of the 1989 Charles Douglas-Home Memorial award for a study of Britain and 1992, of which his contribution in this book forms part. Author of *Dismantling European Border Controls* (Pinter, forthcoming) and of *Reluctant Europeans: Britain, the British and European Integration* (Macmillan, forthcoming).

Jutta A. Helm is Professor of Political Science at Western Illinois University in the United States. She studied political science in Berlin, Innsbruck and at Duke University and the University of North Carolina, where she received her doctorate. Her research has focused on issues of participation and on the connection between economics and politics. She has published book chapters and articles in Germany, Britain and the United States.

Jolyon Howorth has been Professor of French Civilisation in the Department of Modern Languages and International Studies, University of Bath, since 1985. He has taught at the universities of Paris (1969–76), Aston (1976–85), Madison, Wisconsin (1974–75) and Harvard, Cambridge (1981–82 and 1983–84). He is the author of several books and numerous articles on French history, politics and foreign affairs, and joint editor of *Contemporary France: a review of interdisciplinary studies.*

Eva Kolinsky is Professor of Modern German Studies at Keele University. She studied German, Political Science and Sociology at the University of Frankfurt/Main and at the Free University of Berlin where she completed her D.Phil. She has published widely on the social basis of contemporary German politics and political culture and is general editor of the *German Studies* series at Berg. Her books include: *Parties, Opposition and Society in West Germany* (1984); *The Greens in West Germany* (editor; 1989); *Women in West Germany (1989); Political Culture in France and Germany* (editor with J. Gaffney; 1990); *The Federal Republic of Germany – the end of an era* (editor; 1991).

Mairi Maclean gained an MA and PhD at the University of St Andrews, followed by an MBA at the University of Bath. She has taught at the Université de Paris IV (Paris-Sorbonne) as a Lector (1984–85) and at the University of Aston as a Lecturer in French with International Business (1985–89). Since 1990 she has been a Lecturer in French and European Business Management at Royal Holloway and Bedford New College. Her publications are on various aspects of French business and economics, notably privatisation, and the contemporary French author Michel Tournier (the subject of her PhD). She is the author of a forthcoming book on the French penetration of the British market for public water supply.

Edgard Pisani was formerly a minister under both General de Gaulle and François Mitterrand. He is currently a foreign policy advisor to François Mitterrand and President of France's Institut du Monde Arabe in Paris.

Rainer Riemenschneider, PhD, studied historical science, Romance languages and literature and educational science in Göttingen and Paris. Previously a Lecturer at the University of Caen, in 1976 he became a Research Associate at the Georg Eckert Institute for International Textbook Research, Braunschweig and from 1983 to 1987 was a Research Fellow at the German Historical Institute in Paris. His publications, on the history of nineteenth-century France, on contemporary history and on historical textbook research in Germany and France in the nineteenth and twentieth centuries include: *Dezentralisation und Regionalismus in Frankreich um die Mitte des 19. Jh.* (co-edited with Karl Ernst Jeismann; Bonn, 1985); *Geschichte Europas für den Unterricht der Europäer (Braunschweig, 1980); Geschichte für den Nachbarn* (ed.; Frankfurt, 1989); *Deutschland und Frankreich im 20. Jahrhundert* (co-editor with Andrea Hofmeister-Hunger; Frankfurt, 1989); *La Guerre de 1870/71 et ses conséquences* (co-editor with Philippe Levillain; Bonn, 1990).

Introduction: the 'Old Continent' in Turmoil, a New One in the Making

Mairi Maclean and Jolyon Howorth

> 'History is knocking at the door. Are we going to pretend that we cannot hear?'
>
> (Jacques Delors)

EUROPE IN UPHEAVAL

To discuss the future of Europe when all around us is couched in uncertainty, is an awesome task. *Europeans on Europe* was first conceived in what now appears to be another era, in the last days of a bipolar universe, a global order cast in the mould of World War II, born of the victors' desire for retribution, informed by division and fear, and inflamed by the rival ideologies of the nineteenth century, socialism and liberalism. This Europe rift asunder was all that most of us had ever known.

In 1985, new leadership at the Kremlin was to mark, although few realised it at the time, a seismic shift in East-West relations, and the beginning of the end of the Cold War. Mikhail Gorbachev recognised the impossibility of perpetuating the stale old charades of the cold war era, both in foreign and domestic policy. Yet as *glasnost* and *perestroika* became household words across the world, as breakthrough followed breakthrough at what came to be regular superpower summits (each with its own touch of the miraculous, each unwrapping some new gift in arms control, or even arms reductions), as the feeling began to emerge that it just might be possible to progress in our time beyond a security based on terror and the stockpiling of nuclear weapons, and as the 'iron curtain' began to appear increasingly permeable – nevertheless, few Europeans were prepared for the final and most dramatic breakthrough of them all.[1] On 9 November 1989 what many on both sides of the divide had scarcely dared to dream of actually occurred: the Berlin Wall was breached, and the first euphoric Berliners streamed through. It was not, to use Churchill's words, 'the end, nor even the beginning of the end'; but this profoundly symbolic gesture seemed to herald 'the end of the beginning' of the disappearance of frontiers between countries which had been in conflict for a thousand years. For the first time since Yalta in 1945, it seemed possible to think in a meaningful way of a Europe reaching 'from the Atlantic to the Urals', which might one day become a 'common European home'.[2] The forty year winter in Eastern Europe had been long and harsh. In the end, outworn ideology had been forced to take second place to the rude realities of economic incompetence: more vociferous than those who protested about their lack of political freedom were those who had simply had enough of perpetual penury. The system manifestly was not working and history's summons was becoming strident. But there is a very real sense in which ultimately, the breakthrough was primarily due to just one man. Whatever else may subsequently have transpired, there can have been few more deserving winners of the Nobel prize for peace than Mikhail Gorbachev in 1990.

Meanwhile the West struggled to formulate a cohesive response to a situation for which it was inherently unprepared. As the former Soviet Foreign Minister, Eduard Shevardnadze, commented during one of his frequent visits to the US, 'We have deprived you of your much needed enemy' – echoing the Egyptian poet Constantine Cavafy: 'What's going to happen to us without barbarians? They were, those people, a kind of solution'.[3] However, warmer relations with the East did not bring in their wake the security and stability one might have expected to follow. Lending an ironic new twist to the 'domino theory', the dismantling of the wall triggered a chain reaction, unleashing pent-up energies and emotions previously held in check. As the bell tolled for hard-line communism throughout the Eastern bloc, cries for the right to political pluralism and self-determination rose from every corner of the Soviet empire itself.[4] It was difficult to persuade those peoples who had been incorporated into the USSR, sometimes in living memory and always against their will, that what had become normal elsewhere could not be countenanced at home.

Meanwhile Gorbachev hung on to power by the skin of his teeth, treading a delicate tightrope between conservatives and radicals, as he sought to implement a reform programme which pleased nobody. *Glasnost* proved too far-reaching for some, too limited for others, while *perestroika* failed singularly to get food into the shops. Poor distribution chains left the fruits of bumper harvests rotting in railway sidings, and dearth turned to famine in the cities. Christmas collection boxes for a superpower in distress made a curious sight in European highstreets. The Soviet Union appeared more than ever as a web of contradictions, held together by threads of gossamer.

As 1990 turned into 1991, Europe was in turmoil. Ethnic unrest was unravelling her eastern expanses, threatening massive destabilisation from the Baltic to the Adriatic and on to the Caspian. On her southern doorstep, the Maghreb was in ebullition and the Middle East blown apart. Muslim fundamentalism – a stark contrast to Western materialism and East European atheism – continued to spread. Saddam Hussein's invasion of Kuwait led inexorably to war, a war whose consequences now bear heavily on the redefinition of the Continent. Inside Europe, the kaleidoscope had turned for the first time in almost half a century, causing long-standing alliances to splinter and new allegiances to form, old boundaries to blur and others to be redrawn. Fears of Soviet strength were replaced by anxiety about the consequences of Soviet weakness. The ideological adversaries of yesterday became the economic partners of tomorrow. The very word 'Europe' acquired a new definition and a new scope as people remembered – or realised for the first time – that Prague and Warsaw, Budapest and Bucharest and even Leningrad were great European centres.

In this maelstrom, the one element of stability seemed to be the calm confidence of the European Community (EC). Yet events in the East soon impacted on the West. For many who had seen West European integration almost as the end point of history, the prospect of rethinking the grand design of 1992 was anathema. But for others, the European Community had itself always been something of an artificial construct, a product of the Cold War, the child of conjuncture rather than the grandchild of culture. A battle soon developed between those who feared that the federal objectives of Brussels (immediate, limited to twelve western nations, understood and realisable) were being undermined by loose talk of a transcontinental confederation (long-term, vast in scope and size, ill-formulated and seemingly utopian). New configurations of actors began to appear in France and in Britain as Gaullists, communists and pseudo-Marxist socialists began applauding each other's speeches, and as Mrs Thatcher and Norman Tebbit started being polite to Eric Heffer and Denis Skinner. At the heart of the dilemma, because at the heart of Europe, lay Germany, the new continental giant, powered by economic rather than military muscle, but potentially even greater than a Soviet Union in disorder and retreat.

EUROPE'S GULLIVER UNCHAINED

After the Fall of the Wall, the centre of gravity within the European Community itself began shifting away from the Paris-Bonn axis. As 1989 turned into 1990, it seemed for a while that the emotional pull from the East had temporarily dislodged the Federal Republic from her position as co-driver of the single market locomotive, causing her to reshuffle her priorities and refocus her attention inwards and eastwards. It was almost as if the political upheavals in central and eastern Europe were conspiring to pull the rug from under the feet of single market architects, demonstrating the infernal, eternal triumph of the 'slip 'twixt the cup and the lip'. The Schengen agreement between the Federal Republic, France and the Benelux countries, which had aimed to abolish checks at all road frontiers by 1 January 1990, was one of the first casualties of the new order. It had originally been agreed in June 1985, when German unification – with Honecker still in the saddle and reform nowhere in sight – was little more than a twinkle in Helmut Kohl's eye. Clearly, however, the easing of internal border controls depends directly on the strengthening of external frontiers. And whereas for the first thirty years of its existence the EC had never had to choose where to draw the line that formed its eastern frontier, by December 1989 this was no longer the case. In the event, West Germany proved understandably unwilling to regard as 'external' the border which until 3 October 1990 continued to separate the two Germanies. Since unification, the former GDR has enjoyed full membership of the EC with the Federal Republic. But the problem has not been solved; the question of German nationality remains inherently unstable. The Federal Republic may have recognised as external the border which divides her from the former German territories of Silesia and Pomerania, now part of Poland. The '2 + 4 Treaty' of September 1990, agreed by the two Germanies and four victorious powers of the last war, made it clear that the land beyond the Oder-Neisse line was strictly out of bounds. But as the Soviet empire implodes, what of the German minorities held within its perforating boundaries – the three million *Volksdeutsch* in Russia, Czechoslovakia, Rumania and Hungary? If the fall of the wall has shown one thing, it is that 'people power' can prove stronger than political programmes or even political will.

However, by 1991, fear of German distraction from the process of EC integration by events in the East had largely subsided. Chancellor Kohl's commitment to Europe seemed stronger than ever, in part reinforced by Germany's increasing need for European assistance. Kohl believes the course towards integration to be unstoppable. He compares it to the inexorable flow of the River Rhine, a powerful symbol in German culture: 'It flows in one direction and I have never found anyone who could make it flow in the other. Nobody can dam it, and so it is with Europe. If anyone were to make a dam it would burst its banks and bring destruction all around'.[5] Most Germans, moreover, do not desire a German Europe, but rather a European Germany. Foreign minister Hans-Dietrich Genscher has insisted that the Germans must never appear as an obstacle to the prosperity of Europe but rather as a benefit for the whole.[6] Many both inside and outside Germany believe that the best way of achieving this is to bind her monetarily and politically into a community with a system of rules sufficiently strong and wide-ranging to ensure that all its nations can live together at peace.

But fear of German self-absorption soon gave way to another: the fear – or rather the certainty[7] – of German domination within the community. The new Federal Republic comprising both post-war German states occupies the political and commercial vantage-ground at the centre of Europe, enjoying privileged relations with the nascent democracies and budding market economies of the East. Economically, it unites the community's highest per capita GDP with a combined workforce some eleven million greater than the next largest in the EC. Linguistically, the relative importance of German within the EC has increased, rising overnight from third place to first equal with English; it is now between these two languages that the contest for the coveted prize of business language of the community will take place, fuelling French fears of marginalisation. Although, militarily, this united Germany has been kept artificially restrained,[8] and although it is likely to be economic muscle which packs the hardest punch in the years and decades to come, the question can no longer be avoided: how will the German superpower, having recovered complete national sovereignty, face up to the diplomatic, political and security challenges posed by a continent rediscovering adolescent growing pains? How will she cope with the new international responsibilities, not only in Europe, which fate has suddenly dumped in her lap.

REACTIONS FROM THE NEIGHBOURS: THE UNCORDIAL ENTENTE

The fear of German domination of the community has been felt particularly keenly by the French, who have seen their country invaded three times in the last century by German armies. President Mitterrand – like de Gaulle before him – spent eighteen months in German prisoner of war camps. France's 'German policy' is not motivated by European altruism or national disinterest. Political and particularly monetary union is seen by the French as a way of locking Germany into Western Europe, and thereby minimising, if not entirely eliminating, the danger. From France's position on the map, moreover, it is clear that, unlike Janus-faced Germany, she can only look one way – towards her partners in the European Community. To the south, her former colonies in North Africa are now seen as more of a latent threat than as cultural outposts or market outlets: Muslim fundamentalism is sweeping the Maghreb, whose populations are growing strongly. After the opening of the Brandenburg Gate, what French defence experts had for some time been muttering in private rapidly turned into a public chorus: 'The threat lies to the south!' Few realised at the time how portentous that much repeated injunction was to prove to be. There can be little doubt that the repercussions of the Gulf War will continue to have a major effect on the history and the geography of the continent.

It has not been easy for France to accept the diminished role of a second rank power which the post-war world has offered her. But she has been quick to realise that French and European interests share much common ground, and that through playing a leading and constructive part in the community, she can transcend her national limitations and enjoy an amplified role on the world stage, thus retaining more control over her own destiny than geopolitical and historical considerations alone would logically have allowed. Appropriately entitled *La France, l'Europe: le Xe Plan 1989–1992*, the Tenth plan highlighted the fact that Europe for France is nothing less than an 'ardent ambition'. As such, nothing must be allowed to put a spoke in the wheel of the single market engine before it has reached its historic destination. On this, François Mitterrand and Jacques Delors, President of the Commission, are united. For them it became all the more imperative in 1990, precisely because of the uncertainty enshrouding Europe, that the EC should press on with its goal of integration – economic, monetary, political, even embracing defence and security affairs – so that at least one anchor might remain, an Ark on troubled waters. For both, and particularly for Mitterrand, the objective of a deeper European federation of the Twelve does not preclude that of a wider European confederation involving both neutral and former Warsaw pact countries. Knowingly to create, just as the Cold War had ended, a greedy West European bloc, heedless of the plight of its economically disadvantaged neighbours, the post-war dispossessed, would have been to put in place a potentially tragic imbalance for the future, and thus in some way to fail history. But a European federation is nevertheless seen as a vital staging-post in the creation of any future 'common European home'. The debate between 'federalists' and 'confederalists' is rampant in France, more so perhaps than elsewhere in the community. But there is nevertheless a strong feeling amongst a majority of the French that until the existing community is made to work effectively and current goals achieved, projects for the enlargement of the community must be kept on the back burner. Yet a strong and increasingly vocal constituency also exists in France, comprising Gaullists, left-wing socialists and communists, which sees the construction of a federal West Europe as a historical error serving only to replicate the division of the continent, this time between haves and have-nots. As usual in France, the debate on the 'architecture' of the continent is being conducted with passion and imagination.

In this respect, France contrasts strikingly with Britain. A latecomer to the community, well known as a reluctant and difficult member, Britain has clung to an old island mentality of 'splendid isolation' while slipping further down the path to economic decline. By the late 1980s and certainly by the autumn of 1990, however, British attitudes to Europe had begun to change – not sweepingly but nevertheless significantly – in favour of greater cooperation with Europe. A Gallup poll conducted at the time of the June 1989 European elections discovered that a majority of Britons (55 per cent) considered EC membership to be a 'good thing' (the highest score recorded since Britain's entry into the community in 1973), while 72 per cent of interviewees saw no alternative to full participation in the EC if Britain's prosperity and position in the world were to be safeguarded.[9] Conservative campaign leaders badly misjudged the prevailing mood in the country in 1989. The unfortunate advertisement, 'Stay at home on June 15th, and you will live on a diet of Brussels', badly backfired when Tory voters did precisely that. The conservative vote collapsed, leaving the remaining 32 conservative Members of the European Parliament (MEPs) feeling betrayed by their own party. A rift had clearly opened up among conservative ranks between those who supported Mrs Thatcher's view of a Europe of sovereign states as outlined in her 1988 Bruges speech, and those who did not.[10] Ranged against her were former prime minister Ted Heath and a growing number of senior ex-Cabinet Ministers, including her erstwhile Defence Secretary Michael Heseltine, the lion who was soon to make the kill . . . for another to enjoy.

Britain's belated entry into the exchange rate mechanism (ERM) of the European Monetary System (EMS) at the beginning of October 1990 was generally seen as 'too little too late' both by the business community it was intended to appease, and by growing sections of the electorate who wanted to play a greater role in the construction of Europe when it mattered, rather than after the event, when the rules of the game had already been agreed. But the level at which sterling joined the ERM suggested that entry had been little more than a cosmetic change, designed to woo voters rather than to mark a change of heart. The pound was to be kept 'strong', and exports expensive. That there had indeed been no change of heart – at least on Mrs Thatcher's part – was confirmed only days later, when at the Rome Summit the then prime minister, with 'finger wagging and [. . .] passionate no, no, no',[11] ridiculed the idea of a single currency, dismissed the notion of an independent European central bank, rejected any move toward closer European cooperation. At Rome, Mrs Thatcher painted herself into a corner. At Westminster, she painted herself out of the picture. Seemingly unaware of the evolution of public sentiment over Europe after more than eleven years as prime minister, possessed of what Sir Geoffrey Howe later described as a 'nightmare image' of a continent 'positively teeming with ill-intentioned people scheming, in her words, "to extinguish democracy", "to dissolve our national identities", to lead us "through the back door into a federal Europe"', Margaret Thatcher's lonely stand in Rome became an even lonelier one back home.

The end, when it came, was swift. Less than six weeks after Rome, a quickly appointed and little-known dauphin (John Major) had replaced her as prime minister. It was a surgical cut of extreme precision, pin-pointing the source of conservative unpopularity. While Mrs Thatcher's own head rolled, her government was preserved virtually intact.

What will be the future role for Britain in Europe, as 1992 beckons? Immediately upon securing his succession to Downing Street, John Major strove to portray himself as his own man, not just the faithful chauffeur to a formidable 'backseat driver', but rather as someone who firmly believed that Britain could not influence the building of Europe from the terraces; she had to be out there on the pitch, playing hard. It remains to be seen, however, whether this change of tone will be coupled with a change of substance. The attitude towards Europe, both of the British political class and of the general public, remains fundamentally ambivalent. They fully recognise the importance of the stakes, but cannot somehow quite bring themselves to enter into the spirit of Euro-construction. As has so often been the case in the past, pragmatism will, at the end of the day, triumph over lack of historical imagination. But at what price for Britain's future place in the new world order?

EUROPEANS ON EUROPE

Project 1992 – designed to lead by 31 December 1992 to a community-wide internal market characterised by the free movement of goods, capital and people – began with a whimper rather than a bang. In Britain, its passage through Parliament in 1985 went unnoticed by the majority of the population, who remained magnificently unaware that their train had just acquired a new locomotive and direction. There was no blaze of publicity; that came later as member states and government bodies began to feel in need of 'catching up', concerned that what had been mistaken for window dressing might turn out to be a brave new world. The sound and fury of the DTI's campaign, 'Europe open for business', masked the massiveness of British complacency: a 1988 survey revealed the proportion of British firms with a strategy for the internal market to be less than half that in France.[12]

When *Europeans on Europe* was first conceived, there were many who were still saying that 1992 would not change attitudes and habits, only laws, and that restrictive practices and national preferences were bound to persist. Scepticism as to how its proposals were to be implemented was also rife. After all, the 1957 Treaty of Rome had paved the way for an internal market which twenty-five years later had still failed to materialise. In the past, of course, the use of the veto by individual members had often led to the paralysis of the decision-making apparatus, while the Single European Act (SEA) of 1987, which revised the original treaty, speeded up the process through the introduction of qualified majority voting, making it harder for governments to block proposals to which they were opposed.[13] Nevertheless, when representatives of the twelve member states of the European Community joined together to approve the new Act, no one could have imagined that the path to market unification would be anything but tortuous. With major obstacles to surmount, such as the dismantling of internal border controls, the harmonisation of laws and standards – soon replaced by the more readily achievable goal of approximation – it was clear from the start that the way ahead would have all the ups and downs of a roller-coaster ride.

By 1990, however, it was fast becoming obvious even to the most sceptical observers that in fact the Single Act was dynamite. Not so much because of its 279 proposals (more than two thirds of which had been formally adopted or provisionally agreed by member states), but rather because in pushing through the objective of trade liberalisation, it had cleared a path for other agreements transcending it in importance: on economic and monetary union (EMU) on the one hand, cemented by a single currency, and on political union on the other, with closer cooperation in matters of defence finally on the agenda.

It is these three fundamental aspects of European union that the present volume sets out to discuss. *Europeans on Europe* offers a transnational comparison of the hopes, fears, expectations and preparedness of three key European countries – France, Britain and Germany – in these three vital domains, and at a crucial point in history when the old order is giving way to the new.

ECONOMICS AND BUSINESS

In the field of economics and business, the three stories are significantly different. France's main assets are a small number of pioneering world leaders, particularly in high technology industries. But for them, Europe is already too small an arena. Confident to the point of indifference, there are even those national champions for whom 1992 is 'the great non-event'.[14] Their bravado contrasts markedly with the vulnerability of a large number of both second-rank industrial sectors and small and medium-sized businesses. The latter can ill afford the expenditure on research and development needed to keep ahead of the rest, and as protected local markets are opened up to foreign competition, survival depends largely on securing a market niche. But the key area of uncertainty is perhaps the following: how will French business respond to the reduced role for the state – the traditional support system for both winners and losers, through investment policy and protectionism – which post-1992 Europe offers?

Germany, regarded by many as the 'miracle man' of the post-war world, is already showing some signs of fatigue. Having benefitted greatly from new state-of-the-art industrial plant in the fifties, she now faces the urgent need to rationalise and restructure her traditional industrial priorities: those sectors in which she is dominant tend to be markets of the past (cars and machine tools), now characterised by low growth, while her share of high technology markets is in decline. To all this was added, in 1990, the enormous challenge of incorporating the former GDR. Nevertheless, by geography, by business culture and by experience, Germany remains the most visibly successful of the three nations. In the eighties, West Germany discovered that her strong economy might enable her to pursue her national interests more vigorously; there is little reason to suppose that Germany will be a net loser from 1992.

Britain's recent massive economic and industrial reorganisation makes prediction hazardous. The eighties saw the industrial heartlands of the Midlands and the North turn to industrial wastelands. Mrs Thatcher, who presided over their demise, insisted that it did not matter, that the British should have a service-based economy. 'What that means', retorted her predecessor Mr Heath, 'is that we do our own washing; but we have to buy the washing-machines abroad!'[15] It is said – not without good reason – that Britain's main asset is her financial services sector. But the insistence of government on having a strong currency – coupled at the end of the decade with high interest rates – has proved doubly crippling to major British exporters: it has meant less overseas revenue and tougher competition at home. Since 1983, when for the first time in her history Britain imported more than she exported, the balance of payments deficit has continually worsened. By the end of the eighties, Britain's exposure to foreign competition had made her the primary target for cross-border takeover bids in Europe. It is too late to pull Britain back from the brink of recession; but her future may largely depend on the forging of a more constructive relationship with her European partners.

FOREIGN AND DEFENCE POLICY

In the field of foreign and defence policy, the uncertainties in which Europe is shrouded are at their greatest. The picture is one of three nations used to pursuing different objectives, but which are now being forced, through the realities of international relations, into a cooperative mould which none of them really welcomes and none knows how to handle. France, for twenty-five years the Gaullist maverick, began to recognise the very real limits to 'national independence' at precisely the point in time when her four main political parties were engaging in self-congratulation about the creation of a 'Gaullist consensus' on foreign and defence policy. As national independence gives way to European interdependence, France's long-standing nuclear priorities are clearly in question. No other European country shares France's enthusiasm for the *force de frappe*, and nobody in France knows what future there might be for conventional forces. On foreign policy also, there is confusion over how to effect the transition towards a European role, the precise parameters of which remain ill-defined. Although clearly France shares with her community partners many common interests throughout the world, at the same time she considers, with reason, that in the Arab world, in Africa, in the Pacific and South East Asia, she has special historical relationships which give her a rather different slant on developments.

Germany, meanwhile, is increasingly aware that the Washington apron strings to which she has clung for forty years are rapidly being untied. Towards the end of the eighties she hesitated for a time between the perils of *Ostpolitik* and the uncertainties of exchanging an Atlantic support system for a much more problematic European one. But the nineties have brought new conditions. Given German unification and the consequent need to reassure Europeans that they have nothing to fear from their former aggressor, and given the unequal response of EC countries to the crisis in the gulf, Germany is now firmly behind community initiatives to bring defence within the new treaty on political union. At the same time, given her new-found sovereignty and the sudden emergence of unstable political regimes on almost every one of her eastern borders, her dilemma is in fact even greater than before. Loath even to contemplate re-emerging as a military power, Germany must grapple with the unprecedented task of consolidating her European leadership in the field of security through economic and industrial influence rather than through the sword. Geographically situated at the hub of the continent, she is obliged to look both East and West at the same time. Imagination and subtlety have not characterised her approach to this dilemma in the past. This time around, they must.

Britain is slowly beginning to appreciate the genuine limits of the 'special relationship' with the United States (which was given a new lease of life by the Gulf War), and to understand, if somewhat reluctantly, that her future can only be a European one. Yet nothing in her diplomatic or military past prepares her to play a truly European role. She shares with France a problematic nuclear posture which most other European nations, including Germany, fail to appreciate. And yet the prospects for cooperation even with France on this issue seem fraught with problems. All three of our countries face budgetary constraints which make cooperation inevitable. 1992 has proved to be the impetus which has forced them to go beyond lip service and to initiate genuine measures of cooperation. Yet paradoxically, the most urgent necessity of all – rationalisation and restructuring of a huge and tentacular armaments industry – which, in the first instance, concerns Britain and France, may well prove to be most 'beneficial' to Germany, the one country of the three which has hitherto undervalued this particular card. But here again, cultural divergence over the last forty-five years may well militate against any easy or rapid harmonisation of plans or objectives. On an issue as fundamental as the development of a new fighter aircraft for Europe, the three countries have revealed over the last decade that they have irreconcilable differences of opinion. It has often been said that, on foreign and defence policy, the community is in a vicious circle: without central (federal?) political institutions, no harmonisation of diplomacy or security is possible; yet it is precisely the reluctance to yield sovereignty in these areas which makes the emergence of central political institutions almost impossible to achieve. Once again, the imperatives of pragmatism in an increasingly multi-polar world will, no doubt, eventually generate a solution. But how long can the world wait for Europe, which everybody recognises once again as a major actor, to get its act together?

POLITICS AND POLITICAL CULTURE

The erosion of sovereignty which populist politicians in all countries have denounced, seems almost a foregone conclusion. Despite the new buzz-word 'subsidiarity' – the principle that decisions should be taken at community level only if there is clearly a need to do so – an increasing number of decisions are bound to be taken in Brussels rather than London, Paris, Bonn or Berlin. One possible repercussion of this shift is that the German political framework, with an important regional role for the Länder, may well become the model for other nations. Over the last twenty years, the Federal Republic's apprenticeship in democratic processes has been passed with flying colours. Her closer association with the two main democratic nations of the old continent cannot but enhance this process and consolidate a model for the whole of Europe.

In Britain, where traditions of decentralisation are not entirely moribund, such a model would not be difficult to apply. The corollary of distant macro-political decision-making is likely to be the growth of a new identity with the political region for micro-issues. Many in Scotland – and not just the SNP – feel that this old European nation, now perceived as a disadvantaged region of Europe, will get a better deal from Brussels than it ever has from Westminster, and will, at the same time, be able to foster once again its own cultural identity. Britain is clearly hamstrung by what would appear to be a psychological nostalgia in and about Westminster, which the last prime minister attempted to turn into a national crusade. But in Rome Mrs Thatcher met her Waterloo and her successor is unlikely to be able to forget this. The institutional issues involved in generating a new political framework for Europe are legion – although less numerous than the solutions currently being proposed. The most urgent task is to reduce the 'democratic deficit' experienced by the European Parliament and to introduce some real measure of control and accountability. Britain has much to offer in this respect, but it is inconceivable that the process will not have a boomerang effect, with profound consequences for the future of political institutions in the UK.

It is possible that Britain will adapt more easily to the twofold structure of future European politics than her nearest neighbour across the Channel. There, the sheer historical weight of the central state will be far more difficult to dismantle. In one sense it could be argued that since so many local issues have traditionally been resolved in distant Paris, they could in future just as easily be resolved in distant Brussels. In practice, however, this is unlikely and the fact remains that, where France is concerned, neither of the two current loci of political power (the state and the local community) is quite appropriate for the political structures of the next century. Moreover in France, the dangers of 'regionalisation' are far greater than in either Germany or Britain. For two hundred years, Jacobinism has striven to eradicate the fissiparous tendencies of Girondism. If that process were reversed, where would it end? Bretons and Corsicans would not be the only groups to welcome the advent of greater autonomy. Many in the south west of France can look with real feeling towards Barcelona as the obvious regional centre. And how, given a genuine absence of external constraint, would the inhabitants of Alsace prefer to carve out a new European identity? Lotharingia, for many in the Eastern parts of France, is not simply a lost kingdom from the later dark ages. And then, there is the increasingly bitter dispute over the future site of Europe's political institutions, with the status of Strasbourg the stakes in a furious tug-o'-war between Paris and her partners.

In all three countries, however, political parties are likely to harmonise ideologies and policies as a result of European practices and transnational cross-fertilisation. The likely outcome of operating within clearly recognised and internationally imposed constraints in this way will be the consecration of centrist opportunism and the marginalisation of extremes. But if 'scientific management' within externally imposed parameters is to be the future lot of politics, what place is there to be in this new scheme for dreaming? In his Foreword to this volume, Edgard Pisani provides an object lesson in the peculiarly French capacity for the deployment of the creative imagination in politics. In the Europe of tomorrow, there will be many who concern themselves only with the technical performance of the locomotive. But those who care about the ultimate destination will surely be even more important.

A EUROPEAN FORUM

In conceiving this volume, the editors wished above all to bestow upon it a genuine *European* flavour. We could not attempt to cover all European countries, nor did we wish to produce a random sample. The concentration on Britain, France and Germany is therefore justified quite simply by our desire to examine several countries in some depth and to attempt an element of cross-fertilisation. In all three countries, but particularly in Britain, the 'debate' on Europe is all too incestuous. There is an urgent need, in the words of Robert Burns, 'to see ourselves as others see us'. From this derived the principle of inviting contributions from scholars in France, Germany and Britain who are essentially specialists on a country other than their own. We have stuck almost rigidly to this principle, not because we feel that 'outsiders' can know us better than we can know ourselves (both perspectives may be equally valid) but because this seemed the most promising way of creating a rich variety of opinion. We thus have, among the contributors to this volume, three Britons, three French and four Germans – a symbolic balance? All three Britons currently live in England, although one of them defines herself as Scottish, has a life-long love affair with Germany and currently specialises on France; one has lived for almost ten years in France and likes to feel that his analyses benefit from the knowledge of the insider and the distance of the outsider; and the third (who constitutes the exception to our rule about looking in from the outside) is one of that rare breed in the UK: a life-long committed European, whose scholarly writings encompass the entire community but who also combines, in his approach to Britain, the science of the academic with the commitment of the political activist. Of the French contributors, one lives on the Breton periphery and is ideally suited to analyse both British and French developments in a cross-national perspective; one lives in Brussels, works in Paris and is a specialist on Germany; the other – who was born in North Africa, held ministerial office under both de Gaulle and Mitterrand, has been a European commissioner and is currently a foreign policy adviser to the President, as well as Director of France's ambitious Arab World Institute – is very much at home embracing concepts of universal sweep. Of the four 'Germans', two live in Britain, one in the United States (another exception which proves the 'European' rule behind this book) and the fourth in Germany . . . but married to a French woman. The four German contributions are more difficult to classify. One, written by a resident of the UK, addresses a British topic; a second, equally by a UK resident, studies Germany (from the inside-outside). A third performs the same function but from transatlantic distance, while the fourth German contribution studies France. The result is for the reader alone to appreciate.

HISTORY IN THE MAKING

This book was submitted to the publisher in January 1991 as the two inter-governmental conferences of European Community leaders were beginning, in Rome, their historic task – one to determine the political constitution of Europe, another to establish a single European currency. History was daily in the making and the editors had no illusions about the rapidity with which the ideas, opinions and analyses presented in this book would be overtaken by the pace of change. However, it is our belief that the picture presented in its pages will stand as a valid cross-national interpretation of the way ten separate Europeans perceived the reality of the continent as it entered the watershed year leading up to 1992. The strange meteorological phenomena which have borne down on the old continent over the past two years have produced accelerated changes on the surface of the terrain: divisive geological features have been subject to rapid erosion, unified expanses of territory have been battered by the fissiparous pressures emanating from the gusty squalls of renascent nationalism, rivers and waterways which had laboriously been bridged (or tunnelled) over the previous thirty years, have seen their significance reinforced by the strangeness of the climate, and their links called into question. Everybody has been asking: where is it all going to lead? To seek answers to those questions, the contributors to this volume have tried to burrow deep into the cultural geo-strata underlying the surface of the continent. At this level, permanence is much more noticeable and it is in that permanence that we have sought to identify clues to the eventual shape of the future. But the book is not intended to be a crystal ball. It is a snapshot of a continent as it embarks on its biggest ever adventure.

NOTES

1. The former French president, Valéry Giscard D'Estaing, had predicted shortly before the fall of the wall that German unification was at least a century away. His successor to the Elysée was somewhat closer: François Mitterrand thought that East and West Germany might be united within a decade.
2. The respective visions of General de Gaulle and Mikhail Gorbachev.
3. Constantine Cavafy, 'Waiting for the Barbarians'.
4. See Hélène Carrère d'Encausse, *L'Empire éclaté* (Paris, Flammarion, 1978); *La Gloire des nations ou la fin de l'Empire soviétique* (Paris: Fayard, 1990).
5. Quoted in 'The snowballing power of the superstate', *The Independent on Sunday*, 9 December 1990, p. 19.
6. Cited in 'Delors, the history man', *The Economist*, 21 October 1989, p. 68.
7. Dominique David, in a paper entitled 'La France, l'Europe et les enjeux stratégiques des années 90' presented to the 1990 annual conference of the Association for the Study of Modern and Contemporary France

(ASMCF) Wolverhampton, commented that, in all the uncertainty which we in Europe have experienced since the fall of the wall, there is at least 'une petite certitude': that of German domination.

8. The Paris Conference on Security and Cooperation in Europe (CSCE) in November 1990 placed even greater military constraints on Germany than before, reducing her military hardware by half.
9. See 'Poll shows British want integration in Europe', *Facts*, July 1989, p. 1.
10. Backing Mrs Thatcher were the Bruges group, named after her attack on a federal Europe delivered in Bruges in September 1988, and more ignobly, the editor of the *Sun*, who ran a vulgar front-page anti-Delors campaign throughout the month of November 1990.
11. A brief extract from Sir Geoffrey Howe's resignation speech to the House of Commons on 13 November 1990, *The Independent*, 14 November 1990.
12. Consensus Research survey commissioned by management consultants Ernst and Whinney. See 'British not prepared', *The Times*, 2 March 1988, p. 2.
13. With the exception of those proposals which concern the free movement of people, and financial or monetary issues.
14. Personal interview with a number of leading French industrialists, November 1990, Paris.
15. Question Time, BBC 1, November 1990.

Part I
Economics and Business: New Worlds to Conquer

1 The Unfinished Chrysalis: Market Forces and Protectionist Reflexes in France

Mairi Maclean

> 'Priorities! Priorities! There are so many that none really counts. And yet can there be any other dimension for any man or woman in a position of responsibility – particularly if they run a company – than Europe, France and Europe, France in Europe, Europe in the world?'
>
> (François Mitterrand)

The bicentenary year of 1989, and the months and years of preparation which led up to it, formed a long drawn-out celebration of France and of her past. But with 1992 shortly to become a reality, self-obsession and retrospection gave way to a new focus on Europe and on the future. In the words of President Mitterrand, 'France is our country, *Europe is our future*'.[1] And as the last echoes of the Marseillaise died away, a new refrain was heard in France: 'On va gagner!'

The profound transformation of France's economic and business institutions during the 1980s has turned this country of 'capitalists without capital' – for such was France in the days of Giscard – into the major cross-border acquirer in Europe. And the full significance of the failure of the Mitterrand-Mauroy experiment of 1981–82, which sought to solve France's problems purely at the level of the nation through a go-it-alone reflation of the economy – at a time when Britain and West Germany were pursuing austerity programmes – has literally yet to be realised. For when it ran into the sand (as it did as early as June 1982), the evaporation of a dream which had been carefully nurtured for a generation gave way to a pragmatic realisation that the state's powers were severely curtailed. The interdependence of France's economy with those of her economic partners in the European Community could no longer be ignored, and the French began to look seriously towards Europe to see what it had to offer. There is a very real sense in which they have never looked back.

By the late 1980s a new obsession held top French companies in its grip: that of rapid expansion within – and without – Europe. Yet beneath the confidence and the bravado – 'we must believe', Mitterrand insisted, as if only through faith could the prophecy be fulfilled – there was an awareness that success in Europe's open market of the future was anything but guaranteed. There were nagging doubts concerning France's ability to rise to the three great challenges of the new decade: the fight for market share in Europe, and for the business 'clout' which the French seemed to believe only size could bring, in the teeth of a new – enlarged – German threat; the battle for world market share amid growing competition from Japan; and the race to capture virgin markets in the East.

Certainly, French business could take heart from its recent vote of confidence by the Organisation for Economic Cooperation and Development (OECD). In April 1990 the Paris-based organisation predicted that France would continue to enjoy healthy growth and low inflation for the foreseeable future – but without the inflationary virus sapping the British economy (which, with the double blows of the 'poll tax' and crippling interest rates, was experiencing in late 1990 the worst inflation since the crisis-days of 1982) and threatening to undermine that of the former West Germany as it strove to integrate with the East. Nevertheless, France's performance in the more rigorous competition of the single European market remains a major uncertainty. And if the general anxiety which prevails could be attributed to a single cause, it would perhaps be this: how will French business respond to greater exposure to market forces given the reduced role for the state – the traditional support system for both winners and losers, 'national champions' and 'lame ducks', through investment policy and protectionism – which the post-1992 world offers?

This essay explores the strengths and weaknesses of business and the economy in France today in relation to the external threats and opportunities which are in the process of shaping tomorrow's world. It also seeks to evaluate the goals and objectives formulated by French government and business leaders to bridge them. Finally, it highlights those issues which may play a key role in determining France's prosperity – those differences which may make a difference – in the decade ahead.

THE ECONOMIC BALANCE SHEET: ROSY OR GREY?

Perhaps, as a *Financial Times* editorial suggested in April 1990, the key political legacy of the 1990s will be neither Reaganism nor Thatcherism, but Mitterrandism. For the tight monetarist policies which France has pursued since the U-turn of 1983 have gone a long way towards improving her standing in Europe and in the world. Wage restraint (especially for blue-collar workers) and a strong franc anchored within the European Monetary System – increasingly recognised as both anti-inflationary and an effective guarantee of monetary discipline for those countries which are members – helped to create the conditions for economic stability, driving down the French inflation rate to within a hair's breadth of West Germany's. At the same time, necessary measures of liberalism, a revamped Bourse and a new enterprise mentality added an element of 'spice' to that stability, enhancing France's attractiveness to the international investment community. François Mitterrand steered a middle course between deregulation on the one hand, where obstacles to the free play of market forces were removed, and *dirigisme* on the other, where the state decided which economic objectives were to be privileged and pursued. The result was two years of healthy economic growth in excess of 3 per cent, and forecast to remain at that level throughout the early 1990s. And if on this side of the Channel high wage claims are repeatedly blamed for exerting inflationary pressure on the economy, socialist Prime Minister Rocard need have no such worry. Inflation has been estimated to run at a mere 2.9 per cent in 1990 (a prediction admittedly made in sunnier climes, prior to the autumn's oil price hike), while salary increases in France's extensive public sector were fixed at a modest 2.5 per cent for the year.

One of the most dramatic developments to have occurred in France during the past decade has been her final, belated awakening to the importance of equity capital in an increasingly internationalised and open economy. In 1981, after a generation of rule by the Right or Centre-Right, investment in business and industry was still regarded as the responsibility of the state. Private-sector firms sought loans from public-sector banks whose 'civil-servant' managers were often in the pocket of whichever government had appointed them. Almost the last place prospective fund-raisers would think of looking would be the Bourse, which had stagnated throughout the 1960s and 1970s. Perhaps the most telling comment on its importance at the time was its total capitalisation, which was equal to a mere two-thirds of that of a single American company of the scale of IBM.

During the 1980s, however, France has increasingly become a property-owning democracy. Shareholders have swollen in number from one million in 1978 to almost eight million ten years later. And whereas in 1979, 20 per cent of households admitted having unearned income, by 1984 – prior to the privatisation programme implemented by the Chirac government – that figure had risen to some 28 per cent. By 1989 the market capitalisation of the Bourse had grown to $267.6 billion, in hot pursuit of Frankfurt with $268 billion (although Frankfurt had a higher turnover), but still some way behind London, with a capitalisation of some $796.5 billion. It is in part the new viability of the Paris Bourse which has made possible the costly series of takeovers on foreign soil prompted by the imminence of the 1992 deadline.[2]

Meanwhile, high technology continues to flourish in France. Success in the international business environment of the future will depend on swift communication, whether of transport (with European manufacturers increasingly operating just-in-time production lines) or of information, and France is determined to be well placed in both. A new Paris-Strasbourg line for her enormously successful high-speed train, the TGV (*train à grande vitesse*), is due to open in 1997. And in the pioneering telecommunications field of optical fibres, France-Télécom is well on the way to making France the 'optical heart' of Europe, with a total of 350 000 kilometres of cables expected to be installed by 1995.

Both projects were originally government-sponsored. Such state-led initiatives, particularly in fields considered to be of strategic importance, have served France well since her humiliating experience during the Occupation, when much of her infrastructure was destroyed. It has been said that France's defeat in 1940 was not so much a defeat for the French army as a defeat for her technology. Determined never to give history the opportunity to repeat itself, France has used that defeat positively as a spur to great technological achievements. The contrast with Britain is startling. Fibre optics was a British invention. And for want of government foresight and subsidy, Britain's high-speed Channel tunnel rail link lay foundering on the beaches of Kent – never to relieve commuter congestion into London, nor allow outlying regions of this island on the periphery of Europe to reap the single market benefits they so desperately need – until its last-minute rescue by the new man at No. 10.

Old habits of thought die hard. France, according to the Dutch sociologist Geert Hofstede, is a society with a deep-seated need to avoid ambiguity; and perhaps the state derives some of its power and legitimacy from this basic need for security.[3] Yet the notion of 'national interest' is not one which can be easily reconciled with that of an open market. State aid is far from being a thing of the past in France. But it has been correctly identified by the Commission as another barrier to trade, another means of preserving chronic inefficiency and over-capacity among European firms; it has therefore been outlawed as incompatible with the single market programme. Longstanding dependencies, particularly where they have proved fruitful to both parties, may be difficult to dislodge. The stark contrast between them and Europe's unprotected market of the future means that the outlook for France, however rosy, cannot be guaranteed.

ALARM BELLS: TRAINED MANPOWER AND MANUFACTURING INVESTMENT

The Achilles' heel of the French economy is without doubt France's high level of unemployment, which in May 1989 dropped into single figures for the first time in four years, and which by mid-1990 stood at 9.3 per cent.[4] Half a million jobs were created in the two years from 1988–90, yet there was little erosion of the unemployed population. This was partly due to the continuing rise of France's active population, anticipated to swell from 24.2 million in 1987 to 24.8 million by the turn of the century, by which time those of Britain and especially the former Federal Republic will have undergone significant decline.[5]

But the fact that steady growth should have left some two and a half million out of work is indicative of a more serious structural weakness: the acute shortage of skilled workers in France which, if it persists, cannot but act as a brake to future prosperity. Ironically, the problem got worse – not better – with the return to economic health: by the autumn of 1989 as many as 44 per cent of companies were experiencing recruitment difficulties, representing a threefold increase since the spring of 1987.

Paradoxically, social inequalities have grown in socialist France. The gamut of incomes widened, as economic growth – the creation of wealth which, ideally, everyone should enjoy – replaced taxation as the favoured means of redistributing wealth in society. The unemployed were worse off than before, and for longer, with the average period out of work lengthening from 370 days to 385 days. And perversely, the so-called minimum wage, the *Salaire Minimum Interprofessionnel de Croissance* (SMIC), was increasingly regarded as a maximum, a ceiling and not a floor as it was intended when first introduced in 1970. Provided that some seed falls on good soil and produces a crop, does it matter if other seed falls by the wayside?

Yet it is misleading to discuss these weak spots as if they were separate and autonomous, for everything is interrelated. France's shortage of qualified workers and high unemployment, for instance, are part of the same equation which has to do with the fact that that country's educational establishments are inadequate and ill-adapted to her needs. The French car industry in particular suffers from its reliance on low-skilled labour.

Education Minister Jospin decided that 80 per cent of school-leavers should have the *baccalauréat* by the year 2000, but how this was to be achieved given chronic overcrowding in French schools – poor conditions provoked a pupils' uprising in the autumn of 1990 – was unclear. The French university system remains overutilised but undervalued. The *grandes écoles* produce too few graduates each year, and too few engineers in particular. And with the emphasis firmly on the cultivation of the intellect, they offer future government and civil service elites neither practical training in managerial decision-making nor technical skills. Their main benefit to companies lies in their rigorous recruitment procedures; but those embittered students who see their career prospects wither when they fail to qualify for selection to the *grandes écoles* represent an enormous waste of talent. There is a widening gap between the worlds of education and business which must be bridged if France is to compete in Europe on an equal footing with Germany, where apprenticeship and vocational training are more common. What will differentiate European firms and nations in the months and years ahead, according to Industry Minister Roger Fauroux, is the value they place on their human resource, the extent to which they are willing to invest in their own personnel in terms of offering relevant, motivation-enhancing education.[6] That process of differentiation has already begun, and in France the education-enterprise partnership has been designated a priority area, as has training in general. It remains to be seen how that priority will be translated into practice. Britain is similarly blighted by a scarcity of skilled labour; but its government seems unable to decide whether or not to leave training entirely to market forces. The result has been half-hearted dithering, abortive schemes for young people and an ineffectual and emasculated Manpower Services Commission.

The greatest underutilised source of human capital in both countries, however, is women. Just over 60 per cent of women of working age work in the UK, and just under 60 per cent in France. With problems building up for the future in the form of a declining workforce and growing longevity, the need for women to join – and particularly to rejoin – the British labour market is greater than ever before. Yet mothers seeking to do so have been confronted with a dearth of child care facilities, coupled with exhortations on the part of former prime minister Mrs Thatcher to stay at home and look after baby. (To add insult to injury, the minister responsible for the family, Angela Rumbold, suggested that they should be paid for doing so!) If crèches are more plentiful across the Channel, however, the undervaluing of female labour is nonetheless apparent in the fact that women, who represent only one-third of the working population (36 per cent), account for some 60 per cent of those earning the SMIC.

Of concern is also the substantial trade deficit which France has been running with the community in general, and with West Germany in particular, since 1987.[7] By the end of the eighites both had begun to narrow, and in February 1990 an improved seasonally adjusted monthly figure of FF 961 million for the community as a whole (about £10 billion for the year) was regarded as 'encouraging'. Again, the trade gap is symptomatic of an underlying and more serious vulnerability: the chronic lack of investment in manufacturing industry by successive governments over the past twenty years, which has disadvantaged French industry vis-à-vis her economic partners. And if the agro-food and service sectors continue to earn huge surpluses (the former raking in more than FF 5 billion for the month of February 1990 alone), that too may be interpreted as a structural defect, suggesting as it does that the picture-postcard image of France as a country of cheese, wine and tourism may be uncomfortably close to the truth. Pointing out that manufacturing industry contributed a mere 20 per cent to France's GDP (compared with 30 per cent in the former West Germany), Roger Fauroux drew the conclusion that 'France was not yet an industrialised nation'. The reason, he said, was simple: 'France hasn't invested enough in the past, and when she has, it has been in nuclear power, roads or telephones, and not enough in factories'.[8] While the former were associated with national prestige, to engage in manufacturing industry in France was regarded even in 1981 as an unworthy activity, as 'dirtying one's hands'.

A measure of industrial investment in France can be gleaned from the number of new products or inventions patented there each year. Product innovation is not an area in which the French excel. France's 13 000 patents for 1987 were a pale shadow of West Germany's 32 200, and a mere drop in the ocean when set against a staggering 311 000 Japanese patents for the same year. (There had been only a slight increase since 1982, when France's 11 000 new products had been fewer than those of a single Japanese company, Hitachi, which patented 12 000.) Again, France's industrial research has tended to be concentrated in a small number of national champions from those high-technology sectors designated of national importance (with state procurement providing a powerful motor), in striking contrast to the 'technological desert' of small and medium-sized firms in traditional industries. Fauroux is currently trying to bridge the technological gap through a new *projet de loi* on innovation, promising greater diffusion of information on new inventions and financial incentives to inventors. Perhaps what France lacks most, however, is a structure of organisation designed to accommodate the irrational and foster the creative. These benefit from flatter, more flexible structures than are the current norm in France, where work relations are hierarchical, impersonal and partitioned, and where communication tends to be top-down, discouraging a bottom-up flow of ideas from shop-floor to boardroom. One thing is clear: where inventiveness and creativity are lacking, technological dependency, trade deficits and ultimately 'subcontractor status' are likely to follow.

The financial health of French firms improved considerably in the late 1980s, due to higher profit margins and above all to greater access to equity capital, as companies sought stock market flotations or carried out rights issues; or, if they were in the public sector, devised ingenious equity substitutes in order to raise much-needed private funds. Debt to equity ratios peaked at 62.6 per cent in France in 1985. (In the Federal Republic they had never been higher than 52.1 per cent, and that in 1981 when the second oil crisis was biting hard.) Thereafter, French managers became almost obsessed with reducing their levels of debt. Curiously, however, the recent wave of foreign acquisitions has had the effect of rehabilitating debt in French eyes. Given the relative smallness of the Paris Bourse and the recency of its promotion to being a serious world stock exchange, given too the vastness of France's public sector, nominally prevented from raising funds through equity sales on the market, it is clear that such a costly spate of takeovers would not have been possible without further borrowing. Interestingly, it is France's nationalised and newly privatised companies which have emerged as the most aggressive cross-border acquirers. Privatisation in particular released a pent-up potential for international expansion frustrated in the years spent in the state sector. Yet the relish with which French firms have taken to launching foreign bids is also a reflection of their former insularity: there is a great deal of catching up to be done, and very little time now in which to do it.

INTERNATIONAL CHALLENGES: THREAT AND OPPORTUNITY

It is remarkable that the now widely discredited 'certainties' of marketing management should have survived so long in France, given that France was one of the last countries to embrace them. When marketing made its debut there in the 1960s, those businessmen who chose to embrace its Anglo-Saxon teachings (and many did not, for France has traditionally been more concerned with producing than with selling) did so unquestioningly. According to the original precepts, customers were targeted, their needs scrutinised, and everything done (in theory if not always in practice) to ensure that the product-client match should be as perfect as possible.

But the evil spirits of the fairy tale – the company's competitors – were ignored. Or if they were included in the idyll, it was as friendly rivals, members of the same 'club', all playing the same game. And market share, it was assumed, would grow of its own accord.

Those days are gone. Growth in the triad markets of Japan, Europe and the USA is all but exhausted, and market share can only be gained there at competitors' expense. The *real* commercial opportunities lie elsewhere, above all in the huge, virgin markets of the East, where markets are immature and as yet unfractionalised, and unsophisticated consumers hungry for all that the West can offer.

It is extraordinary that the French should have woken up so late – albeit still incompletely – to the rude realities of strategic marketing: to the fact that its ultimate objective is the elimination of competitors. But as 1992 looms large, there is a growing awareness that it is time to take the war to the enemy. Two threats in particular dominate the horizon: within the community, Germany, Europe's economic engine and its historic monetary anchor; and without, but determined to force her way in, the economic might of Japan. The Germans may still be playing the same game; but they have found other playmates. The Japanese are not playing the same game. Their markets are closed and cartelised. They have no sentimentality about their international competitors. They are, quite simply, at war.

One of the great French fears, heightened by the single market programme, is that of being left behind at the starting-block while her German partner and rival trail-blazes her way to the finishing-post. This is not a groundless fear; there are statistics in plenty to reinforce it. Whereas the average turnover of the top 250 West German firms in 1987 was $2.2 billion, the equivalent number in France averaged only $1.3 billion. While French firms have just over a thousand subsidiaries in the former Federal Republic, West German companies have twice as many in France. Moreover, West German firms spend about twice as much on research and development as their French counterparts.[9]

So the need for French companies to establish themselves in the new, expanding markets of the East is more urgent than ever. There are obvious opportunities for the French agro-food sector, for instance, in markets where foodstuffs have for so long been lacking in choice and in supply. If the French fail to seize such exceptional opportunities, they will be left even further behind by the Germans, for whom market entry is facilitiated through unification with the GDR. With each passing day, more and more businesses from the Federal Republic start up in the East. But France has no obvious point of entry, with overall French market share there running at only 7 per cent in 1990 – behind Italy, the US, Japan and Austria and well behind the Federal Republic, with a large and growing 30 per cent slice of the action. The French government is therefore urging those firms which do have German subsidiaries to use them as springboards for expansion eastwards. And if the indebtedness of the Eastern bloc is off-putting, those companies which can afford to do so are asked to take a long-term view and get a foothold *now*, before markets are wrapped up by competitors.

While there is a general consciousness in French business circles of the commercial possibilities opened up by changes in the East, an attitude of prudence nevertheless prevails. France has been slower to react than other countries in the OECD. By December 1989, 800 joint ventures, formed by public actors from the East and private companies from the West, had been established in the Soviet Union. The French were involved in as few as 35 of them (putting France in an unimpressive ninth place behind the Federal Republic, Finland, the US, Austria, the UK, Italy, Switzerland and Sweden). Nevertheless, the following year Elf-Aquitaine won a major contract for the exploration and production of oil on Soviet territory, the first time such a contract had been agreed; and the Renault 19 became the most popular foreign car in the former GDR. The general feeling, however, was that the East was far from being an Eldorado: the Berlin Wall might have fallen, but the administrative system survived intact. The 1980s in France had seen the rise of a new enterprise mentality, a new taste for risk; but there were some new worlds which French entrepreneurs did not yet feel equal to conquering.

But the West German threat is not without its silver lining, potentially at least. Over the last forty years France has had great difficulty in coming to terms with her role as a second-class world power. One reason why she is now such a *committed* member of the European Community, in marked contrast to Britain, is precisely because she has come to see Europe as a means of achieving *national* objectives, political and economic. (The same is true for Germany, as Jutta Helm highlights in Chapter 2.) Something of a national consensus has emerged which conceives of the single market as an opportunity for France to reaffirm her historic role in Europe and in the world. For Europe, according to the Tenth National Plan, is 'above all the lever for a better position in the world economy'. The formula devised by Prime Minister Rocard epitomises the new French dream: 'A united France in a victorious Europe'. As Eva Kolinsky argues (see Chapter 8), the economic dominance of a united Germany in Europe is virtually guaranteed. The question is: will German success help fellow members in the community, or will it be at their expense? In fact, German economic strength is unlikely to increase Europe's share of world markets after 1992 because those sectors in which she is dominant tend to be markets of the past, now characterised by low growth (cars and machine tools), while her share of high technology markets, the high-growth sectors of the future, is in decline. Nevertheless, the win-win situation within Europe which Rocard's formula implies can only be achieved if Europe is to pull together to counter growing economic threats from the USA and especially Japan. And as the 1992 deadline approached, the French obsession with the latter heightened, its focus increasingly the battlefield of the European car market.

A survey on French attitudes to Japan conducted in January 1990 discovered that a majority of French people (55 per cent) feared its economic muscle. The same survey showed that there was genuine cause for concern: only 46 per cent of interviewees expressed opposition to the eventuality of purchasing a Japanese car.[10] The fear is that mounting deregulatory pressure may liberalise European markets before French companies – with their fragile financial structures and public sector dependencies – are ready to compete. In 1989, Japanese firms (Toyota, Nissan, Honda, Suzuki) held a 10 per cent stake in the European car market. If nothing is done to turn the tide that stake may rise to 25 per cent or even 30 per cent by the year 2000. Given that the European car market is expected to grow by no more than 1 per cent per annum, the price of larger market share for Japanese producers can only be the demise of one of Europe's existing manufacturers. And as European markets are prised open, perhaps prematurely, Japanese markets remain virtually impenetrable: for every 30 small and medium-sized Japanese cars imported into the EC, only one European car secures a passage to Japan.[11] The problems and prospects of the European car market, according to Jacques Calvet, chairman of Peugeot SA, epitomise those confronting Europe as a whole: 'It needs time to consolidate, and it would be absurd to open the door before the house is built'.[12] Hence the ten-year breathing-space requested from the Commission by Fauroux, before the European car market should be fully opened to outsiders, and during which quotas observed were should include those cars produced by Japanese manufacturers within the community or in third countries. Hence, too, the stance assumed by Edith Cresson, French Minister for European Affairs, for whom protectionism still has an important role to play: 'France will never let its car industry be destroyed. She will take unilateral measures if necessary. We are ready to open the market, but not at any price'.

The price of liberalisation may be high indeed: at best, one European job for every 7 Japanese cars imported into Europe; at worst, technological dependency and subcontractor status, ignominies the French are determined to avoid at all costs. The examples of British industry in general, dominated by Japanese and American subsidiaries,[13] and of Nissan's Tyneside assembly plant in particular – denounced by the French as a 'Trojan horse' affording access into mis-named 'fortress Europe' – give stern and unequivocal warning. Additional sectors in which France, according to Edith Cresson, is courting national disaster thanks to Japanese penetration include computers, electronic chips and high definition television.

THE NEW FAITH: BIG IS BEAUTIFUL

How then are European firms to meet the challenge of mounting global competition? While Japan and the US operate as nation states, Europe remains a plurality, 'a mosaic of little stones with a bit of cement around them rather than the rock it ought to be', as one of Renault's senior managers expressed it.[14] As Suzanne Berger points out, the days of national champions – often too small for global competition, yet too large to be supported by domestic markets alone – are definitively over. If European firms are to compete effectively at international level, then, as Sharp and Shearman argue, Europe needs to find some means whereby some of its minnows can grow into bigger fish, even at the expense of others going to the wall.

As 1992 approached, the belief that 'big is best' regained popularity in France. A 1989 survey of 300 large and medium-sized French industrial and services companies revealed size as the key strategic objective of 38 per cent of the sample, a throw-back perhaps to the 1960s when improving international competitiveness was believed to rest on acquiring critical mass.[15] But the concentrations of the sixties led, in the seventies, to companies encumbered with debt and inflexible structures. Hopefully this time the pitfalls might be avoided. (Towards the end of the eighties, France's world-leading glass manufacturer, Saint-Gobain, was busy setting up foreign subsidiaries; but the centre was kept lean, with a staff of just over two hundred.) Expansion, of course, does not need to be home-grown: size can be bought in, through takeovers and mergers. In 1989, a staggering 1721 successful takeover bids were launched by French companies, 480 on foreign soil and 73 per cent of this number in Europe. Those top companies which took part in the survey anticipated acquisitions to account for as much as 75 per cent of their growth from 1988 to 1992; and most of these acquisitions (70 per cent) were expected to concern a foreign prey.

There is a growing belief, however, that the future of Europe will be dominated by *alliances* between different international groups. In a complex, uncertain world, characterised by converging consumer tastes, turbulent technology and escalating fixed costs, it is better not to go it alone. Partnerships are reciprocal arrangements where two parties collaborate for mutual benefit from a position of comparative equality. They do not require the vast financial resources exacted by costly foreign acquisitions. (In the first six months of 1989, French companies spent Ecu 4.1 billion – about FF 600 million – on foreign takeovers.) Teaming-up facilitates pre-competitive research and product development, which, with shortening product life cycles, might otherwise prove prohibitively expensive, particularly in the more capital-intensive industries (helicopters, trucks, cars etc.). Collaboration, as Sharp and Shearman point out, is also something of a 'half-way house', providing a modicum of protection while at the same time confronting firms with more competition than hitherto, as domestic markets are opened up to Europe; it is therefore a most useful means of introducing firms used to cosy national markets to the harsh realities of global competition, and hence perhaps especially suited to France.

MARKET FORCES AND PROTECTIONIST REFLEXES: LIBERALISING THE STALEMATE SOCIETY?

When Renault teamed up with Volvo in April 1990, the alliance broke the mould of the French state-owned company. For Renault was a public sector flagship. The largest of France's nationalised firms, Renault was to some extent the concretisation of Resistance and Liberation ideals, having come to symbolise the marriage of state and industry on the one hand, and French self-sufficiency on the other. Certainly, the *régie* had been through difficult times in the past, and in the late 1980s it had undergone painful restructuring in order to cut out excess capacity. By 1990, however, the future had begun to look bright again. Thanks to the success of the Renault 19, the company increased its share of the European market for the first time in ten years.

But when, in April 1990, Renault lost the privileged bankrupt-proof status it had enjoyed as a publicly-owned *régie* to become a limited company, ceding 25 per cent of its voting shares to the Swedish car manufacturer Volvo, a new statement was made to the world. The alliance was a public acknowledgement of the fact that, with the opening up of markets, state ownership was no longer deemed sufficient to guarantee survival and prosperity, even in better times.

Prior to 1973, business life could to a large extent be planned. But the shock waves which travelled through the industrialised world in the wake of the first oil crisis gave rise to a situation in which unpredictability became the norm. The greater exposure to market forces which the single market carries with it, and the escalation of economic warfare with Japan in particular, have added to that uncertainty. Centralised control has fulfilled a critical purpose in France. Without it, the national project of reconstruction which set France's economy on the right track in the years following the Liberation, and kept it there through state planning, could not have been coordinated. But it is no longer enough simply to hold the ship on course. Only a decentralised approach and the devolution of power which accompanies it, can allow the rapid managerial response – characterised by flexibility and adaptability – which increasingly internationalised markets exact. Today, there is even the suspicion that the restrictive control which state ownership implies can only be an enormous handicap. Granted, in 1990 the chairmen of public-sector firms are no longer the political puppets they were even two years ago. If their companies are doing better, however, it is largely due to their greater managerial autonomy, to the fact that the state is tending to keep out of their affairs.

In his presidential campaign for a second term in the spring of 1988, François Mitterrand promised that there would be no further nationalisation nor privatisation. 'Ni ni' as it came to be known was intended as a truce, a means of stilling the age-old public-private debate which had been heightened by the privatisation programme of 1986–88, and in particular by the domination of the hard cores of stable investors of newly privatised firms by right-wing RPR (Rassemblement pour la République) sympathisers. What it meant in fact was stalemate. The 'ni ni' rule has hung like a millstone around the necks of those nationalised companies which, because of the October crash and because the Chirac government ran out of time, were left stranded in the public sector when what they needed most was private funds and private friends in order to grow. When news of the Pechiney insider-trading scandal and the Société Générale *dénoyautage* fiasco (the unsuccessful state-backed attempt to break the bank's *noyau dur* master-minded by Georges Pébereau) broke in the winter of 1988–89, it became imperative that the state be seen to be above such marketplace fiddling. Attitudes hardened, 'ni ni' became even more inflexible, and a wedge was driven between the public and private sectors. The former was obliged to resort to ingenious stratagems in order to get what it needed within the rules of the game. State-owned parent companies such as Rhône-Poulenc issued new hybrid securites – forms of share but without voting rights attached. Nicknamed 'Canada Dry' these had, as a *Financial Times* journalist wrote at the time, 'the same colour and fizz as a whisky and soda but none of the kick'. Public-sector companies also changed their structures, decentralising their activities in order to maximise speed of operational decision-making at lower levels. Meanwhile acquisition activity on the part of their subsidiaries, not subject to the same restrictions, was astonishing. Nor is it by chance that one of the largest takeover bids ever launched on the Paris Bourse should have come from a newly privatised company, Suez, freed from public sector constraints.

What the high-profile alliance of Renault and Volvo signified, then, was a new chapter in state-industry relations. It acknowledged the limits to the power of the state and demonstrated the willingness of the French government to collaborate with private European firms. It was followed in the late spring of 1990 by an equally symbolic gesture at home, when the national constructor of nuclear power-stations, Framatome – which would once have been regarded as a repository of national interest – was divided among public and private actors.[16] If state and business are not entirely reconciled, at least they have agreed to compromise in the national interest. It seems then that the powerful external threats of an enlarged Germany within a single European market and the growing economic strength of Japan may have served as powerful unifying forces at home. Today, there is not a single company left in France's extensive public sector which continues to be wholly owned by the state.

With the forging of alliances between public and private actors in preparation for 1992 a new type of mixed economy is developing in France. *La mixité* or *le mixage* is in vogue, giving rise to new sectors such as *bancassurance*, where public insurance firms have allied themselves with private banks (UAP with Suez, AGF with Paribas). Yet by its very existence, it calls into question the point of having a public sector in the first place. For it is the private sector – not the state – which has what these state-owned companies need: money. Funds for France's nationalised sector, which accounts for 30 per cent of GDP, are in limited supply. Membership of the EMS may well have driven down inflation; but it also imposes strict constraints on state expenditure, and France has one of the highest ratios of public spending to GDP of any country in the community (45 per cent), with an annual budget deficit of FF 100 billion to boot. Nevertheless yesterday's luxuries – product development, investment abroad, and the wherewithal to clean up one's act in an increasingly environmentally-conscious world – are the necessities for survival in the 1990s. France's state-owned companies are highly geared, and with the mad scramble for acquisitions in Europe and the US which characterised the end of the eighties, their need of funds became greater than ever before – particularly since they bought when prices were high, before the recession began to bite. The idea that the same shareholder-state which both prevented them from raising core equity from private investors and perhaps made them unattractive to prospective corporate partners, could ever again be their motor for prosperity, appeared to be something of a contradiction in terms. In April 1991, the door to private capital was officially, if only partially, opened, signifying a major turnaround in government thinking.

If it is still occasionally said in France that the state is the main guarantor of growth, those who believe it are diminishing. And with unemployment running at 9.3 per cent despite healthy growth, fewer still believe the state to be a guarantor of employment. Renault shed a total of 37 000 jobs in the five years which preceded its alliance with Volvo. A survey of 200 former workers at the soon-to-be-closed Billancourt plant carried out by the Confédération Française Démocratique du Travail (CFDT) revealed the extent of the culture of dependency which had been bred in them: 'The conclusions are catastrophic. We have found people who, having left behind an existence where they were taken in hand, are completely dependent and sometimes incapable of looking for another job.'[17] The welfare state was a victim of the failed 1981–82 experiment, and the 'competition state' rose like a phoenix from the ashes. But the mentality which the socialist government has sought to inculcate *borrows something from both.* As President Mitterrand said when he promised aid to farmers in the drought-stricken south-west in the spring of 1990: 'It is only to be expected that you should count on the state, but do not count on it beyond what is reasonable.' The message is one of shared responsibility between state and individual, rather than an abdication of government responsibility in favour of market mechanisms.

Undeniably, the sheer enthusiasm with which France has embraced both the concept of a unified European market and even its free-market spirit is something of a revolution. The Gallic tug of war between state and economic liberalism is an old and enduring one; but it is one in which market forces stood little chance of ever gaining the upper hand, until recently. Published in 1989, the tenth plan – entitled *La France, L'Europe, le Xe Plan 1989–1992* – was the first to accord a lower priority to the state than to private enterprise.

Yet the transition to a market economy of the Anglo-Saxon type remains incomplete. The state still controls, directly or indirectly, almost a third of the 890 companies listed on the first and second Paris markets. Its liberal credentials, moreover, have yet to be tested by the hostile foreign takeover of a major French company. That none has as yet arisen is largely due to the fact that the same French firms which are frantically purchasing businesses abroad are protected at home through *autocontrôle* (where the company's shares are safely held by its own subsidiaries), crossed shareholdings (where allies hold major stakes in one another), secret shareholder pacts and corporate structures which radically reduce shareholders' powers. Such protection, however, comes only at the price of share sclerosis, and carries with it the danger that inept management will be shielded from legitimate assault. And although the French Senate voted to outlaw *autocontrôle* in 1989, the new law was not due to come into effect until July 1991, by which time, it was hoped, companies would have mobilised alternative takeover defences. It would seem that the old protectionist reflexes are still in place: *dirigisme* is being held in check, but there is no doubt that is still survives, even if its methods are more subtle than before.

How much, then, has changed in France? After all, this was the country dubbed by Crozier in 1970 the 'société bloquée', a stalled society giving rise, according to Hoffmann, to a nation held almost in limbo, having emerged from a rural past, yet held back in fear on the threshold of an industrial future which might be expected to lay greater store by the market, a development for which it was culturally and psychologically unprepared. There is no doubt that the role of the state in France has been reduced, while that of business and the financial markets has been increased. It is more generally accepted that companies should be responsible for their own investment strategies, and that for this they require unrestricted access to capital. And in this transition towards an enterprise culture, the state has hastened the pace in the interests of international competitiveness, paradoxically acting as a lever for its own undoing through both the deregulation of the financial markets and the dramatic incitement to form international alliances provided by the Renault-Volvo pact. Yet it has not let go entirely.

So the question perhaps needs to be rephrased. Might not this half-way house, this unfinished chrysalis of a mixed economy, represent the best way for France? The French state has ceded its place on centre stage to the institution of free enterprise. However, as we so often forget on this side of the Channel, there is such a thing as 'market failure'. By remaining in the wings, ready to intervene if necessary to correct the short-sightedness and short-termism of individual firms and markets, the state ensures a continuing long-term perspective and a continuing responsibility. Between the undiluted free-market ideology of Adam Smith embraced by the present governments of the UK and the US and the concerted economies of West Germany and Japan, France is engaged in the difficult process of finding her own path, her own cultural model. No doubt she will make mistakes along the way. But liberalism – like *dirigisme*, and like 'tactical intervention' as the new role for the French state might be called – is only as good as its results.[18] If, in January 1990, the Rocard government offered French railways a massive FF 38 billion debt write-off, counter to EC policy, it exacted in return the modernisation of the existing rail network, improvement to the Parisian suburban railways and the extension of the TGV. Britain, on the other hand, may well have pursued the most unadulterated free-market policies of the twelve member states. But her infrastructure is not being renewed in vital areas. In pre-1992 empire-building, she emerged as the major target of cross-border bids. As well as 'market failure', there is also 'institutional failure'.

Free-market ideologues may have more to learn from the French than they think. If the enemies without show no willingness to disarm, does it make sense to lower one's guard?

NOTES

1. New Year's address to the nation, December 1986.
2. In the first half of 1989, French companies launched a total of 157 successful bids. French investment abroad has increased fourfold in three years, from FF 20 billion in 1985 to FF 76 million in 1988, well in advance of foreign investment in France, which rose from FF 19 billion to FF 43 billion throughout the same period.
3. In the 1970s, Hofstede compared work-related values within matched samples of people working for one multinational across 40 and then 50 countries. Of the four value patterns to emerge, France scored particularly highly on the uncertainty avoidance index.
4. This compares with just under 5 per cent in the UK and just over 6 per cent in the former FRG.
5. The former West Germany's labour force is expected to decline substantially, from 28.2 million in 1987 to 25.7 million by the year 2000, while the decline of Britain's active population will be more gentle, sliding from 27.8 million to 27.3 million. See 'A policy of prudence and caution', *Financial Times*, 28 June 1989. The growth of the French population for the year 1987 was, at 4.3 per cent, the highest of any country in Western Europe.
6. 'L'écart de performance au sein de l'Europe industrielle trouve son explication en priorité dans l'organisation et la préparation des hommes'. See 'L'Industrie veut faire école', *Le Monde*, 29 March 1990, p. 13.
7. France's trade deficit for the years 1987 and 1988 was FF 87 billion and FF 90 billion respectively.
8. Cited in 'La France n'est pas encore un pays industriel', *Le Monde*, 4–5 January 1990, p. 13.
9. In 1983 West German firms accounted for 35.6 per cent share of European R & D expenditure against 18.7 per cent for France.

10. ESOP survey January 1990. See 'On peut craindre les Japonais et avoir envie de leurs voitures', *Le Monde*, 30 March 1990, p. 35.
11. In 1988, 1212 000 Japanese cars were imported into the EC, compared with 111 500 European cars exported to Japan. Two thirds of the latter were at the top of the range, a segment of the market in which the Japanese were not then present. Hence the ratio of 30:1.
12. Cited in 'L'Europe, forteresse de sable', *Le Monde*, 6 January 1990, p. 2.
13. Scotland's 'Silicon Glen' failed to take off due to its domination by assembly plant subsidiaries, which do not create entrepreneurial spin-offs.
14. Personal interview with the author, November 1990, Boulogne-Billancourt.
15. The management consultancy firm, Bain and Co., was commissioned by the Ministry of Industry to carry out this survey.
16. CGE, la Compagnie Générale d'Eléctricité, has been the main beneficiary.
17. Cited in 'Renault esquisse un nouveau modèle social', *Le Monde*, 12 April 1990.
18. Philip G. Cerny refers to this new role for the state as one of 'arms-length *dirigisme*'. See P. G. Cerny, 'From *Dirigisme* to Deregulation? The case of financial markets', in P. Godt (ed.), *Policy-Making in France* (London: Pinter, 1989), p. 158.

2 Germany: the Ambivalent Insider

Jutta Helm

How will West Germany's economy and industry fare in post-1992 Europe? Will her high wage labour force and her large conglomerates concentrated in the traditionally dynamic sectors (engineering, cars, electrical and chemical industries) experience the strains of an ageing giant? Or will her workers and her industries adapt successfully to the new economic order? Answers to these questions have become even more difficult as a result of the rapid and unexpected crumbling of the Iron Curtain in 1989. The European Community as a whole is challenged to redefine its relations with Eastern Europe. West Germany is already consumed by efforts to develop a new relationship with what rapidly ceased to be the East German state, its society and economy. East and West Germany have united, but the nature of this enlarged state, its economic agenda, and the international framework of which it will be a part remain unclear. We can be sure that West German policy-makers and business leaders will shift their attentions from the challenges posed by 1992 to those offered in the East as the difficulties involved in unifying two rather different sets of economic structures unfold. To some extent this has already happened. From November to February 1989–90, twelve issues of the popular news magazine *Der Spiegel* carried only four articles on European Community matters. Articles on East German politics and economics and on the newly developing relationship between East and West were legion. Proceedings at recent EC Summits have been overshadowed by developments in East Germany, even though the agenda regularly includes several issues central to the completion of Project 1992.

As a result of these dramatic events, the tone of this essay will be somewhat speculative, hedged with qualifiers. Two years ago, nobody could have predicted the changes in Eastern Europe. At that time the German press was full of reports about the preparations of West Germany's business community for 1992. There was a consensus about the challenges and opportunities that would result from the removal of internal barriers to trade, capital and services. German business attitudes have, of course, long been very pro-European. European and German business elites were intimately involved in the deliberations preceding the famous 'White Paper' issued by the European Commission and its President, Jacques Delors, in 1985.[1] For German business with its strong export orientation, the stakes in the success of the single European market are very high. At issue are not only the opportunities for greater productivity and trade, which are opened up by the removal of the remaining internal barriers, but of potentially greater significance is the challenge for a united Europe to play a larger role in shaping the international economic order. This will have consequences for Europe's place in world trade, its access to high technology, and its control over monetary resources.

With half of West Germany's exports going to the EC market, it is not difficult to see why German managers are 'bullish' on the single market. A representative survey of managers in 1988 showed two-thirds expecting higher sales and only four per cent fearing losses. What is the basis for such optimism? An examination of several West German industrial sectors will show the real strengths of their position in the EC. In subsequent sections several special concerns, including the unification issue, will be analysed.

WEST GERMAN BUSINESS IN THE EC

It is a truism that West Germany has benefitted enormously from her participation in the European Economic Community. Membership paved the way for her political reintegration into the community of nations. Economically, she quickly became the dominant industrial power. Her liberal economic policies encouraged business to compete in international markets. Soon this brought high earnings from trade and high levels of economic growth, particularly in the 1950s and 1960s. These were the years of the 'Economic Miracle' with its enviable combination of full employment, growing real wages, and low levels of inflation. The fact that West Germany was also a net contributor to the EC budget during that time was more than offset by the earnings of her export industries. Even the dislocations of the international economic order in the 1970s – the collapse of the Bretton Woods system, repeated oil price shocks and stagflation – were better digested by West Germany than by her European competitors. It was only in the late 1970s and continuing through to the mid-1980s that growth rates plummeted and unemployment soared. West Germany could not escape the harsh effects of the global recession leading many commentators to pronounce the end of the 'German miracle', and to predictions of 'Eurosclerosis' and 'Europessimism'. Today these forecasts seem rather dated. When the global recession had run its course, growth in productivity, exports and earnings resumed. Since 1986 preparations for 'Project 1992' have reinforced the renewed optimism, and today the vital statistics for the West German economy are positive. Even the October 1987 crash on Wall Street did not derail the continuing recovery. High unemployment (as in France) remains a significant exception, however.

It is virtually certain that after 1992 the Federal Republic will continue to depend on exports. Export dependency results from two factors, namely the need to pay for imports (raw materials, finished and semi-finished goods) and the 'relative over-industrialisation' of her economy. As Christian Deubner has pointed out, West Germany's industrial labour force, as a portion of the total labour force, is between eight and ten per cent higher than in her major competitors (France, the United States). In the 1970s, a fifth of all jobs were export-dependent; today a fourth of the labour force is tied to exports. Efforts by the Social-Liberal coalition government to reduce export dependency through the stimulation of domestic demand had to be abandoned. They threatened the stability of the coalition government as well as the stability of the currency. Since then, virtually all sectors of the economy favour trade.

EC membership has assured German industries a market for about half of their exports, particularly in the more technologically advanced sectors, with exports to the EC growing faster than those to third countries. For a couple of years now firms in these export sectors have been positioning themselves to take advantage of growth opportunities in the completed internal market. Volkswagen for example is strengthening its European orientation with the recent purchase of SEAT, the Spanish car manufacturer. Siemens and Daimler have acquired Dutch and British firms. Hoechst, the chemical giant, is entrenched in several European firms. The list of the world's twenty largest industrial corporations includes eight European firms: five German, two Dutch, and one Italian firm. They are likely to be among the companies that will improve their market share through the Europeanisation of production and the resulting economies of scale. Aided by new communication technologies, decentralised production systems will emerge, allowing businesses to take advantage of different production costs, skill levels, and other variables in different locations. This may well lead to some loss of employment in West Germany. Volkswagen, for example, no longer produces its low-cost Polo in West Germany. As the European production facilities are more closely integrated into its competitive strategy, other cost-saving measures such as outsourcing (the increasingly common strategy of producing fewer and fewer parts within the firm, and buying more and more from independent suppliers) and the relocation of production will follow. For Volkswagen this strategy is probably unavoidable if it wants to maintain its European market share against Japanese competition.

In contrast to large firms with sizeable market shares, the prospect of small and medium sized firms benefitting from the opportunities of 1992 are less certain. However, some also doubt the competitiveness of Germany's industrial giants. How strong are they in high technologies and new products? Several studies by the European Commission and the German Economics Ministry have raised this question. It seems ironic that claims about the future of the German economy should rest on the shoulders of the same industries which led the industrialisation and modernisation effort in the nineteenth century: metal working and mechanical engineering, and the electro-technical and chemical industries. As an American observer of the economic scene put it, Germany 'continues to make the best nineteenth-century products on earth'.[2] Two pillars of the industrial revolution, the coal and steel industries, have already fallen behind and are now shrinking. Just how modern is the German economy, and how well has it adapted to the third industrial revolution? Patent registrations are one indicator of the capacity for innovation, and here the Federal Republic does well. Relative to population size she scored a strong second (after Switzerland) in the number of patent applications filed in two or more countries in all technological sectors. Overall, she was responsible for a fifth of all patents registered, about the same proportion as Japan.[3] But these data alone do not tell the whole story. The actual application of new technologies is of even greater significance. While German firms do not pioneer many new technology products, they are very advanced in applying new technologies to traditional products and production processes. This diffusion-oriented strategy has ensured the competitiveness of a number of economic sectors, foremost in the engineering and chemical industries.[4] Diffusion also requires a commitment to a highly skilled workforce, often cited as another ingredient of Germany's export competitiveness. A close look at three sectors which have long been the backbone of the Federal Republic's industrial strength will illustrate these points.

The automobile industry has over time weathered considerable shocks. In the early 1970s Volkswagen was the 'sick giant' of the industry. The company had delayed product innovation and sales suffered. Together with other car manufacturers it was hit by the oil price hikes and the resulting doubts about the industry's future. Today, however, the car industry alone generates eighty per cent of the Federal Republic's export surplus. Over half of its exports are absorbed by the European Community. According to Wolfgang Streeck's analysis of the car sector, this dramatic turnaround was based on a cooperative labour relations system, a long-term investment perspective, and the de-Taylorisation of work organisation combined with rapid absorption of technical change. And although the German market is wide open to foreign competition, German producers have held on to two thirds of that market.

In the future, that may be more difficult to achieve. Japanese producers for example have now moved into the production of more expensive cars, a market in which German firms have long had a secure niche. Moreover, it is quite possible that globally the car industry suffers from overcapacity. But based on their past performance, there is little reason to fear that German producers are directly threatened. Future crises will, in all likelihood, be met by a new mix of the strategies which were effective in the past: the restructuring of production, retraining of the labour force, and cost cutting through new technology.

The chemical industry also experienced the drastic oil price increases as a watershed. More recently the industry has come under increasing political scrutiny as a result of the environmental movement. Its responses have been similar to those of the car industry; faster innovation, more training for a highly skilled labour force. Dominated by three giants (Hoechst, BASF, Bayer), which account for about a third of total sales and employment, the West German chemical industry remains the strongest in Europe. It has strong market shares in the EC, but the big three firms especially define their interests in global rather than European terms. They have increased their American investments, a move that might provide some protection if environmental regulation in Europe were to threaten their international competitiveness. Overall, Christopher Allen's concept of 'fragile strength' captures the industry's dynamism without ignoring its dependence on imported raw materials (notably oil), its export dependence, and its need to accommodate the demands of an increasingly skilled labour force. At this time it is difficult to see the German chemical industry as a likely loser of Project 1992.

The mechanical engineering industry also seems well positioned to thrive in the internal market. It is a very diversified industry, with more than four thousand firms producing over seventeen thousand types of machinery. For much of this century the industry has been Germany's leading exporter. As recently as 1986 it produced a fifth of all exported goods, most of them sold to European customers. Japan is another major machinery exporter, but most of her sales go to markets in Asia and the third world where German producers have only begun to compete. The success of the German machinery industry rests on its strength in the production of one-of-a-kind or small series batches of very specialised high technology craft products. Interestingly this strategy has been successful in two rather different types of machinery firms, namely large firms incorporating most of the production stages under their control, and small, decentralised producers, often family owned, who developed craft production into a high technology specialisation. Both have become experts in the application of new technologies.

If these are the success stories of German industry, what about the losers? The steel, coal and shipbuilding industries have been in a prolonged state of crisis. As these industries are regionally concentrated in the Saar and Ruhr (coal and steel) and along the coast (shipbuilding), their decline had a dramatic impact on local economies. Steel weathered its crisis rather more successfully than coal and shipbuilding. Over fifteen years, it shed forty per cent of its workforce and large portions of its production capacity in a peaceful restructuring process. This became necessary due to world-wide excess capacity that coincided with a decade of stagflation and global recession during the 1970s and 1980s. With government subsidies well below those of their European competitors, West German steel producers are now much smaller and more efficient. They lead the EC in the production of oxygen steel and the adoption of continuous casting technology. As a result of these adjustments, the West German industry has been profitable since 1984. In the past, German producers have opposed EC-wide crisis cartels which attempted to stabilise the industry through production quotas and limits on subsidies. The future of the steel industry depends to some extent on political decisions. Will barriers and trade restrictions (subsidies, quotas) be completely removed after 1992? If competition prevails, German producers are likely to prosper.

If the story of steel shrinking to a healthy size is a relatively happy one, this cannot be said of shipbuilding and coal. Commercial shipbuilding seems to be dying, and government subsidies serve only to cushion the blow for the employees. Over the last fifteen years the industry has reduced employment by two-thirds from its 1975 level of 80 000. It appears that only military production and refitting will survive. Neither the industry's owners – steel corporations and the governments of the Länder – nor the federal government are willing to reverse the decline.

The story of coal is relatively more complicated due to its rather politicised nature. The fact that the industry is the centre of parity co-determination, with equal numbers of labour and capital representatives on the Board of Directors, has required government involvement in several crisis solutions. Over the last thirty years the industry, now dominated by the Ruhrkohle conglomerate, has closed over a hundred mines and shed 240 000 jobs, almost exclusively through attrition and early retirement.

But it has never regained profitability in spite of tremendous productivity growth, and has required continued subsidisation. These subsidies – primarily to coal-burning power stations – have been criticised by the European Commission, and the federal government is likely to respond to these pressures. Today the future of the coal industry remains uncertain. Factors like the world oil price and the fortunes of the nuclear power industry will influence that future. Growing economic cooperation between the European Community and Eastern Europe may lead to increased Polish coal imports, which would further dampen the prospects of Ruhrkohle.

The picture of other losers in the internationalisation of the West German economy are more complex. The textile industry, for example, eliminated many jobs, primarily in small firms. The remaining firms invested in state-of-the-art equipment and have become extremely productive, specialising in up-market, fashionable goods. They have invested abroad in low-wage countries, re-importing their products for the domestic market. (This, incidentally, explains the fact that German textile producers have not supported the calls for protectionism which could be heard from other sectors.) The non-durable consumer goods sector has adjusted in a similar fashion. Third country imports now make up a sizeable portion of the German market in textiles and light consumer goods.

Overall, it appears that the most dynamic sectors of the West German economy are likely to benefit from the completion of the internal market. In these sectors economies of scale and reduced transaction costs will increase profits and perhaps even market shares. In weak sectors like coal and shipbuilding, 1992 is likely to accelerate the long process of decline. Other sectors like textiles and steel will encounter vigorous competition.

In the business community the prevailing mood is one of optimism. The business sections of West German papers are filled with reports about mergers and acquisitions. For corporate managers, 1992 has already become a reality as they race to position their firms ever more advantageously. Outside corporate headquarters, however, there are concerns about the costs associated with the completion of the single European market. The concerns focus on the concept of 'social Europe', monetary stability and the unification of East and West Germany.

SOCIAL EUROPE VERSUS *STANDORT BUNDESREPUBLIK*

There are very real fears that the enhanced efficiency and productivity achieved by German firms in the single European market will result in losses in employment. Even the rather optimistic Cecchini Report predicts short-term increases in unemployment.[5] This prediction must be seen in the context of even the most dynamic sectors of the West German economy not adding enough new jobs during the last decade to absorb workers who became redundant in the declining sectors. Fears that Project 1992 will only reinforce what Germans call the 'two-thirds society' cannot therefore be dismissed. Current unemployment levels are around seven per cent, lower than the EC average but well above what its considered socially acceptable. Particularly alarming is the increase in long-term unemployment. So far only the Greens, trade unions and the Republicans have politicised this issue, albeit for different reasons. They all criticise what they perceive as the construction of 'a Europe of corporations', moving to the beat of multinational firms and their priorities.

In addition to growing unemployment, critics also fear what they call 'social dumping'. It is a fact that wages, social benefits and labour law (including employee representation) diverge considerably. With hourly labour costs at $18.17 in Germany and $2.96 in Portugal (figures are for 1987), might not German firms have good reason to move production to Portugal to get the benefits of a low-wage area? Or, alternatively, will business use the Portuguese data to pressure German unions for concessions on wages and working conditions? How secure are the gains which the West German labour movement has achieved during the last forty years, since pressure is likely to brought to bear on German firms to reduce their labour costs? Of course, labour costs alone do not determine business decisions. If that were the case, industrial investors would have deserted West Germany long ago. The qualifications of the workforce, infrastructure, research and development spending and monetary stability also play a role. Moreover, costs are not only determined by wages, but also by social regulations and social security financing. If these factors are taken into consideration, the picture becomes much more complicated. Several Mediterranean EC members, for example, put drastic limits on business flexibility in the hiring and firing of labour. Employer shares of social security contributions are higher in southern EC members than in the high-wage north.

The European Commission rejects the 'social dumping' charge and points to the 'social dimension' of the European market spelled out in the Single European Act and the Treaty of Rome. So far efforts to translate the social dimension into a set of binding minimum standards in the form of a European social charter have been foiled by the British veto. Trade union spokesmen actually charge that this absolves the West German business community from taking a stand. At its 1989 Strasbourg summit the Council was only able to adopt a non-mandatory, much diluted social charter.

Experts outside of trade union circles suggest, however, that 1992 will not bring massive social dumping. Instead, they predict pressures for the dilution of labour norms which business finds particularly burdensome. The German Trade Union Federation fears for the future of co-determination, its unique model of employee representation, among other things. But it is not obvious that even a binding social charter would secure the strong position of West German workers. Any EC standard that does not incorporate West German regulations fully would leave the door open to downward harmonisation. Labour movements in low-wage countries, on the other hand, will resist upward harmonisation because it would rob them of their one competitive advantage.

An underlying issue in the debate about 'social dumping' is the fact that in the past West Germany's high trade sectors were able to export unemployment. Will German workers be willing to sacrifice their gains for the sake of a more equitable division of labour which allows the poorer regions to catch up? Or is the problem rather the dual economy within the Federal Republic? Increasingly workers who do not find employment in the growth sectors of the economy find themselves locked out of productive and secure employment. The influx of large numbers of East Germans, unfamiliar with and presumably hostile to the experience of long-term unemployment, may help to politicise this issue in the major parties.

On the other side of this debate are business concerns about 'Standort Bundesrepublik' (the 'Garrison Republic'), which stem from the relative un-attractiveness of the Federal Republic for business investors. In the eyes of prominent representatives of the business community, West Germany suffers from a competitive disadvantage due to high wages, rigid labour laws and stiff environmental regulation. Research institutes have come out with reports on this subject, with conclusions both for and against. But regardless of the accuracy of this charge, many corporate executives do not perceive the Federal Republic as an attractive production site. Japanese investors, for example, have avoided West Germany in their rush to establish European subsidiaries before 1992. Similarly, American multinationals have been reluctant to expand their West German investments. To some extent this perception is the product of the dominance of radical liberal economic thinking in Great Britain and the United States. This approach also has supporters in some German circles. The Institut für Weltwirtschaft in Kiel (the Institute for International Economics) and its former director, Herbert Giersch, have frequently called for the loosening of restrictions on competition and growth (such restrictions include labour regulations and job protection). The concept of the European social charter is anathema to Giersch and others; they can be very blunt in tarring it as an obstacle to economic and social progress.[6]

It is certain that the debate between advocates of radical liberal economic thinking and supporters of a mandatory social charter will continue. Many employees are already apprehensive about their job prospects. This is particularly true in the former East Germany where the survival of whole industries is now threatened. Some have asked whether the extension of West German labour law to the East would undermine the attractiveness of the East for West German and other EC investors. So far new investments in the East are below expectations. And there appears to be an asymmetry between the advanced state of economic integration and the rather rudimentary state of integration in social matters. Is this an indication of the international unity of capital and the fragmentation of the international labour movements? Observers who have argued that Project 1992 would have been impossible had it not been for the weakening of the European Left seem to have a point.

TOWARD EUROPEAN MONETARY UNION

Current preparations for the completion of the internal market include plans to move from the European Monetary System to Economic and Monetary Union. EMS was established in 1979. It links ten of the twelve EC currencies in a stable exchange rate system, with the Deutschmark serving as the anchor currency. This system has created greater monetary stability in Europe with lower levels of inflation, as well as some protection against the fluctuations and uncertainties of American monetary policy. For EC members it also has meant that their room to manœuvre in independent monetary policy has been greatly reduced, obliging them to accept the stability norms of the Bundesbank.

With the ratification of the Single European Act in 1987, the member nations agreed to expand monetary and economic cooperation with the goal of eventual monetary union. A first step was taken with the decision to remove all restrictions on capital movements in the group of ten members, completed on 1 July 1990. A second step was the decision to plan for the intensified cooperation of European Central Banks, to be achieved in several stages. The 'Delors Report' of May 1989 presented such a plan.[7] In early 1991 amendments to the Treaty of Rome allowing for the creation of a European Central bank system are to be adopted.

The impression that all this is rather technical and non-controversial is mistaken. For the Federal Republic at least two extremely difficult issues are involved. First, there is the issue of the stability of the Deutschmark. Since 1948 monetary stability has been one of the most important guide-posts of economic and fiscal policy in West Germany. Some experts even argue that it was the single most important maxim, due to the collective memory of hyperinflation and its destructive consequences in the 1920s. How effectively will the Bundesbank be able to ensure the stability of the German currency within the future European Central Bank system? These concerns have led some financial leaders to suggest that community-wide financial structures are not really necessary. Karl Otto Pöhl, the President of the Bundesbank, has expressed reservations about the Delors Report, even though it goes some way toward allaying German fears about the priority given to monetary stability. Related to this is the issue of periodic currency adjustments within the EMS. There are some indications that German financial leaders would like to revalue the mark. At issue here is the huge export surplus and the distorting effects of an undervalued mark on the structure of the economy, which could become even more export-addicted. Other EMS members reject this argument, however. They fear the consequences of a *de facto* devaluation of their currencies should the mark be revalued.

The second thorny issue is the impact of intensified monetary co-operation on the pursuit of a growth-oriented economic policy. There is widespread agreement that such a growth-oriented macro-economic policy is necessary to achieve the goal of eventual economic convergence within the EC. Several studies have shown, for example, that coordinated growth policies supported by appropriate steps in all or at least several member nations can achieve a multiplier effect. This combined effect would maximise growth and minimise potential negatives like budget deficits and inflation. Post-Keynesians in the German Trade Union Federation believe that above-average growth rates in post-1992 Europe require such a supportive macro-economic policy. They also worry, however, that such a policy will be derailed by the Bundesbank with its strong voice in any European Central Bank system.

How much scope is there for growth-oriented strategies such as public investments in the economically weaker regions of the community and spending for environmental protection and transportation systems? Such strategies would acquire added urgency if there should be another economic recession. The Delors Report stresses the need to coordinate economic and monetary policies. It is too early to tell whether effective structures for such coordination can be created and maintained. And the Federal Republic's past record is not promising. Her support for the community's regional fund – designed to accelerate growth in depressed regions – has been tepid. At the same time German policy makers join in the verbal consensus that the Single European Act must be supplemented with more active regional initiatives, just as they agree to the need to supplement the Act with a European social charter. In practice, however, both initiatives are likely to be severely diluted. Current uneasiness about the development of European monetary union is at least partly governed by German concerns about monetary stability. Will Bonn (or Berlin?) and Frankfurt (seat of the Bundesbank) be able to agree on a coherent policy? Will disagreements about the course of monetary policy create temptations for the Federal Republic to pursue national solutions to monetary policy problems? This is unlikely. But there is much scope for conflict.

GERMAN UNIFICATION AND 1992

In the spring of 1990 the emerging relationship between East and West Germany raised new questions about the completion of the single European market by 31 December 1992. Early fears that German unity would lead to the Federal Republic's withdrawal from the community, however, have proved groundless. Even a united Germany can probably advance her international economic goals more effectively within the EC. But there are questions about the pace of the integration process and about the nature of the German role in a united Europe. Indeed both questions have already been raised by Western leaders. The rapid development of events in East Germany and Eastern Europe caught the Western allies off guard. In Strasbourg in December 1989 François Mitterrand, the French President, insisted that German unification could only take place within the EC. In Germany the Foreign Secretary, Mr Genscher, is most strongly identified with this strategy of embedding unification within the European framework.

This strategy will, however, bring delays in the integration process. The European Commission has already adopted two-thirds of the approximately three hundred regulations needed to complete Project 1992. But the member governments, including Germany, have been slow to ratify these regulations, as required by the Treaty of Rome. German unification will cause further delays. Delors, among others, has warned that the integration process is not yet irreversible and insists that the 'deepening' of the community and its 'widening' to new members and associated nations are not alternatives. On the contrary, he envisages rapid integration as a prerequisite for the eastward extension of the community. This perspective is certainly a logical one, but logical solutions do not inevitably prevail. The little known 'Schengen Agreement' is an example of the kinds of slowdowns that are ahead. This 1985 agreement provided for the removal of all border controls between France, Belgium, the Netherlands, Luxembourg, and the Federal Republic by 1 January 1990. Recently its implementation was seriously delayed due to disagreement on the status of GDR citizens. West Germany refused to classify them as foreigners while the other signatories refused to classify them as German citizens for the purpose of border crossings. Agreement was only reached in July 1990. Disputes of this sort will put Mr Delors' timetable for the completion of the 1992 agenda severely to the test. There are those, however, who believe that failure to ratify the harmonising regulations in time will not do great harm. Herbert Giersch, for example, insists that productivity arises from diversity rather than uniformity and that harmonisation will evolve to the extent that it is needed and desired. 'The best that Europe can expect . . . is that the harmonisation agenda will remain unfinished on December 31, 1992, and that border controls will be removed just as governments have promised'.[8] It is not clear how much support this view enjoys outside radical liberal circles.

More important than the exact timetable of the integration process is the question of the united Germany's role within the community. Will the size of the new Germany fatally unbalance the community? In view of her almost eighty million inhabitants and her huge industrial resources, assumptions that Germany's role will not change are naïve. Will Germany become the leading power in the community, perhaps akin to the role of the US in NATO? Or will she rather be the ambivalent insider, too preoccupied with national issues to assume the role of a pace-maker? Does her past reluctance to assume a leadership role (except for the creation of the EMS) provide any guide-posts for the future? The last question will be taken up first.

The literature on West Germany's role in the EC has emphasised the fragmented and often contradictory nature of Bonn's policy-making on EC issues.[9] Various causes have been cited, namely the sectorisation of the West German policy process, the strong position of several independent actors (the Bundesbank, for example), the power of entrenched interests (i.e., agriculture), and the lack of coordination between federal ministries. West Germany's EC policy has been reactive. The fact that there is relatively little pro-European ideological fervour (note the declining turnout in European elections) has contributed to this. Contrast this with the intensity of pro-unification sentiments. In 1979 Werner Feld concluded that '. . . the basic strength of support for reunification appears to be greater than that given to European unity'.[10] The emotional climaxes of East Germans crowding West German embassies in the autumn of 1989 and eventually crossing the Berlin Wall have certainly intensified this. Equally striking is the feverish activity of West German politicians preparing for closer economic and political ties between East and West. Is it unreasonable to conclude that West German priorities will shift from Project 1992 to Project Unification?

It is not difficult to foresee new conflicts over German issues on the EC agenda. Take the subject of regional funds as an example. The single European Act calls for major increases in support for depressed regions. In the past the Federal Republic has been a net contributor to this fund, albeit somewhat reluctantly. In the not too distant future German politicians may well demand regional fund allocations for East Germany. Objectively there are many areas in the East that would qualify for such aid. As a result, Portugal, Greece, Sicily, Scotland, Ireland and the north of England will receive less aid from the regional fund. This is not likely to be acceptable to the affected governments. If their opposition is very strong, Germany might scale back her contributions to the EC budget. After all, East German needs are urgent and huge sums are needed. The economist Paul Zieber estimated that one trillion Deutschmark will be needed just to repair the basic economic infrastructure. This will put enormous strains on the German banking system, with repercussions on EMS. How much support will Germany provide for the continuation and expansion of the community's research and technology projects? Once the East German research establishment is joined with its Western counterpart, interest in EC-wide programmes may decline. The agricultural industry sector will also be affected by unification. How much of the Western surplus can East Germany absorb? How will this influence German support for the common agricultural policy of the community? In all of these areas policy-makers in Brussels, Bonn and/or Berlin will be sorely tested to design effective and equitable solutions.

Beyond that, German unification will require agreement on all sorts of special exemptions from EC regulations for Germany, or at least its Eastern parts. This could easily lead to chronic irritation on the part of other EC members. In other words, Delors' vision of the need to anchor a united Germany in the European Community may not be strong enough to handle the multitude of conflicts that will emerge in virtually all areas of EC jurisdiction. This is the greatest threat to Project 1992. And it is not conducive to a German leadership role in the community.

There is another scenario, however, in which such a role is not only possible but necessary. It is no secret that West Germany has been flexing her economic muscle in the recent past. 'An indication of how far the world balance has shifted is Germany's assumption of the role of world financial and economic preceptor. With the foundation of a strong economy, Germany can now tell the world how to behave'.[11] What would be more logical for a united Germany than to assert her leadership within the European Community? Is there a more effective way for Germany to pursue her global economic (and political) interests than by playing a leading role in the EC? An enlarged global role for Europe was, of course, one of the objectives of Project 1992. Are German and European interests in the global economy compatible? And how will German/European interests in the global economy be defined? The scenario most frequently mentioned by foreigners, 'Fortress Europe', is not a very likely one. German as well as British views run counter to this concept, and in the other EC countries there is also considerable opposition to protectionism. A second scenario is Europe as a relatively open trade region, adjusting to the pressures of the global economy as needed. The third option is somewhat of a compromise between scenarios one and two. Here, Europe would consciously adopt policies for its own benefit.[12] This might entail trade relations based on a mix of open competition, reciprocity, and developmental strategies in sectors that are not (yet) globally competitive. This scenario would require a more cohesive European role in the world economy, and Germany's size and export dependence may move the community in this direction. In the process, Germany might push for accelerated integration of European monetary policy or the coordination of macro-economic policy.

The political obstacles to a German leadership role in the EC should not be underestimated. At this time it may be impossible to find a single EC member to endorse this. But we cannot rule out developments that might lead them to acquiesce in a German leadership role.

CONCLUSION

The examination of West Germany's economy and industry in relation to Project 1992 has turned up a rather complicated mix of unqualified support along with barely concealed ambivalence. Corporate West Germany has already anticipated 1992 and established itself in virtually all European markets through acquisitions, mergers and cooperative deals. There are a number of sectors which stand to gain considerably from the single European market. There are losing sectors as well, including agriculture, shipbuilding and coal, as well as much of the East German industrial arsenal. Their economic (but not political) significance has been shrinking and 1992 may well accelerate this process. While there is some concern that the biggest industrial giants will reap the lion's share of the benefits from economic integration to the detriment of smaller and medium-sized industries, the business community shares a sense of excitement and anticipation in regard to 1992.

This rather optimistic picture requires qualification, however. What will Germany's workforce gain from 1992? The prospect of lower inflation and an even greater variety of consumer goods at lower prices cannot compensate for the very real fears about 'social dumping'. Will the single European market result in pressures for the downward harmonisation of wages, social benefits, and labour regulations? If this should be the case, increased social conflict is likely, and German EC membership might no longer be supported by the 'permissive consensus' of the past. European monetary union raises apprehension among monetary policy specialists, a small group of strategically placed experts who are likely to insist that German concerns for monetary stability be given pride of place in the European Central Bank system of the future.

Finally, the unification of West and East Germany raises a host of thorny questions. Just what role will a united Germany play in the EC? Her economy will continue to be export-dependent, even though new markets in Eastern Europe might reduce the significance of EC markets for German industry. Political realities make German withdrawal from the community improbable. The greatest danger would seem to result from the new pressures and conflicts which unification is likely to inject in the agenda for European integration. These are reasons to anticipate a more ambivalent outlook on the EC in the minds of German politicians and perhaps even business leaders. But it is also possible to imagine a united Germany assuming a locomotive role within the community, accelerating the integration process. In the 1980s, West Germany discovered that her economy might enable her to pursue her national interests more vigorously. Is it inconceivable that the 1990s will bring German assertiveness in the regional and global economy?

NOTES

1. Commission of the European Communities, Completion of the Internal Market: White Paper from the Commission to the European Council (Luxembourg, 1985). The White Paper sets out the liberalisation and

deregulation agenda and suggests almost 300 measures to realise the internal market.

2. Bruce Nussbaum, *The World After Oil: the Shifting Axis of Power and Wealth* (New York: Simon and Schuster, 1983), pp. 83–4.
3. The data are cited in 'The Competitive Position of German Industry in the High-Tech Field', IFO DIGEST 11 (1988) 1: 40.
4. This interesting distinction between 'shifting' and 'diffusion' is developed by Gerd Junne, 'Competitiveness and the Impact of Change: Applications of High Technologies', in Peter J. Katzenstein (ed.), *Industry and Politics in West Germany* (Ithaca and London: Cornell University Press, 1989), pp. 250 ff.
5. Paolo Cecchini, *The European Challenge, 1992: the Benefits of a Single Market* (Hounslow: Wildwood House, 1988).
6. Herbert Giersch, 'EC 1992: Competition is the Clue', *European Affairs* 3 (1989) 3: 15–16.
7. Ausschuß zur Prüfung der Wirtschafts- und Währungsunion, 'Bericht zur Wirtschafts- und Währungsunion', *Europa-Archiv* 44 (1989) 10: D283–D304. This is the so-called 'Delors Report'.
8. Giersch, op. cit., p. 13.
9. Simon Bulmer, William Paterson, *The Federal Republic of Germany and the European Community* (London: Allen & Unwin, 1987), pp. 20–1.
10. Werner J. Feld, *West Germany and The European Community* (New York: Praeger, 1981), p. 121. Feld's argument is disputed by other researchers, notably Gebhard Schweigler.
11. Harold James, *A German Identity* (London: Weidenfeld and Nicolson, 1989), p. 208.
12. These issues are explored more fully in the excellent article by Wayne Sandholtz and John Zysman, '1992: Recasting the European bargain', *World Politics* 42 (1989) 1: 94–128.

3 Britain: Financial Sophistication and Industrial Wastelands

Maurice Baslé

On 29 April 1989, *The Economist* credited the Iron Lady (a latter-day Joan of Arc in English colours) with having restored the confidence of Britain's captains of industry. The article stressed the shift in mentality which had taken place, rather than statistical data or the concrete performance of the British economy. I would not disagree with this particular judgment. It is not the long-term statistics or even the short-term originality or relevance of Mrs Thatcher's policies which lead me to believe that, in revolutionising attitudes, the former prime minister has indeed emerged victorious. However, I would argue that, despite Britain's good economic showing in 1985–89, the slow decline of her manufacturing economy continues and the prospects of the single European market and the opening to the East will only partially reverse the long-term trends in the productive system. Indeed I would add that the real mental leap on the part of Britain's managers (which can be attributed mainly to Mrs Thatcher's stubbornness) has not succeeded in mobilising all the technological, cultural, social and industrial resources which the dynamism of capital requires to accelerate growth and extend the sphere of an efficient, productive, profitable and socially useful accumulation. The reason for this, in my view, is the shift towards a finance-based economy.

A LONG-TERM OVERVIEW OF BRITAIN'S 'GENTLE BUT IRRESISTIBLE' INDUSTRIAL DECLINE

Unfortunately, the long-term figures are eloquent. In the interests of objectivity, I have taken the statistics for 1900–87 published by *The Economist* on 21 October 1989. They are harsh and irrefutable: in long-term growth performances the United Kingdom comes 19th out of the 24 countries examined. Worse still, since 1960, disparities in growth have remained considerable. Japan, of course, has done more than catch everybody else

TABLE 3.1 *Comparative real growth in several large industrial nations (1960–1987, average annual growth rate, in percentages)*

	UK	FRG	USA	France	Italy	Japan
Real GDP	2.4	3.0	3.2	3.7	4.0	6.5
Real per capita GDP	2.0	2.7	2.1	3.0	3.5	5.5
Real value added in industry	1.3	2.6	2.6	3.9	4.3	8.2
Real value added in manufacturing industry	1.3	3.0	3.5	4.1	5.5	9.5
Real value added in services	2.8	3.5	3.7	4.0	4.2	6.4

SOURCE: OCDE, Historical Statistics, 1960–1987, Paris 1989.

up (its GDP has multiplied by 5.83). Italy (×3) and France (×2.76) have shifted into high gear. Even the USA (×2.42) and the Federal Republic (×2.29), which have been generally sluggish, have done better than the UK (×1.97). Even if economic and social life has been radically transformed right across the British Isles, the UK, relative to other countries, continues to slip down the table of GDP per head of population and does even worse in terms of real added value in industry and particularly in manufacturing industry. To adapt the motto of the city of Paris, *Fluctuat et mergitur*.[1] Even the real added value in the service sector, which is particularly decisive for the post-industrial economy that Britain aspires to become (having had a head start, two centuries ago, in the snakes and ladders of capitalist industrialisation), has not shown any sign of rapid development over the long-term. Worse still, the economic recession between 1973 and 1982 hit harder in the UK than elsewhere, despite revenues from North Sea oil (see Table 3.1).[2]

It is true that things went much better between 1983 and 1989, particularly on the unemployment front. Business began to pick up and the British threw themselves into a new round of consumption, as well as fuelling a real estate boom which lasted until 1988. But the 1990s came in with a *continental* fanfare: political turmoil in Central and Eastern Europe, Italy overtaking the UK, Germany poised for a new explosion of business activity. Will Britain – as has usually been the case in this type of European development – continue to take a back seat? A first reading of the evidence forces us to conclude that 'British particularism' (that virus so feared by the French who are themselves constantly torn between their Atlantic and their European aspirations) is alive and well and living across the Channel. Mrs Thatcher has even transformed it into a new national sport by periodically anathematising the EC (without of course rejecting the sizeable rebates she extracted from the common agricultural policy).

Despite the continental attraction exerted on the south-east of England (fortunately we shall soon have the tunnel which Michel Chevalier so craved in 1860), Britain alas remains, for most of Europe, an island disconnected from the mainland. Indeed, she has become, even more than in 1960, the 'aircraft carrier' allowing for the rearguard invasion of Europe by American and Japanese capital and goods. The tunnel may simply replace the pontoons of the GIs! The Trojan Horse scenario is particularly acute in the field of cars and electronics. It began with the greater openness and freedom of exchange noticeable after 1979. The UK, like Taiwan in the Pacific, offers the Japanese – who now have more than sixty major industrial plants in Britain – scope for short-circuiting EC regulations. UK imports, which are competitive on the British market for reasons we shall examine later, have widened penetration of the internal market and undermined traditional British industry. Leaving all ideology aside, it is obvious that the advantages of liberalism can only be enjoyed under certain initial conditions. The forward rush towards the high-tech sector, despite certain well-known successes, still looks a little like a wild goose chase.

On the monetary level, the pound continued until October 1990 in glorious isolation, blissfully unaware of the international credibility of the ECU and that the EMS goes from strength to strength. In London, the pound is believed to be 'strong'. But in 1960, £1 was worth \$2.8 or 11.75 DM or even 13.80 FF. For the City, there is a feeling that only in London can certain financial or insurance transactions be properly carried out.

The long-term trends have therefore not been reversed since 1979. Britain remains a prisoner of her former roles even if certain images have changed in the economic landscape and in certain high-tech agglomerations such as Cambridge. And yet there were those who believed, during Mrs Thatcher's first term, that she possessed the 'magic potion'. In fact, even if one looks at the new recipes for short-term political management and for the control of the 'commanding heights' which were going to replace the defunct 'stop/go' precepts of Keynesianism, Mrs Thatcher has by no means slain the dragon.

SHORT TERM POLITICAL MANAGEMENT: RETURN TO SQUARE ONE

The one hundred and forty months of Thatcherism, viewed through a kaleidoscope, appear above all as a series of actions intended to serve a single objective (even if, in day-to-day terms, they turned out to be contradictory): the struggle against inflation.

The frontal attack was first of all *monetarist*: everything had to be done to break the back of inflation, which was ruining the image of the UK and was inexorably destined to kill off the pound – just as the DM or the Yen or even some European currency was rising like some new star to the East of the City. Monetary control, tax rises in Mrs Thatcher's first term coupled with indirect taxes, a draconian strategy for financial strait-jacketing of the short-term economy (the 'Iron Corset'), liberalisation, deregulation, increased competition, all this was to converge on the ground to peg down prices. And the constant repetition of the same drastic deflationary message was intended to stifle at birth the inflationary expectations of the various actors, bringing about a general transformation of attitudes, both on the part of the man in the street and among captains of industry. But the facts remained obdurate.

By 1982, the recession was so intense that this monetarist approach was relegated to the rank of intermediary instrument, the new objective becoming what it ought never to have ceased to be: *the exchange rate* (history, however, does not indicate at what level). The government profited from the sale of assets to the private sector, from taxes on North Sea oil. It began the attack on 'public waste' (the evil of vested interest) and on monopoly overpricing. The upturn in the US economy after 1983 was at first an asset on this side of the Atlantic. High interest rates could be maintained and deployed in the service of defending the pound without nipping growth in the bud. All this was achieved.

Oddly enough, however, at this point short-term political management became more routine. The strategy on sterling was slightly relaxed at the end of 1984 and above all in 1986–87. Chancellor Lawson even began to attempt to anchor the pound to the Deutschmark. The effect in terms of the reduction of imported inflation, at first quite visible, tailed off rapidly however while tension on the salary front remained high. Inflation, which had fallen until 1986 (3.6 per cent), crept up to over 6 per cent by 1988 (twice the rate in most other industrial countries) and 10 per cent by 1990.

And so, in terms of politics, it was back to square one, all the more so in that the balance on the current account had worsened since 1981. After 1983, there was a trading deficit in manufactured goods. After 1986, the balance of payments went into the red, reaching a deficit of about 4 per cent of GDP by 1989–90, despite the massive net export of oil (16 per cent of all exports). The surprise caused by this return to 'Go' provoked major tension within the government and Nigel Lawson stormed out of the cabinet.

In fact, deep down, while the British experience was comparable in certain respects to a Scandinavian model (relatively small country, relatively open market with intense struggles over pay), what is lacking is the main asset of such a model, *sufficiently dynamic exports*, even if Britain's share of world exports in manufactured goods reversed its decline in 1985–87 and even if the 1990s – prior to the onset of the Gulf crisis – seemed to offer favourable prospects for manufacturing exports (see Table 3.2).

The UK is therefore living way beyond its means. British households are at the forefront in this expression of preference for the present: household savings are at their lowest level for over a decade and in January 1990, as in January 1980, according to *The Economist*, 'the economy as a whole is facing a bleak year' (6 January 1990). Which turned out to be the case.

Economists no longer bother to look for the original features of short-term political management in the UK. There is none. The economy of the slow decline is overheating. The landing looks no more interesting. To quote *The Economist* (6 January 1990) once again: 'the economic downturn in prospect for 1990 looks like a soft mirror-image of the one in 1980–81. Better-off people, rather than the poor, are being hit; small service companies are suffering more than big export-geared manufacturers; the south-east is doing worse than other regions'.

And yet, pessimism is hardly rampant in Britain; nor should the shift in the slow decline or the return to square one on the political front conceal the fact that there has indeed been an attitudinal transformation, albeit one

TABLE 3.2 *Data relating to the openness of economies, terms of exchange and relative exchange rates (1960–1987, in percentages)*

Degree of openness measured by:-	UK	FRG	USA	France	Italy	Japan
ratio of imports to GDP	22.4 –27.4	16.5 –23.7	4.4 –10.8	12.4 –20.7	13.5. –18.9	10.2 –7.3
ratio of exports to GDP	21.1 –26.4	19.0 –28.7	5.2 –7.4	14.5 –20.8	13.0 –19.6	10.7 –10.5
Terms of exchange in national currency*	–0.1	+0.4	–1.3	–0.4	–0.2	–1.5
Rate of exchange *from*:	£0.357	4.2 DM	–	4.94 FF	624LI	360 yen
to:	–£0.612	–1.8DM	–	–6.01FF	–1296LI	–145 yen

* average annual rate of growth.

SOURCE: OCDE, Historical Statistics, 1960–1987, Paris 1989.

which is perhaps not as *industry-centred* as some people would have us believe.

SOME THOUGHTS ON THE BRITISH REVIVAL

Let us first establish a method of assessment and, in order to do so, take a small detour.

Most economists have in mind an *implicit model* of the performance and dynamism of the great economies of today. Although this is partially hidden from view, it is nevertheless the one factor which allows a given economist to make sense of his or her data and also, at the end of the day, to judge the macro-economic performance of a given nation and thereby to take sides on the economic policies of the government producing such results.

As far as the UK is concerned, one's first impulse is to rely on the models and conclusions of the home-grown economists. These, after all, whether close to government or to the opposition, are best equipped to appreciate the mechanisms at work, the factors inhibiting or unleashing economic activity, are best able to interpret the welter of economic data coming from every direction. Unfortunately, from the perspective of analyses conducted in France of work published in the UK, the picture is disappointing. Such work seems either too journalistic in style or too confined to a particular punctual phase of the period since 1979, too lacking in objectivity or else overly systematic. With respect, it seems that certain British economists are (or have been) too close to the corridors of power to be taken at their word (thus Alan Walters, claiming an 'economic revival' in 1985).[3] In the same way, certain economics institutes have been too close politically to Thatcherism (the Institute of Economic Affairs, founded in 1957 or the No. 10 Downing Street Policy Unit, founded in 1974). Others have failed to produce a panoramic synthesis of the Thatcher years (the Centre for Policy Studies, founded in 1974, or the Adam Smith Institute, founded in 1977). Other economists have above all been fired by critical opposition, to the neglect of constructive counter-proposals (like the 364 economists who, headed by N. Kaldor,[4] published a much discussed letter in *The Times*). Finally, other institutes appear not to have had either the ability or the presence of mind to adopt the necessary critical distance in relation to the long-term growth of the UK economy (neither the minuscule Social Market Foundation nor even, on the left, the Institute of Public Policy Research).

Are we therefore to conclude that there is no valid synthetic reference model for the British economy? Seen from across the Channel, the Liverpool model in particular seems, to put it mildly, at best exotic, at worst a series of exaggerations, claiming more substantial 'wealth effects' than normal, a far too *ad hoc* definition of private supply (which is in any case in contradiction with taxation and public spending policy) and a prices-wages approach which seems to be based on wishful thinking (prices and wages are so flexible that pressure of demand has immediate repercussions on inflation) and, last but not least, the belief that the government can stifle the inflationary activity of the various economic agents.[5]

Clutching at straws, one has to fall back on a makeshift analysis, which is all the more sensitive an operation in that the debates on Thatcher-Joan of Arc are particularly rough and tumble. Such a makeshift approach has to rely on the necessary distance (for want of an appropriate wide-angle lens). As a doctrinal compromise, I would suggest that the dynamism of the good ship Albion, and therefore the quality of those who, aboard her, must underpin capital accumulation, can best be gauged in terms of the respective strength or 'latent heat' of the engines highlighted in three groups of theories:

(i) The theory in which the real growth factors are *demographic, geographic or technological*, in other words, factors outside the economy in the strict sense of the word. This theory extends the boundaries of production potential. With population growth, economies of scale, an improvement in training, better organisation of the productive cycle, good substitutions, and a sensible division of labour (and nothing else), growth is inevitable. The principle can be briefly stated: 'Produce more and better'. This vision will be considered by economists as neo-classical and optimistic: a vision of huge outboard motors and competent pilots. It allows one method of judging whether Mrs Thatcher's United Kingdom has improved its performance.

(ii) The classical theory, essentially British (in fact Ricardian) but also widely adopted in Germany and even in France, stresses the primacy of equitable wealth distribution as a guarantee of growth. 'Give me a country with social peace and you will see that the motivation to produce will be strong and there will be surplus enrichment'. The axiom here is that wage, profit and interest rates are the foundation stones of the social edifice. Without any *a priori* attempt to set such rates by conventional means, the overall structure remains fragile. On the other hand, with good compromises on the wages front or over the division between finance and industry, in short with a good wages policy or a type of workforce management involvement such as exists in Scandinavia or Germany, the market economy runs itself. All that is required is administration: apportionment between present and future and the function of savings become self-correcting. Labour, capital, credit and the state all have a guarantee of performance and a joint interest in growth. How does the Iron Lady stand when judged by this criterion?

(iii) The *Austro-Keynesian theory* (elaborated by Schumpeter and Keynes) which also has a long British pedigree (thanks to the glorious ancestry of Adam Smith) as well as French connections (ever since J. B. Say and Saint Simon, even if they remained in the shadow of Colbert). According to this theory, the dynamism of capital can only wrench itself free from the sclerosis of the stationary state if the 'entrepreneurial party' or the 'industrial party' (employers, scholars, artisans and artists according to St. Simon, innovators in the view of Schaffle and Schumpeter, captains of industry as defined by Veblen or 'animal spirits' as seen by Keynes and Robinson) is free to formulate in the secrecy of the boardroom and to impose upon the whole of society (indeed in the name of society) a wager with the radical uncertainty of the future by investing along new 'flight lines' or 'technological trajectories with all their inherent risks', and by avoiding too much hesitation at the crossroads. With such a theory, one can easily understand the general interest in a policy of high-level training and research and development. It is also clear that credit, banking and the financial markets should serve industry and not vice versa. This is a third type of analysis for gauging the attitudinal revival which could have taken place in Britain and which could have brought the country back onto the razor's edge of unstable progression which characterises truly dynamic economies.

Let us now examine these three visions in turn.

UNCHANGED GROWTH FACTORS BUT A TRANSFORMED ORGANISATION?

According to the neo-classical vision, Britain could produce more over the next decade and arrest her slow decline if she were better able to mobilise her resources, weave her way through the new technological maze and bring about a better organisation of the productive cycle. How has she fared?

(a) As far as *land*, a limiting factor, is concerned, scarcity has increased. Urban and even semi-rural ground rents have increased, especially in the south-east. Land prices have become so high in London that jobs have begun to be relocated away from the capital.

Oil revenues have played the opposite role as a factor of abundance. The UK, like a small oil emirate (albeit with marginally higher production costs), has assumed some of the features of an economy based on surplus finance capital. Yet the relaxation of overall budgetary constraints has produced some astonishing results. On the one hand, the state, as beneficiary of oil revenue taxation, has begun to spend less! On the other hand, the current account balance has gone from bad to worse, particularly with countries like the Federal Republic, Japan and even Italy, France or Holland, the latter having overcome its 'Dutch syndrome' which was linked to a dependence on gas to the neglect of the rest of the economy.

(b) *Demographic trends* are hardly improving. The old-age dependency ratio was higher in 1986 than that of either France or Germany and the youth dependency ratio is lower than that of France. Overall population growth is close to zero. The only factors which continue to help matters are a *female participation rate* in employment which is higher than that of France or Germany, a slightly higher number of annual hours worked, a high level of immigration from the Indian sub-continent bringing with it an industrious, entrepreneurial and ambitious work-force, but which all too often exists in closed circuits in a small number of large towns. The number of graduates in engineering and technology at all levels (craftsmen, technicians, bachelors, masters and doctorates) is still grossly inadequate (142 per 1000 as against 268 in France and 310 in Germany according to the National Institute for Economic and Social Research [NIESR]). The Youth Training Scheme (YTS) produced mediocre results and employers are insufficiently interested in appropriate training.

(c) *Job creation* between 1984 and 1989 and the development of the self-employed have indeed shown evidence of better mobilisation of the productive forces. And yet the overall number of employed people scarcely tops the 1975 figure of 25 million. The fall in unemployment after 1986 was considerable but the true measure of this was obscured by new regulations on entitlement to unemployment benefit. Between 1963 and 1986, according to calculations made in France by J. M. Jeanneney's *Observatoire Français des Conjonctures* (OFCE), the number of employed persons in the UK remained more or less stable.[6] As for industrial jobs, Britain holds the European record for destruction. Even if the dividing-line between industry and services is shifting, the low level of industrial activity is an indicator of a general lack of economic dynamism.

(d) *Consumption of non-residential fixed capital* was fortunately very high in 1984–85 and after 1987. This is a sign of modernisation, even if the growth figures of 1966–79 were never subsequently attained. When combined with a high degree of selectivity of the most talented and effective sections of the labour force, this factor facilitates the incorporation of new technologies and hence the shift to a better trajectory and to an increase in growth. The 'pure productivity effects'[7] stemming from this are a move in the right direction and can be chalked up on the credit side of industry, not only in the oil and gas industries. But results are very uneven depending on both sector and region (with very weak levels in Ulster, for example, in textiles and shipbuilding).[8]

(e) *Direct Japanese and American investment* in the UK has had some measure of responsibility for this 'springtime' of British production (mainly in cars, microchips and consumer electronics). Even if one were to analyse it as Britain's contribution to the construction of a world economic network planned elsewhere by non-Britons, it nevertheless has important dynamic effects at home. In particular, a secondary effect is the spread of new attitudes to work, new potential qualifications for young people and less obsolete plant and production methods.

(f) Despite such progress, the mobilisation of these growth factors has nevertheless proved inadequate. But Thatcherism has created a new game plan in market organisation and competitiveness.

The first aspect of this concerns the *rights to property of the means of production*. The leitmotiv was the rapid extension of the market sphere (which has traditionally known ups and downs over the long-term) at the expense of quasi-markets (where prices do not cover costs) or of non-commercial public services. Thatcherism wanted to be rid of the tentacular state with all its pockets of under-productivity.

The results here are relatively positive. The private sphere has increased, with sales of assets rising from £2 billion in 1985 to £7 billion in 1989. Fifty-four companies have been sold off since 1979, among them world leaders such as Rolls Royce, British Steel, British Airways, British Telecom, the water and electricity companies (but not nuclear energy!). And yet the difficulty remains that these sales have not been accompanied by the expected rise in productivity, nor has the change of ownership substantially altered competitiveness, while shareholders are clearly expecting dividends, which will represent profit unavailable for investment. More extensive accumulation (a bigger market) does not necessarily mean more rapid accumulation. The quicksand of an ossified public sector has certainly been avoided. But it is too early to claim victory for the whole of the economy.

The second aspect concerns *market deregulation and the development of competition*. The Monopolies and Mergers Commission had its work cut out given the initial situation: long-established corporatism in certain sectors, price fixing and so on. The significant move towards mergers and concentrations in 1987–1988 (£37 billion) only made the task more complex. The basic idea remains that of ensuring that the best man wins – so that the best can remain best and growth can rise as fast as possible. But the results of Thatcherism can clearly only be mitigated and provisional, competition, like the rock of Sisyphus, having to be continually renewed.

On the whole, the neo-classical approach to growth suggests that, despite a number of positive factors, the UK has hardly been able to count on the development in sufficiently large numbers of new (reserve) growth factors. Consequently, it is only the transformation and extension of the market, through restructuring and potential productivity gains, which can help to overcome the dead weight which acts as a brake on the revival of growth in the British economy. And even then the return on the new capital in the new sectors will have to be as encouraging as was initially anticipated, which itself suggests that investment will have to take on board more new technology in order to show greater increases in productivity than is currently the case.

ENHANCED 'SOCIAL PEACE', BUT TO WHAT END?

'Social corporatism', it is said in Great Britain, 'is what existed before Mrs Thatcher. It's already been tried. It doesn't work.' Something else has to be tried and in particular greater dynamism brought to the market, without compromising on incomes. Such arguments seem perfectly reasonable but in fact it is difficult to know how far British originality can go in this direction. Can Britain escape the continental, Scandinavian or Japanese models of social economy?

It should not be forgotten that Labour fought long and hard over the closed shop during the Heath government of 1970–74, and won. Labour also won on the issue of an incomes policy (1975–78). This makes the success of Thatcherism all the more remarkable and all the more surprising. Indeed few were more surprised than the Tories themselves. But it remains to be seen whether social peace has really arrived, and what has been made of it. The price paid during the miners strike (1984–85) was exceptionally high. Since then, the unions have been further weakened and other wedges driven into the shaky structure of union practice. *The number of days lost through strikes* seems to have reached an all time low (3 million as opposed to 12 million in the 1970s). The world of labour has been opened up. Yet the government still has much to do. TUC membership dropped from 12.2 million in 1979 to 8.7 million in 1988, but the rate of unionisation is still higher than 40 per cent. The public sector, even in its reduced form, continues to be a hotbed of collective bargaining on salaries. Has this been realised? What adaptation is taking place? A new Employment Bill has been prepared with measures against the closed shop, trade union immunity and unofficial strikes. But it is hard to believe that, in Britain, the labour market will be deregulated. That would constitute a considerable step backwards.

In any case, if social peace has been restored, what use has been made of it? Let's look at *salaries*. The rapid growth in unit wage costs (wages related to productivity) has had no equal anywhere in Europe for many years. The nearest comparison is the former situation in Italy! The price-competitiveness of British products has to cope with the consequences of these wage rises both internally and externally. There appears to have been no solution once the soft option of devaluation was ruled out.[9] *Inflation* has therefore taken off again since 1986, and is well above the average for the EC, almost as if the infernal couple of wages and inflation were a fixture in the UK. Employers seem to give in on wages in a way which might suggest that constraints on their prices were not tough enough. The unions play on comparisons and interregional contagion, having abandoned strikes based on solidarity. The overall impact leads to spirals which are unknown in economies as corporatist as those of Sweden, Austria, Japan or Germany!

Since such wage trends do benefit wage earners, are there any signs of a healthier attitude towards productivity? Unfortunately, increased wage earnings are, in the long-term, wiped out by inflation and the slow decline of the pound. They do not represent a fundamental stimulus to increased performance. At the same time, the massive development of home-ownership has brought in its wake, owing to rising prices between 1985 and 1988 and interest rates far higher than the European average, a crushing burden of mortgage repayments and a much more sceptical view of the prospect of personal prosperity.

Besides, the *rate of household savings* has fallen regularly since 1980 (from 13 per cent to 4 per cent of available income). Consumer credit has risen massively (British households owe, on average, 15 per cent of their available income) as has financial speculation (20 per cent of households hold shares or some other form of investment equity, as against 7 per cent in 1979 and almost 2 million wage earners hold shares in their own company). The net wealth of British households rose steadily from 1981 to 1987, but it was accompanied by a parallel rise in debt and inflation. At the same time, inequality is on the rise, as measured in terms of gross weekly earnings. In 1979, as a percentage of the annual median figure, the figures for the two extremes were 65 and 150. By 1989, they had stretched from 60 to 180. On the whole, the preference for the present is an extremely visible feature of British society: an anti-Victorian and anti-Schumpeterian situation if ever there was one!

Macro-economics can only be made to work because the savings of the private sector are topped up by self-financing on the part of firms operating a cost-plus policy in order to generate the necessary margins. The overall picture is therefore one of weakness compared with Germany or Japan and even the much heralded reversal of public sector borrowing, now in surplus, cannot really compensate.

Managing the 'income-finance-available funds investment' circle has not therefore led to improved performance in terms of inflation and growth. There are many reasons for this. Mrs Thatcher seemed to be unable to vanquish monetary illusions while retaining the sort of degree of confidence which Jacques Delors enjoyed in France in 1983 when he imposed de-indexation. This betokens a strange type of chemistry in social relations in a world where social peace, popularity and re-election in no way suggest that the 'just economy' (as defined by J. Meade) has been achieved and that it is possible, in Britain, simply to get on with producing more and better. The UK is in a better state, but inflation remains a significant symptom of macro-economic disequilibrium.

THE AUSTRO-KEYNESIAN 'ENTREPRENEURIAL PARTY' EXISTS BUT IS TOO RESTRICTED TO FINANCE

It is well known that innovation breaks down routine, and that risk-taking increases the sense of responsibility. The economy of efficient markets, even if this notion is sometimes too readily assimilated to a Hayekian economy of the casino, does stimulate – and concentrate – the mind. Thatcherism, by insisting on all this, did manage, between 1975 and 1985, to revive *certain dynamic principles*, even at the risk of upsetting a sector of the establishment which favoured the classical-Keynesian rules of the game (after the example of Germany).

But the art of Saint Simon or of Veblen has not been properly assimilated. There is much more to it than there is in Hayek. In particular, care should have been taken to protect the true captains of industry, instead of simply engaging in sterile doctrinal squabbles over the role of the state.

To this extent, Mrs Thatcher's onslaught against the civil service ('If one is truly talented one does not go into the civil service, one goes into the private sector') retains echoes of France in 1890 when Paul Leroy-Beaulieu, Professor of Economics at the College of France, said: 'It is better to have fewer, many fewer, and only the best'. The first effect of massive reductions in the number of civil servants was merely to reduce the quality of the public services. Only later did it contribute, marginally, to the spread of Schumpeterian norms. Basic services, education, the quality of water and the environment hardly lend themselves to the brutal laws of the market. Reform and restructuring of the public sector was essential.

But was it conducted in optimal fashion by Thatcher's frontal onslaught? If quangos had their uses, why not deploy them instead of waging open warfare? In short, should 'anti-constructivism' not have been replaced by institutionalism?

By the same token, *the campaign against vested interests*, all dear to Veblen's heart, can be useful from time to time, but it is well known that this rarely leads to greater efficiency and it should not be pushed too far. A. Marshall, long ago, has opened our eyes to the essential generalisation of monopoly elements and their corresponding incomes.

What Saint Simon and Veblen taught us has in fact been missed: *the most important point is the culture which brings together employers, but also scholars, researchers, intellectuals, artisans, artists*. Today, in Great Britain, what of culture? Is there indeed a common culture? How is it deployed in choices about the present and the future, about growth, about freedom and justice? There is no obvious reply to this question. Yet, for many analysts, today's Britain is as uncertain of its route, despite all Mrs Thatcher's efforts, as the continental Europe of bygone days, and is certainly far removed from the aspirations of the former prime minister. The education system has long been a major problem in the UK. Yet the upper reaches of the system used to be considered reasonably effective. Today, however, the most prestigious universities find their students more interested in finance and speculation than in engineering and management. The great attraction of the City clearly plays more than its normal role. Has the 'entrepreneurial party' not gone too far down the road of financial services? Here, the answer needs to be carefully weighted.

Basically, it is quite logical that the UK, like the USA, should show a *preference for the economy of the financial markets* (rather than for a debt-based economy as in France or Germany) and for the professions corresponding to it. Share capitalisation in the UK is 85 per cent of GDP (as opposed to 20 to 25 per cent in France and Germany) and corporate debt as a percentage of equity (characteristic of the situation known as 'banked') is only 15 per cent in the UK as opposed to 23 per cent in France and 30 per cent in West Germany. The Anglo-Saxon model involves much more equity capital and more responsible shareholders than the German model based more on loan-finance and the solid links forged between banks and industrial firms. Lord Keynes brilliantly anticipated the consequences of this drift.

But the British entrepreneurial party nevertheless remains too weak and the nerve centre of the economy and of the market society remains in the City (rather than with the heads of industry). This is not all negative. Here we must give credit where credit is due. The City remains a major cathedral, rejuvenated by the Big Bang and by the financial culture which it has cultivated. All of this is without parallel on the continent. London remains the *biggest share market in the EC* (40 per cent of all share transactions in French companies take place in the City) with some of the biggest actors being the life insurance companies, pension funds and other collective investment vehicles. It is also *the foremost exchange market in the world* with 34 per cent of the global turnover in April 1989 (as against 24 per cent for New York, 21 per cent for Tokyo, 10 per cent for Zurich and 5 per cent for Paris). Finally, it is the *main centre for the issuing of Euro-money*, totalling 75 per cent of all issues. The City remains more than ever a stronghold where the international stock exchange has adapted to international financial mutations (computerisation of transactions, existence of world markets, acceleration of the development of financial bonds and bills).

This makes London a unique centre in Europe and puts it in a good position to engage in American style takeover bids (that is to say with high-risk borrowing techniques). It is also in a good position to concentrate henceforth on financial surpluses rather than industrial turnover, and to prepare itself for the arrival of unrestricted Japanese finance. A *high-productivity post-industrial activity* is firmly in place and is a fine asset in the British game plan. Yet a glance at the international financial press calls for a more measured analysis. Already Japanese finance is more powerful because it can rely on an unrivalled national financial capacity. More and more loans are underwritten by Tokyo even if the UK remains a net creditor. The toughest competition will come with the carving up of positions in world financial structures and it is already beginning with questions about the quality of the services provided, about the future development of the insurance markets and about prospects in low-profit or high-risk geographical areas (Eastern Europe, China, Third World). On these three issues, the British will have a very hard time, despite their in-built historical advantage.

CONCLUSION

Among all the variables we have been discussing (absence of 'growth reserves', insufficiently rapid evolution of productivity, squabbles over distribution, lack of incentives for the appropriate preparation of the future, diversion of too much energy towards the City), the positive elements of Thatcherism seem thin indeed. The home-spun Anglo-Saxon model of market regeneration hardly shines by comparison with the German or Japanese model. In the UK, the financial markets alone have any real uniqueness.

And there remains the most important handicap of Thatcherism: its absence of leadership in the construction of Europe. The philosophy of integration has passed Britain by. It remains to be seen whether her new prime minister, John Major, will mark a change of substance in Britain's relationship with the EC, or merely a change of tone. The EC cannot be a mere zone of free capital flows. By the end of the century, it will have to have a common currency, it will have learned to recognise its financial leaders, its best commercial banks, its main industrial companies, its principal technological programmes. As far as the last two are concerned, Britain is far too noticeable by its absence. The surprise departure of Chancellor Lawson in 1989 seems to have been accompanied by renewed confusion over Europe. Why have the major European choices not been made? The deep-rooted reasons are legion. The main one is undoubtedly mutual lack of confidence. One remedy might be to revive the spirit of Adam Smith who understood the irreplaceable and leading role of the extension of markets.

Shouldn't the continental countries make better use of British talent and vice versa? Who has yet calculated the benefits of a division of labour over a vast geographical area? Are we seriously considering suppressing the opportunity costs of 'non-Europe', as proposed by Pablo Cecchini? The time for mutual concessions is surely approaching and we must accelerate integration in order to ensure that it does not become an unintended victim of the political implosion in the East. Is the UK not, once again, able to offer an Atlantic counterpoise to the already emergent German financial and industrial hegemony? The peripheral regions of Western Europe (Scotland with four regions, Wales with two, Northern Ireland, the south-west of the UK with three regions, Ireland, Lower Normandy, Brittany, the Loire Valley, Poitou-Charentes, Aquitaine, Galicia, Asturia, Cantabria, the Spanish Basque country, Portugal) surely have a card to play together if only because of their relative distance from the main European axes. Why look so resolutely to the past when the economic life of Europe is being recast with new patterns in response to new forms of solidarity? The challenge of the single market is crucial and the UK cannot afford any more than France not to rise to it. A pinch of constructivism and institutionalism would be welcomed.

NOTES

1. The motto of the city of Paris, *Fluctuat nec mergitur*, can be roughly translated as 'Beaten by the waves but not going under'. The emblem of Paris is a sea-going vessel.

2. See S. Dowrick and Duc Thoniguyen 'OCDE Comparative Growth 1950–85: Catch up and Convergence', *The American Economic Review*, 1988.
3. A. A. Walters. *Britain's Economic Renaissance – Margaret Thatcher's Reform 1979–1984* (Oxford: Oxford University Press, 1985).
4. N. Kaldor. *The Economic Consequences of Mrs Thatcher* (London: Duckworth, 1983).
5. See the presentation, utilisation and critique of this approach in the review *Economic Policy*, October 1987, in particular K. Matthews and P. Minford, 'Mrs Thatcher's Economic Policies, 1979–1987' and the discussion of this article by S. Nickel of Oxford University and E. Helpman of Tel Aviv University.
6. *Lettre de l'OFCE*, Paris, no. 56 (1988).
7. See W. H. Buiter and M. H. Miller, 'Changing the Rules: economic consequences of the Thatcher regime', *Brookings Papers on Economic Activity* (1983), and also K. Matthews and P. Minford, *op. cit.*
8. W. L. Hitchens and J. E. Birnie, 'Productivity levels in Northern Ireland Manufacturing Industry: a comparison with Great Britain', *Regional Studies*, no. 23 (1989).
9. See A. Dunnet, 'The Role of the Exchange Rate in the Decline of UK Manufacturing', *Royal Bank of Scotland Review*, March 1989. See also the Cambridge theory on these problems of competitiveness in R. A. Becker, 'International competition, income distribution and economic growth', *Cambridge Journal of Economics* (1989) 3: 395–412.

Part II

Foreign and Defence issues: Beyond NATO . . . to What?

4 France and the Defence of Europe: Redefining Continental Security

Jolyon Howorth

GAULLISM AND THE DEFENCE CONSENSUS IN FRANCE

For over a quarter of a century, France has basked in the tropical sunshine of 'Gaullism'. After the hurricanes and earthquakes of the 1940s, which brought in their wake war, occupation, devastation and humiliation, and the chill winds and hailstorms of the 1950s, which engendered retreat, indignity, fear and insecurity, President de Gaulle swiftly brought about a radically different security climate. The 1960s offered a traumatised nation the twin benefits of national independence and an end to military conflict. Two innovations were sufficient to effect this revolution: the institution of a strong executive presidency, and the development of an independent nuclear deterrent. The very existence of each reinforced the credibility and enhanced the political function of the other. It was a symbiotic relationship in which both were permanent winners. In the maelstrom of post-war history, the major issue for France was the redefinition of her international role. This quest precluded for several decades any structured relationship with her European neighbours

Gaullism, in its defence and security dimensions, embodied three key principles. First, the need for an *independent strategic nuclear arsenal* with which to 'sanctuarise' France's national territory. *Sanctuarisation* was underpinned by a declaratory approach which insisted on the *deterrent* function of nuclear weapons and which vehemently denied the very principle of their use in a battlefield situation (the scenario which was central to NATO's doctrine of 'flexible response'). Second, a strategic discourse signalling the *total independence* of France's military options, while at the same time pledging (in times of crisis) *unspecified conventional support for allies* – particularly in the European theatre – but refusal to take up a permanent front-line position alongside the Allies. Third, the determination to play a *world role*, with major 'out of area' commitments in Africa, the

Indian Ocean, the southern Caribbean and the South Pacific. This overall strategy was codified in the 1972 *Livre Blanc sur la Défense Nationale*, and was popularised in the theory of the 'three concentric circles' formulated by General Lucien Poirier.[1]

In order to bestow even greater force upon this potent combination, de Gaulle also felt the need to link it to a constant discourse and an occasional practice which, on the face of it, challenged the very foundations of the post-war world order. He anathematised the bloc structures and mentalities of the Cold War, inveighed against American hegemony in Western Europe, expelled NATO headquarters and all foreign troops from France, withdrew his country from the integrated command structure of the Alliance, eulogised a largely mythical cultural entity which he perceived as stretching from 'the Atlantic to the Urals', courted Eastern Europe and the Third World, and generally drove home on every occasion the new message that decisions concerning France's relations with the remainder of the world were made in Paris and only in Paris. A lively debate still persists concerning his true intentions, many 'Anglo-Saxon' commentators believing that he seriously intended to destabilise the Atlantic Alliance, while his more sympathetic critics argue that he was merely doing what had to be done to restore France's standing in the world and that, if anything, the Alliance actually benefited in terms of diplomatic openness and strategic diversity.[2] Whatever the truth about his intentions, it is beyond question that his approach depended for its very existence on the historical conditions which prevailed at the time: a period of strategic calm after the Cuban missile crisis, marked by superpower détente and arms control talks; the maintenance of the American nuclear 'umbrella' over Western Europe; the division of Germany and the welding of the Federal Republic to NATO; and the total absence of any coordinated defence and security arrangements among the Western European nations.

Gradually, Gaullism created around it a political consensus embraced by all four of the major parties in France (communists, socialists, liberals and Gaullists), albeit to differing degrees and for different reasons. Under the presidency of Giscard d'Estaing (1974–81), the traditional Atlanticism and Europeanism of the liberals and Christian-democrats might have been expected to lead to a break with Gaullism. To some extent this happened in the field of European integration. On the defence and security front, however, Giscard's predilection for a more overtly integrated European defence system was kept firmly in check by his Gaullist parliamentary allies as well as by the awesome impact of the presidency itself upon the incumbent. By 1974, the fears of both liberals and Atlanticist socialists, originally convinced that de Gaulle would destroy the Atlantic alliance, had disappeared. NATO's Ottawa declaration of that year accepted France's maverick stance as representing a consolidation of the alliance, and thereby lifted a major political burden from the shoulders of former anti-Gaullists. Recent revelations have shown how, behind the declaratory façade of total independence, all French presidents from Pompidou onwards engaged in intense but highly covert cooperation with the White House and the Pentagon on military – and particularly nuclear – planning and coordination.[3] At the same time, within the Socialist Party three separate developments guaranteed a move towards the consensus. The Ottawa declaration assisted the conversion to 'Gaullism' of a presidential aspirant and life-long Atlanticist such as François Mitterrand, as well as of the former 'NATO lobby' under men like Robert Pontillon. Second, the latent Gaullism (based largely in Jacobinism) of factions around Charles Hernu and Jean-Pierre Chevènement was able, ten years after the General's departure, finally to come out of the closet. Third, the small pacifist wing of the party was so traumatised by the totalitarian revelations of Solzhenitsyn that it was prepared to sacrifice its former anti-nuclear protests to the cause of taming the Russian bear. As for the Communist Party, its initial satisfaction at the General's anti-Americanism, reinforced in the 1970s by the prospect of actually coming to office and wielding power . . . over nuclear weapons (not to mention the job-creating potential of the nuclear industry), proved more than sufficient reason for it to drop its former opposition to France's defence programme.[4] Small wonder that the consensus lasted so long.

Yet, over the course of the last ten to fifteen years, the historical conditions outlined above, which had allowed Gaullism to take root, have gradually disappeared. In 1990, France was faced with nothing less than a strategic revolution. This involved on the one hand the collapse of the bloc system in Europe and the erosion of any serious military threat from the Warsaw Pact, and on the other hand major destabilisation in Eastern Europe, significant withdrawal of the American presence from Western Europe, unification of Germany coupled with uncertainty over that nation's future military options, and the intensification of both Western and trans-European efforts to create a new, coordinated security structure. And yet, on the face of it, Gaullism is still alive and well and living in Paris. Commentators still celebrate the survival of the 'consensus' and ponder over the fact that François Mitterrand, once the General's bitterest critic, has assumed his mantle with both relish and success.[5] This chapter will analyse the extent to which, behind the façade of 'Gaullism' under the presidency of François Mitterrand, France has actually moved towards greater integration of her security arrangements with the other nations of the Atlantic Alliance and particularly with those of Europe.

FRANÇOIS MITTERRAND AND THE EVOLUTION OF FRENCH STRATEGY: TOWARDS A NEW CONSENSUS?

The 1980s saw a constant shift in European strategic thinking towards greater international cooperation. France shared and often generated this thinking. The buzz-word was the 'European pillar' of NATO, a structure more talked about than defined or understood. The impulse for this cooperation was initially based on fear, subsequently on hope. In the first half of the decade, the unpredictable style of American leadership, epitomised by incidents such as the 'Euromissiles' crisis, Reagan's 'Evil Empire' speech and also his Strategic Defence Initiative (SDI), revealed to an anxious continent the extent and precariousness of its dependence on Uncle Sam. In the second half, the advent of Mikhail Gorbachev and the achievement of major arms treaties held out the promise of a totally restructured world order; but also reminded Europeans that, unless they got their own act together, they risked being the objects rather than the subjects of that restructuring. Both developments, added to Europe's own growing wealth and self-confidence, stressed the desirability and/or feasibility of greater West European cooperation in defence and security issues.

The driving force behind these shifts was a restored 'Paris-Bonn axis' incarnated by President Mitterrand and Chancellor Kohl. The two leaders had their own separate reasons for wishing to restructure NATO through the creation of a much stronger, more cohesive and autonomous European component. In Mitterrand's case, the hope was to take advantage of the crisis in the alliance both to forge a more autonomous European security structure and to ensure that France would emerge as the nuclear nerve centre behind it. In Kohl's case, the need was paramount both to respond to mass anti-nuclear sentiment in Germany and to engage in constructive dialogue with the Soviet Union. Both objectives were served by exploring possibilities for greater freedom from the NATO strait-jacket. In the first half of the 1980s, both leaders had to tread extremely cautiously. Mitterrand, whose early governments included communist ministers, felt obliged to 'compensate' Washington for this heresy by a number of spectacular gestures of NATO solidarity, including, in May 1983, acceptance of a joint security statement at the Williamsburg economic summit and, in June 1983, the hosting of a NATO council meeting in Paris (the first time this had happened since 1966). But by far the most significant of these gestures was Mitterrand's unequivocal support for the deployment of Cruise and Pershing Two missiles in Europe, which was accompanied by several highly mediatised visits to Washington (courtesy of Concorde) for working breakfasts with Ronald Reagan. The high point of this 'NATO solidarity' was Mitterrand's January 1983 speech to the Bundestag in which he effectively intervened in the German general election campaign on behalf of Chancellor Kohl's CDU (and against his fellow socialists) by urging the Germans to accept deployment of the 'Euromissiles'.[6]

At the time, most commentators on these developments, naturally preoccupied by the fact that the major item on the international agenda was the superpower struggle over the Euromissiles and the parallel resurgence of anti-nuclear protest in Europe and the USA, tended to interpret them in terms of French alignment with NATO. This was a tactical risk which Mitterrand was prepared to assume. In retrospect, it seems clear that even in the early 1980s Mitterrand's real agenda was the gradual creation of the diplomatic and military conditions for the forging of a new *European* security identity. The centrepiece of this emerged as early as October 1982 when the French president proposed to the freshly-elected Helmut Kohl a reactivation of the moribund defence clauses of the 1963 Franco-German treaty, whose principal intention, at least in the mind of its architect, General de Gaulle, had always been to shore up European cooperation within, but also as far as possible independently of, the Atlantic Alliance. Franco-German defence cooperation was to become the veritable shibboleth of the 1980s, marked at every turn by some dramatic new development: establishment of the Franco-German defence commission (1982–83), the creation of the French rapid deployment force (*Force d'Action Rapide* or *FAR*) intended as a political guarantee to Bonn of French solidarity if ever the shooting started (1983); solemn statements on the unity of French and German security interests (1984 and 1985); intensified joint manœuvres (1985); a presidential promise to consult with Bonn before firing a sub-strategic nuclear missile (1986); the highly mediatised joint exercises involving a German brigade and the FAR under a German commander, codenamed 'Saucy Sparrow' (1987); the creation of a joint ministerial defence council (1988); the creation of a Franco-German brigade (1989). So much has been written about the detail of these developments[7] that it is sufficient here to stress three main points about them. The first is that they were predicated upon the continuation of bloc politics and superpower confrontation in Europe and were at least in part designed to help satisfy calls on both sides of the Atlantic for greater West European burden-sharing in general and for a more cooperative French attitude in particular. Second, their impact was more political and diplomatic than military or strategic, more symbolic than concrete. Nevertheless, they opened up a real agenda for discussions on European defence cooperation and clarified the nature of the problems to be resolved. Thirdly moreover, they laid the foundations for more general moves towards a 'European pillar' and created the impetus for the other major development of these years: the reactivation of the Western European Union.

This again was essentially a French initiative. Western European Union, largely because it had been, virtually since its inception, superseded by NATO, meant different things to different nations. To the British and to the Americans, it has always been somewhat suspect, a quirky distraction from the serious security structure which is NATO. To some extent, those suspicions have been shared by the Germans. To the French, however, WEU has always offered a potential alternative to NATO, or at the very least a forum through which might be generated a distinct European voice on defence and security issues. Various French attempts to revive WEU in the past (notably Michel Jobert's 1973 initiative) had foundered on the reef of 'Anglo-Saxon' hostility. It was therefore in order to short-circuit such objections that in 1983 Mitterrand persuaded the Belgian government to join forces with Paris in pressing for the reactivation of WEU. For different reasons, the seven WEU member-states all felt, at that time, that there was mileage in the proposal. The result exceeded all expectations. From a Thirtieth Anniversary meeting in Rome in October 1984 sprung a series of further meetings (Bonn, April 1985; Venice, April 1986; Luxemburg, April 1987) all of which succeeded in reinforcing both the institutional credibility and the political will of WEU. The high point of these developments was the adoption in The Hague, on 27 October 1987, of the Western European Union's *Platform on European Security Interests* which reasserts the 'common destiny' binding together the seven nations (soon to be nine with the entry in 1988 of Spain and Portugal) and states their collective aim 'to develop a more cohesive European defence identity'. The Hague Platform was clearly perceived as the foundation stone for the much heralded European pillar of NATO and promised a concerted European effort in all areas of defence, arms control and the promotion of the CSCE process.[8]

For a brief moment, this reactivation of WEU promised to create a new defence consensus in France. With the exception of the Communist Party, which had by 1987 reduced itself to virtual insignificance, the other major political formations, including their constituent factions, all saw considerable advantages in the reactivation of WEU. There were those who envisaged it simply as the *European pillar of NATO*, and therefore as a re-cementing of the alliance; there were those for whom it offered scope for a *loosening of the alliance* and the assertion of an increasingly autonomous West European security policy; and there were even a few who already saw it as a useful first step towards a *continental security system* which would one day supersede both NATO and the Warsaw Pact. At this stage, these longer-term aspirations remained more or less concealed as politicians, diplomats, academics and security experts all jumped on to the bandwaggon of an intensified West European defence identity. At issue for security elites was the complex question of managing the transition from one consensus to another, from stated independence to intended interdependence without abandoning the former and without a blueprint for the latter. This involved juggling with three sets of interests (French/European/Atlantic) in a three-point time frame (short/medium/long). It implied that the precarious balances which France had developed over a quarter of a century in her relations with herself, her European neighbours and her Atlantic cousins were impossible to sustain in the medium term and probably irrelevant in the long term. Meanwhile, outside the Western European door, the winds of history were whipping up into a tornado.

Before the tornado struck, however, opinion pollsters had a field-day testing the development of the new consensus. Opinion surveys on defence issues are notoriously unreliable, particularly in France where the monopolisation of strategy in the Elysée palace has stultified debate not only among the public but even among elites. However, as the Euromissile crisis unfolded and French people once again came face to face with issues of war and peace, polls began to appear at an astonishing rate. Their most remarkable findings have to do with French perceptions of the need for a common European defence identity. In 1980, when asked whether they would be prepared to fight for their own freedom, 79 per cent of respondents to a *Le Point* poll answered in the affirmative but only half that number (40 per cent) were prepared to fight for the defence of Western Europe. By 1987, a poll in *L'Express* revealed that 74 per cent of respondents felt France should automatically come to the assistance of West Germany if the latter were attacked and 88 per cent were in favour of a common European defence system. The first time the issue of an integrated European defence was raised in a poll was in November 1981 when interviewees were asked by *Le Figaro* to express a preference between different sorts of military alliances. An alliance with the USA (35 per cent) was clear favourite, followed by those in favour of total independence (24 per cent), advocates of a West European defensive system being the least numerous (22 per cent) – with the exception of the 4 per cent of stalwarts who preferred an alliance with the Soviet Union. Two years later, preference for NATO (39 per cent) and total independence (26 per cent) had both increased, at the expense of a West European alliance (21 per cent) and of the remaining rump of 'Muscovites' (2 per cent).

By 1985, this picture had begun to change dramatically. In a *Le Monde* poll about Franco-German relations, when asked which nation they felt the Federal Republic to be closest to, French respondents saw France (41 per cent) as clear favourite, followed by the USA (29 per cent), the German Democratic Republic (22 per cent), Belgium (21 per cent) and the UK (13 per cent). One imagines these findings may well have raised more than one smirk in Bonn. In the same poll, 57 per cent of the French felt that their country should give Germany an *automatic* guarantee of military assistance if attacked, little realising perhaps that the revised Brussels treaty of 1954 involved just such a guarantee, or indeed that Gaullism implicitly ruled out any cast-iron guarantees at all. As many as 40 per cent of the French were prepared to extend their national nuclear 'umbrella' over the territory of the Federal Republic, a proposal which had been supported by only 14 per cent five years previously. This poll came as a revelation to political commentators who detected in it a sea-change in French feelings about their Eastern neighbour. Whereas previously the predominant perceptions had been negative (German traits were essentially un-French: discipline, efficiency, militarism), now the stereotype of the cold Teuton was seen to be fading in favour of a shared European cultural identity based on the Paris-Bonn axis. As many as 59 per cent of respondents felt that German unification was both legitimate and desirable.

This pro-European trend intensified over the following years. In a four-nation poll published in *Libération* in February 1987, alliance preferences were again analysed, but this time the pro-European lobby had shifted from the weakest position (in 1981 and 1983) to the strongest (35 per cent), while only 20 per cent now favoured total independence and only 26 per cent an American alliance. In June 1987, *Le Parisien* revealed that 71 per cent of the French were in favour of the creation of a single European army and 53 per cent even wanted the merging of the French and German armies. These findings were confirmed in a series of polls testing support for a common European government. In December 1987, *Le Figaro* revealed that France with 60 per cent support for such a government was the second most enthusiastic after Italy with 70 per cent. As to the attributions of such a government, France was by far the most supportive of a common security and defence system, a finding which was borne out by a similar poll in *Armées d'Aujourd'hui*, the armed forces monthly glossy, which in August 1989 revealed 60 per cent support in France for such a notion, well ahead of Italy (40 per cent) or Britain and West Germany (35 per cent).

What is one to make of these findings? Even allowing for the fact that the questions asked were often ambiguous (Gaullists could presumably state a preference either for an 'American alliance' or for 'total independence' according to their interpretation of existing reality) and that the percentage of 'don't knows' in France on defence issues is always far higher than in the rest of Europe (often as high as 20 per cent, compared with a European average of about 4 to 5 per cent – an indication of the extent to which genuine debate about these issues in France has been stifled by the presidential *domaine réservé*), there is a very clear shift of opinion away from the precepts of the previous 'Gaullist' consensus and in favour of a new 'European' one. No poll was ambitious – or foolish – enough to attempt to elicit opinion on the details of these new European arrangements and there can be no doubt that, in expressing preference for them, the vast majority of respondents were merely reflecting shifts in security thinking which had recently dominated the media. Nevertheless, whatever the real impetus behind these shifts, they underscore the reality of two parallel developments. The first is a growing dissatisfaction with the strictures – or ambivalences – of Gaullism as commonly understood. The second is a seemingly deep-rooted desire to bring European institutions into line with cultural perceptions and political aspirations. There was no doubt, prior to the collapse of the Berlin Wall at any rate, that French public and elite opinion in the 1980s increasingly saw West European integration as a development which would allow France a key seat in the control room of the emerging superpower. And defence in particular, with France's clear lead in nuclear and space technology, was the main area offering some compensation for West Germany's commanding position in the field of economics and industry. NATO, it had often been said, aimed to keep the Russians out, the Americans in and the Germans down. An integrated West European defence structure would, it was impressionistically believed in Paris, achieve the same objectives through swapping a waning American commitment for a resurgent French involvement. However, just as the new thinking was beginning to generate a new consensus, history went into the fast forward mode.

THE CRUMBLING OF THE IRON CURTAIN AND THE REDISCOVERY OF EASTERN EUROPE

France's post-war security dilemma barely changed between 1947 and the late 1980s. On the one hand, division of Germany and the imposition of bloc discipline in both halves of Europe considerably reduced Paris's margin of manœuvre. Although this eventually gave rise to Gaullism, the General's response remained a purely theoretical construct in the sense that its military implications were never tested. On the other hand, all talk of German unification seemed predicated on neutralisation of

Central Europe and on the 'loss' of that precious buffer zone between the Rhine and the perceived threat which, throughout France's history, had always been missing. De Gaulle's solution of a Europe from the Atlantic to the Urals was an attempt, based on the assumption of lasting détente, to think through the problematics of subsuming a united Germany into a geopolitical structure vast enough to contain it. The Atlantic to the Urals scenario also implied a strong rejection of West European federalism and the promotion of what the General called *l'Europe des patries*.

With the passing of Brezhnevism and the advent of Mikhael Gorbachev, one dimension of this conundrum changed significantly. It became possible to imagine a solution to the German problem which did not involve neutralisation, or indeed the shifting eastward towards the Rhine of the perceived military threat. At the same time, the rapid acceleration of EC integration seemed to have ruled out the Gaullist recipe for Western Europe. Both these developments, however, conjured up the prospect of the re-emergence in Europe of a powerful and even triumphant Germany wielding unparalleled economic, industrial and eventually political clout. François Mitterrand was the first Western leader to give serious attention to this new situation. As early as 1986, confident that developments in the Soviet Union were transforming the overall situation in Europe, he wrote of a growing consciousness on both sides of the Iron Curtain, 'of belonging to the same continent, of expressing the same civilisation'. Russia, he continued, 'is also a great European country. Her feelings, deep down, are the same as ours . . . the peoples of communist Europe, like Russia herself, possess original values of universal significance. What they lack, Western Europe can supply, and vice versa. To work towards this symbiosis will hasten the hour of Europe, the true Europe, the Europe of history and geography'.[9] Thereafter, on numerous occasions, Mitterrand was to develop this theme into a major component of his utterances on foreign policy in general and European policy in particular. His lead was followed by his senior ministers. By the summer of 1989, the notion of welcoming back Prague, Budapest, Warsaw and Berlin into the arms of mother Europe was a constant in French diplomatic speeches. At this stage, prior to the fall of the Wall, the objective was largely declaratory: to send out signals (to a range of different constituencies) indicating that West European integration, while important and desirable in its own right, was by no means the end of the European story, that Germany should not feel it had to choose between East and West, that the Eastern bloc countries should not despair, that the Soviet Union should give renewed thought to the overall situation of its satellites and that the United States should realise – *pace* Fukuyama – that history was not at an end. It seems clear that no real thought had at this stage been given to the problems of implementing these aspirations should history ever create the appropriate conditions for their realisation. When pressed on the subject during the 54th Franco-German summit in Bonn on 3 November 1989 (less than one week before the fall of the Wall), Mitterrand stated unequivocally that German unification was essentially a matter for the German people, that he personally was by no means opposed to it and indeed that he would be astonished if unification did not happen within ten years. At the time, each of those statements was considered highly controversial.

What the fall of the Wall did was to force all politicians to face up not to some distant abstract aspiration, but to an urgent and immediate reality. It is at this level that their true feelings about 'Europe' began to emerge. For six months, there was generalised confusion (some would say panic) in France and I have studied elsewhere the contours of the chaos created in the wake of 9 November 1989.[10] François Mitterrand himself moved into top diplomatic gear, striving in the first instance, as president of the European Council, to ensure that progress towards the implementation of the 1992 single market be safeguarded, if need be by a process of acceleration. At the same time, he neither reneged on nor forgot his vision of transcontinental reconciliation. In his New Year message on 1 January 1990, he launched the idea of a pan-European confederation which would allow Europe to recover 'its history and its geography', by associating 'every state on our continent in a joint and permanent organisation for exchanges, peace and security'. Clearly, the president finds no difficulty in fitting both the federal West European project and the confederal pan-European project onto the same historical agenda. But it was the tension between these two projects which, in 1990, began to lead to a significant polarisation of French political opinion on the subject of Europe.

EUROPEAN SECURITY AND THE FRENCH POLITICAL CLASS: FEDERALISM VERSUS CONFEDERALISM

In June 1990, the Gaullist deputy and former chairman of the parliamentary defence committee, François Fillon, laid down the security options facing France: 'The choice for France is crucial. Either she plays follow-my-leader and adopts the easy route offered by the reinforcement of NATO and community integration, in which case she will lose her status without gaining in security; or she fulfils her mission and takes the initiative of proposing to the Europeans an end to bloc politics, in which case she will preserve her influence in the world and create in Europe the conditions for a just and lasting peace'.[11] This dichotomy between some form of integrated federalism, confined to Western Europe, and an alternative type of loose confederal structure, theoretically able to contain the entire continent, is a very old one in France. For most of the period since the 1960s, it persisted in the debate over the European Economic Community, but had very little security dimension (largely because NATO was a *fait accompli* and de Gaulle's response to it went effectively unchallenged in France). However, within the shifting historical confines of evolving European issues and parameters, the remarkable feature of French responses to Europe has been the consistency with which the different political parties and/or their constituent units have adopted what, for the sake of simplicity, I shall call either a 'federal' or a 'confederal' position.[12]

The line-up on almost all of the great issues of early European construction – Coal and Steel Community, Treaty of Rome, broadening of the community, direct elections to the European parliament – saw the reappearance of the same fissure running down the middle of both left and right. The federalists are to be found massively within the old MRP (Mouvement Républicain Populaire) or the contemporary UDF (Union pour la Démocratie Française), as well as within large sections of the Socialist Party. The confederalists are to be found within the ranks of the Gaullists, the communists and the remaining socialists. Indeed, the pivot of the whole distinction runs down the middle of the Socialist Party. In the parliamentary division on the proposed European Defence Community in 1954, the official Socialist Party position called for a positive vote. In the event, half the socialist deputies defied the leadership and opposed the scheme. On the other hand, ninety-nine communists (out of ninety nine) voted against, as did sixty-seven Gaullists (out of sixty-nine), while eighty MRP (out of eighty-two) voted in favour. The chances are that, were there to be a vote in 1990 on the creation of an integrated European defence structure, the break-down would not be significantly different. But today, the debate is more complex, the issues more far-reaching, the urgency more compelling.

The real crisis for the 'consensus' in France comes over the new architecture of Europe and the new security arrangements which will accompany it. Here the traditional battlelines are already reconstituting themselves. On the one hand, those who believe first and foremost in the reality of the nation state, who have a trans-European vision and who refuse American (or German) hegemony; on the other hand the apostles of transnational integration, federalism and political unity whose overarching concern is for Western Europe. It is easier, because in some ways more clear cut, to begin with the latter.

THE FEDERALISTS

One large contingent of federalists is to be found in the centre parties associated with the UDF. There are exceptions to this. Men like Alain Madelin and François Léotard have, since the events of 1989, made occasional noises in favour of more pan-European solutions, the former out of a extreme belief in liberalism which, on occasion, rubs shoulders with political anarchism and is intensely suspicious of all centralised political institutions, the latter out of a type of conservatism which prioritises the retention of national tradition. But the predominant tone has been set by men like Valéry Giscard d'Estaing, Jean Lecanuet, Jean François-Poncet and the new rising spokesperson for this camp, Alain Lamassoure. To their ranks must be added socialists in the entourage of Jacques Delors, Laurent Fabius and Michel Rocard, as well as more European orientated Gaullists like Jacques Chaban-Delmas or Michel Noir, and especially Jacques Chirac's former defence minister André Giraud whose closest political colleague is probably Raymond Barre. There are significant differences between these various individuals on the details of a federal Europe, particularly where security is concerned. But it is important to realise that, for all of them (with the notable exception of Giraud), the security dimension, while increasingly crucial, is not the starting point for their reflections: that starting point is economic liberalism and the dream of a great federal West European market. It is also important to bear in mind that none of them currently preaches an American style federalism with the lion's share of decision-making going to the centre. Most federalists in the UDF have eagerly adopted the new buzz-word of 'subsidiarity' which argues in favour of central decision-making only when decisions at a lower level would be inappropriate.

Most federalists became extremely anxious as 1989 turned into 1990. They saw the events in the East and the whole problem of German unification as an immense and potentially catastrophic distraction from what had until only the previous day been the imminent business of completion of the internal market and tentative moves towards political union for the Twelve. There were several reasons why the security dimension crept momentarily to the top of the federalists' agenda in the first half of 1990. First, destabilisation in Europe had become acute and called for attention. Second, it was clear that if there were to be any hope of political unity, then there would have to be some serious thinking about foreign and defence policy. As Alain Lamassoure said in the debate on Europe in the French National Assembly on 10 October 1990, 'either we talk about defence in Rome in December [at the intergovernmental conferences], or we may as well not bother getting together'. Third, NATO had to be re-thought in the context of the new German situation and it was equally clear that much of that re-thinking was going on outside of France, with some real risk – anathema to the federalists – of the break-up of NATO, or, equally bad, of the withdrawal from it of a united Germany. The position of the federalists was therefore sketched out in the context of a fairly muted but nevertheless significant international debate about the essential restructuring of NATO. However, unlike on previous occasions of strategic rethinking, the UDF as a body fought shy of generating a fully-fledged policy statement on security issues. They believed, as 1990 turned into 1991, that events were still moving too fast to justify an attempt to lay down a blueprint for the year 2000.

From the early spring of 1990 to the early summer, there were constant suggestions, mainly from London, but also occasionally from Washington, that the time had come for France to reintegrate NATO's command structure. There were even widespread rumours, subsequently denied by George Bush, that Washington had decided, in order to secure such reintegration, to offer the post of Supreme Commander, Allied Forces in Europe (SACEUR) to a French general. The UDF was the most receptive to these ideas. They believed that, in order to avoid disintegration of the Atlantic Alliance and therefore of Western European cohesion, and also in order to avoid crystallisation of some amorphous pan-European movement, it was essential for France to reintegrate an alliance command structure of some type. In the interests of political cooperation with the Gaullists, the UDF advocated reintegration of a *reorganised* NATO, in which the European component would carry greater weight. Overall command, it was proposed, would rotate between France, Britain and Germany. It was widely felt within the UDF that new European security structures would be established before the end of the year and that it was therefore urgent for France to act rapidly. In this view, the threat from the East had not diminished but simply changed its nature. Gorbachev's siren song about a 'common European home', the massive material requirements of the Eastern countries, and the problem of geo-political destabilisation called for the re-assertion of some *West European bloc* which would be sufficiently strong to put these Eastern distractions firmly to one side until some other solution could be found for them.

This proposal for a transformed, but consolidated and revitalised NATO in which France would play a full, integrated military part was close to, although by no means necessarily identical with, positions being adopted both within the Socialist Party and in sections of the Gaullist RPR. The closest affinity with the UDF was to be found among certain socialists.

Men like Jean-Michel Boucheron, president of the parliamentary defence commission and a close adviser to Laurent Fabius, and Gérard Fuchs, MEP, Socialist Party spokesman on European and security issues and close to Michel Rocard, were saying very similar things throughout much of 1990. The emphasis was always on *West* European integration, on the reorganisation of NATO, on breaking away from 'dogma' (code for Gaullism), on the creation of a European command structure and on the key role which France would have to play within it. This approach was also implicit in the motions for the Socialist Party congress at Rennes in March 1990 put down by the three main tendencies: Mauroy/Jospin, Rocard and Fabius. The most elaborate document available by the end of 1990 was a revised (July 1990) paper which Gérard Fuchs had originally presented to the socialist parties of the Atlantic Alliance in January. This paper was predicated on specific assumptions concerning superpower agreements on conventional, short-range nuclear and strategic nuclear weapons systems. Assuming such agreements were forthcoming, Fuchs anticipated the creation of a genuine European structure of the alliance, with full membership for both France and Spain as well as a European commander of fully integrated multinational forces (which would probably continue to include American troops, especially if short-range nuclear systems had either been eliminated or reduced to minimal levels re-designated as 'pre-strategic').[13] Those socialists who associate themselves with this position are distinguishable from the UDF both in their more relaxed attitude towards Euro-American coupling and in their profession of *eventual* faith in the trans-European confederation – but only once the existing community has been established on unshakeable foundations, consecrated by majority voting on all key issues.

Also close on strategic issues to the federal position, but at least one stage removed from it, is the terrain seemingly being occupied by leading Gaullists such as Edouard Balladur. Although Balladur is basically a liberal, he is not a federalist. His thinking on the overall architecture of Europe is informed by a latent fascination with the prospect of opening up new spaces of freedom in the East, and with the economic and commercial possibilities this raises. But as far as the strategic/security dimension is concerned, his fear of general destabilisation is so great as to turn him into an objective ally of those wishing to reorganise NATO. In a series of articles during the winter of 1989–90, Balladur insisted on the need to ensure that Germany remain within NATO, arguing that, if she did not, then France would have to reintegrate the alliance in order to prevent it from disintegrating. Recent events, he felt, had called for a significant restructuring of NATO, hopefully involving a reunified Germany, but in any case necessitating much greater integration on the part of the main European allies, especially France, Great Britain and the USA. For him, the survival of NATO was paramount.

For a while, it seemed as if Jacques Chirac was going to side with Balladur. In the first half of 1990, he spoke on two occasions in favour of a reorganised NATO with multinational forces and an integrated European command, involving a European defence council made up of the heads of state or government of the alliance countries and of the attribution to the alliance of certain British and French short range nuclear forces. As a sop to the traditional Gaullists, he argued that only France and the USA could take a clear lead in this 'restructured alliance of tomorrow', but there was no mistaking the main strand of his thinking: it was hardly distinguishable from that of the Giscardians and of the 'Atlantic' socialists, particularly in his categorical rejection of any pan-European or confederal security structure, which he denounced as a 'dream' involving immense danger for Europe as a whole. This rejection was all the more significant in that the confederal approach was maturing most steadily and in most elaborate form within the ranks of the RPR (Rassemblement pour la République) itself.

THE CONFEDERALS

The counter-attack was not slow in coming. In June 1990, to launch their new group (Pour un Nouveau Rassemblement), Charles Pasqua and Philippe Séguin asked their defence spokesman, François Fillon, to present their position on European security. Fillon, formerly a Chirac adviser, from 1986 to 1988 the president of the parliamentary defence commission, and without any doubt the most innovative strategic thinker in the RPR, presented by far the most complete, elaborate and detailed analysis of the new situation in Europe to have appeared in France since the fall of the Berlin Wall.

He did not mince his words. For him, the options for France were stark: 'two clear, distinct and irreconcilable conceptions confront one another' – an integrated federal West European bloc or a revival of 'the Europe of nations . . . from the Atlantic to the Urals'. France, he argued, must help forge a new trans-European security structure which would put an end once and for all to the bloc system and enable the Soviet Union to re-engage with the community of nations. To envisage a unified Germany as an integral part of NATO was, he argued, to risk a military coup in the Soviet Union and to put back perhaps for ever the prospect of finding a genuine trans-European settlement. Such a course, he felt, 'would be accompanied by a "Europeanisation" of NATO which would continue to function in an integrated mode'. And in a thinly-veiled reference to Chirac and Balladur he had this to say: 'France's participation in replastering the Alliance, which is presented by some people as a means of forging a new balance within the Atlantic bloc, apart from going in the opposite direction to history itself, would lead at the end of the day to the abandonment both of our world role and of our status as a nuclear power.'

It would, he insisted, be the supreme historic irony for France to contribute to the propping up of the bloc system she had always denounced, precisely at the moment when it was collapsing anyway. The West, he warned, must resist the temptation to see in the events of 1989 a 'victory' and must not lose sight of the chance they offered finally to construct de Gaulle's Europe from the Atlantic to the Urals. Such a structure, he went on, could begin with a CFE (conventional forces in Europe) agreement rendering the prospect of conventional war on the continent almost unthinkable. Thereafter, the CSCE would become the cadre for the institutionalisation of pan-European security arrangements which would do away with the division and the partitioning of the continent. The difference between this view and that expressed by Chirac only two weeks earlier could hardly have been more complete.

The choice between these two 'irreconcilable' visions of a security structure for Europe Fillon saw as absolutely crucial. His concern to avoid the reconstitution of NATO, to prevent the development of a West European federation, his desire to create a pan-European security structure, to allow for the flowering of 'a Europe of nations' and his concern to dismantle the blocs and to bring Russia back into the world community echoed very closely sentiments which had been expressed by a number of socialists in the entourage of the then defence minister, Jean-Pierre Chevènement. Indeed, Chevènement was so impressed with Fillon's paper that he circulated it among his own political followers. The ideas expressed in it were also close in some respects to some of the ideas recently expressed – albeit for different reasons – by the Communist Party.

Nowhere in the publications of the former Minister of Defence or of his faction within the PS (currently called *Socialisme et République* – formerly CERES, Centre d'Etudes, de Recherches et d'Education Socialistes) are these ideas worked out as fully or as coherently as in the Fillon text. Yet dozens of speeches and articles by Chevènement, Didier Motchane, Max Gallo, Jean Gatel and others reiterate the same themes with a consistency which is striking. Virtually nothing in the Fillon text would, I feel, be unacceptable to *Socialisme et République*. This is not to say that the two projects are identical – far from it. The finality of Chevènement's vision is a *social democratic* Europe, whereas that of Fillon is clearly a *liberal capitalist* Europe. But the structural and above all the security arrangements which the two groups see as underpinning the future of the continent are difficult to distinguish from each other. Both dismiss utterly the concept of a narrow federation of the Twelve, both reject transnationalism in favour of 'a Europe of nations', both strive to reconstitute the entire continent, as Mitterrand put it, 'in its history and its geography', both wish to avoid a consolidation of NATO and especially the reintegration of France into any transnational command structure.

The fact that *Socialisme et République* had not at the time of writing (December 1990) produced a blueprint for the institutional framework of the Europe of the future is closely connected with the fact that Chevènement was still defence minister. As such, there was a clear limit to what he could actually say about developments in NATO, especially if they happened to clash with what the President felt. Nowhere in the writings of those belonging to *Socialisme et République*, for instance, is there the *denunciation* of a revamped NATO which one finds in Fillon. But this is simply a question of what you choose to spell out and what you elect to conceal. Both Fillon and Chevènement are in favour of the retention of the Alliance during the period of transition. Both say so. Both are also in favour of transcending NATO. For the moment, only Fillon says so publicly. But in private, many socialists – from both federal and confederal camps – are prepared to say that their vision of a European security structure would be as independent as possible of the United States and would in any case transcend NATO altogether. The die is therefore cast. The identity of the new Europe is fast becoming the crucial fracture line within French politics, one which threatens a radical recasting of the political forces.

Towards the end of 1990, the first major signs of crisis began to emerge. The coalition of opposition parties which had attempted to put together a joint electoral platform under the name of *Union du Peuple Français* collapsed under the strain of the presidential rivalry still opposing Giscard d'Estaing and Chirac. The latent furore in France over the precise function of the French contingent in the Gulf had reopened deep wounds relating to France's independence *vis-à-vis* the United States. This had helped tip the balance within the RPR in favour of the Pasqua-Séguin-Fillon line. After a number of critical and violently animated meetings of the party's national council, the Gaullists adopted, in early December 1990 a text in support of the pan-European confederation and calling for a halt to any further deepening of community integration. The fact that Mrs Thatcher was by that time no longer on the scene to do their 'anti-European' lobbying for them was also a factor in pushing the Gaullists clearly into the 'confederal' camp. Where this will lead, only the next few years will tell, but as Europe embarked on its intergovernmental conferences on economic and political union, the French political class was as split as it has ever been. As Rainer Riemenschneider notes (see Chapter 7), there are indeed two souls to Marianne.

What is the explanation for this deep and lasting division on Europe within the French political class? There are many sides to the problem, but two elements of explanation are paramount. First, at a sociological level, there are three constituencies which feel deeply threatened by a federal Europe: farmers, small shopkeepers and smokestack industrial workers. These just happen to rely for the defence of their interests on the three political parties in France which are the most profoundly anti-European: respectively, the RPR, the FN (Front National) and the PCF (Parti Communiste Français). At the same time, there is no doubt that a second explanation lies in the different starting points of the two sides. For the federalists, the alpha and omega is in fact economics, for the confederals, it is politics; for the former, the creation of a free and largely self-regulating market, for the latter control over national destiny. Where security is concerned, there is now very little margin of manœuvre which would allow for reconciliation of these two approaches. The key, for the moment, lies in the Elysée Palace, where, as we have seen, François Mitterrand believes, as an Atlanticist and a liberal, in the federal project and, as a European and a statesman, in the confederal project.

So what of Mitterrand in all this? The president, as usual, is the most sphinx-like of all the political actors in this particular game. In a sense, he has emerged as the architect both of a federal Western Europe and of a confederal continent. It was he more than anybody who, as president of the European Council in the second half of 1989, accelerated the pace of Western integration. It was he who suggested to Helmut Kohl that the two men put forward a joint proposal on political union for the Twelve in April 1990, which they intensified in November 1990. And it was he, finally, who, in a number of interviews in June 1990, referred to the destiny of the community as being '*à finalité fédérale*' – a comment which was no doubt in part intended to throw the opposition parties into confusion, which it easily succeeded in doing. It was also intended to ensure that the new Germany be subjected to some degree of control from her neighbours and community partners. And yet it was the same Mitterrand who, as early as 1985, called for the solution to the continent's problems to be transcontinental, the reconciliation of history and geography. It was he who, in his New Year message of 1 January 1990, called for the creation of the European Confederation which so many in Eastern Europe have clutched at rather like drowning men to straws. It was also he who, in his meeting with Gorbachev in Kiev in December 1989, proposed the convening of the new CSCE conference which met in Paris at the end of 1990. Where almost all political actors in France see little but contradiction between these two projects, Mitterrand appears to see complementarity. The key, in my view, is his belief that the only way the old continent is going to wrench itself free of American hegemony is through a rapid move towards political unity of the Twelve, this being the most productive development to help foster, in stability, but at a later stage, the transcontinental confederal project. As Europe entered the most ambitious and exciting decade of its history, the French president stood as one of its most discerning and influential architects. The divided and polarised state of the remaining political forces – reflecting the deep and lasting divisions within French culture on this most delicate of issues – bestowed upon the president an extra capacity for control and influence of which he will not hesitate to avail himself in the years ahead.

NOTES

1. For the text of the *Livre Blanc*, see Dominique David, *La Politique de Défense de la France: Textes et Documents* (Paris: FEDN, 1989), pp. 45–63. The three concentric circles are France, Europe and the World. On this, see Lucien Poirier, *Des Stratégies nucléaires* (Paris: Hachette, 1977) and *Essais de stratégie théorique* (Paris: FEDN, 1983).
2. The best expression of this view is in Raymond Aron, *Mémoires* (Paris: Julliard, 1983) Volume II, Chapter XVI, 'Le grand dessein du Général'.
3. Richard H. Ullman, 'The Covert French Connection', *Foreign Policy*, no. 75 (Summer 1989).
4. On these conversions see Jolyon Howorth, *France: the Politics of Peace* (London: Merlin, 1984).
5. See, for instance, the paper read to the centenary colloquium *De Gaulle en son siècle*, held at UNESCO in November 1990, by Professor Jean-Paul Cointet, Ambassador François Puaux and General François Valentin, 'Les suites de l'action du général de Gaulle en matière de politique de défense depuis 1969'.
6. Mitterrand's speech in François Mitterrand, *Réflexions sur la politique extérieure de la France* (Paris: Fayard, 1986), pp. 183–208.
7. See in particular Karl Kaiser and Pierre Lellouche (eds), *Le Couple franco-allemand et la défense de l'Europe* (Paris: IFRI, 1986).
8. See on this, Western European Union, *The Reactivation of WEU: Statements and Communiques 1984 to 1987* (London: WEU, 1988).
9. François Mitterrand, *Réflexions*, op. cit., pp. 70–1.
10. Jolyon Howorth, 'France since the Berlin Wall: Diplomacy and Defence', *The World Today*, July 1990, pp. 126–31.

11. François Fillon, *Sécurité européenne et défense nationale* (Paris: RPR, 1990), p. 30.
12. These labels as such would almost certainly be rejected by most of those to whom I am here about to apply them. They have come to acquire clearer meaning in the course of 1990, but throughout the period under consideration, can be taken as rough code words for, on the one hand, a constructive approach to the EC, including a willingness to promote political integration and an acceptance of sovereignty transfer; and, on the other hand, a suspicion of all things emanating from Brussels, a staunch defence of the nation state and a refusal to countenance any transfer of sovereignty. At a security level, these positions have had less focus, but the essential dichotomy is between interdependence and independence.
13. Gérard Fuchs, 'Quel système de Sécurité et de Défense pour l'Europe de l'Ouest?', PS working paper. I am grateful to Gérard Fuchs for giving me a copy of this paper and for accepting to be interviewed at length about its contents.

5 German Foreign and Security Policy and the European Regional System in the 1990s

André Brigot

One year after the events which transformed the political map of Europe, there is no doubt that their main beneficiary has been Germany. Almost overnight, as if by magic, the German nation was able to reconstitute a unity which even the most optimistic of its advocates had seen as at best a very long-term project. What will be the future of the new Germany's foreign and security policy and what will be the consequences for the rest of Europe?

The foreign policy objectives of the Federal Republic have traditionally been analysed in the following discrete order:

- *Deutschlandpolitik* (German policy *strictu sensu*);
- Security and defence policy guaranteed by membership of the Atlantic Alliance and of the integrated command structure of NATO;
- European policy conducted from the outset in a special relationship with France.

In actual fact, where Germany is concerned, this separation is deeply rooted in an age-old dilemma: can German needs best be satisfied through autonomous policies based on German resources; or through alliances? How can one gauge the consequences of recent events for the answer to this dilemma? How can one measure their impact on the European project and particularly on the organisation of security structures across the continent? And finally, what margin of manœuvre is available to a power which is once again asserting its coming-of-age at the very heart of Europe?

THE GENERAL SITUATION OF GERMAN FOREIGN POLICY

The gateway to sovereignty

However one apportions the responsibility for the opening of the Brandenburg Gate on 9 November 1989 – as between conscious strategy and reactive tactics – the significance of the event itself cannot be overestimated. The date has a very special symbolism in the twentieth century: 9 November 1918 saw the abdication of Kaiser Wilhelm and the proclamation of the Weimar Republic; 9 November 1923 was the date of Hitler's failed putsch in Munich; 9 November 1938 was 'Crystal Night'. In the light of 9 November 1989, the first question to be asked is whether the superpowers which emerged from World War II are any longer able or willing to influence and give direction to the future of European relations? Either the opening of the wall was in large part independent of any conscious political volition, in which case superpower potential for influencing the evolution of the political situation in Europe and in particular in Germany would appear to have weakened if not collapsed. Or the opening of the wall was the result of a conscious decision, by one or other (or both) of the superpowers, in which case its consequence is effectively to restore Germany to the position it lost in 1914 – which immediately poses another set of questions. Why this sudden and unilateral step? Officially, the Western allies of the Federal Republic shared the objective of German unity, although in very different ways and to different degrees. The only unequivocal support came from the United States – and there can be no doubt that the divergent approaches to this question will have an effect on the future internal relations of the alliance countries. The Soviet Union on the other hand had traditionally been opposed to unity if it was to mean the triumph of the West. Yet suddenly this was allowed to happen and Moscow thereby appeared as its principal architect.[1] What pay-off is the USSR anticipating and in what form might the debt be honoured? Finally, to the extent to which the suddenness of these events has forced everybody retrospectively to reposition themselves, what is the current 'state of forces' revealed by the crisis? Although there are no easy answers, these are the questions which have to be asked.

The two superpowers neither foresaw everything, nor did they just let it all happen. The question of their capacity to influence events in Europe is far from academic. For forty-five years, the overall situation in central Europe and above all the foreign policy of the Federal Republic was constrained, indeed totally determined by the respective wills of the superpowers. Whether they (or rather one of them) consciously unleashed the process, or whether they were forced to make the most of an autonomous development, at one level the effect is the same. A certain number of actors, above all in united Germany, find themselves blessed with far greater freedom of action and with the capacity to carve out their own identity. The withdrawal of foreign military forces, which previously ensured a form of protection now seen as dispensable, has unfrozen oppositional and confrontational forces charged with enormous potential. The dilution of the Soviet threat is clearly a problem for an alliance which has lost its main adversary. It is perhaps an even greater problem for the United States which now emerges – witness the Gulf – as the only superpower, but with no further justification for retaining troops in Europe. These changes affect all the European nations, including the USSR. All now have to reorganise the necessary balance of forces.

For the Federal Republic, the reappropriation of sovereignty synchronised with the end of a slow process which had progressively removed the constraints on its foreign policy. The Paris agreements of 5 May 1955 restored Germany's external sovereignty, but the Western allies retained certain rights concerning Germany as a whole (Berlin, reunification, external frontiers and the peace treaty). At the same time, the constant pressure exerted by the USSR on the FRG forced the latter to play ball with the East while clamouring for the support of the West. Given that for forty-five years the main parameters of German foreign policy were externally imposed, the need for alliances, or at the least agreements, is self-evident. Although in the 1950s the SPD (Social Democratic Party) was prepared to go along with the Soviet desire for a neutral and demilitarised Germany, while Chancellor Adenauer and the Christian-democrats (CDU) fought for an alliance with the West involving remilitarisation and continued division, in practice the degree of real autonomy in either of these approaches was very limited. Yet 1989 has now made Germany an actor which is as sovereign as any other in Europe, while doing so in circumstances where the nation also enjoys the only form of power which really seems functional today: economic power. It is this factor above all others which makes predictions about the future direction of German foreign policy so difficult.

In the press conference covering his trip to the Soviet Union on 17 July 1990, Chancellor Kohl stressed that 'the achievement of German unity marks the end of the rights and responsibilities of the four powers both in respect to Germany as a whole and in respect to Berlin. On the occasion of unification, Germany will enter into complete and unlimited sovereignty'. Despite this bold assertion, the full effects of this new situation are yet to be felt, if only because numerous traces of the previous situation remain for the time being. The status of Soviet and allied troops has yet to be resolved. The recognition of the Oder-Neisse line as the definitive eastern border reflected the necessity of taking fully into account the diverse consequences, for Germany's neighbours, of the new order. The financial commitments made to several international actors could prove exceptionally heavy, even for the German economy. After the concessions made to Germany by the Soviet Union, some financial and economic reward became urgent and failure to deliver might have proved dangerous. Moreover, the overall regional environment of central Europe has become uncertain owing to the relative inexperience of several of Germany's neighbours in the field of foreign affairs. Finally, the exercise of Germany's new strength will require a stable world environment because the first victims of any type of tension are the economic and exchange mechanisms. However, once all these elements have been settled and/or stabilised, the full force of German unity-in-sovereignty will be able to make itself felt. Only then will the future become clear.

Is German foreign policy predictable?

Two sets of references are available for crystal-ball gazers. The first involves a reminder of the main lines of German foreign policy before the end of the World War II and partition. This assumes that division was a transitional situation and that the keys to the future can be foreseen in pre-1945 German history. The second, on the contrary, stresses the consequences of the last forty years and seeks in the policies pursued during those years the clues to Germany's future behaviour. This dichotomy of course conjurs up a traditional problem in German politics: the continuity of the German state. What links can be made between the Third Reich and the Federal Republic; between the Third Reich and the Democratic Republic; or between the Third Reich and the Germany which came into being on 3 October 1990? In this respect, it is clearly the Federal Republic, having most fully assumed the political heritage and memory, which has simply 'inherited' territory. But it remains to be seen whether, once the scars of the past have disappeared, the complex concerns of historical continuity will remain, and in what form.

Naturally, the analysts who show the greatest concern (such as Minc, Valence, Dreyfus) attach greatest importance to the most distant period, roughly from Bismarck's unity to the Third Reich. They see the main features as being: the desire for national unity and concern for German minorities; the assertion of economic power and the quest for possible outlets; and a very open-ended approach to alliances which is helped by Germany's position in Europe. Some might argue that this approach amounts to a confusion of different political stances and especially of causes and effects. As the historian K. J. Muller recalls, there have been three constants in German foreign policy since Bismarck: the geographical constant of Germany at the heart of Europe; the demographic constant of eighty million human beings with strong minorities just over the borders; and the economic constant of a lack of raw materials and a corresponding dependence on exports.[2] These characteristics offer Germany the possibility of a 'semi-hegemony' which can exist in two models: either an autonomous great power model, free from external constraint, or alliance with some other power. This choice must now be made once again, this time in a state of full sovereignty.

Those who prefer to base their predictions on German foreign policy since 1945 (experts like Rovan and Grosser) tend to stress five points. Bonn's diplomacy was never autonomous but strove to express German interests from inside multilateral organisations such as NATO or the EC. It always tried to be predictable. Despite the human ties with the East, the FRG remained firmly wedded to the West. Economic ties with the West have been and remain out of all proportion to economic or investment links with the East. One of Germany's major concerns has been to avoid involvement in world affairs and certainly military involvement outside her frontiers. This concern seems to be shared by political leaders and the general population, both of whom are reluctant to be dragged into international conflicts.

Furthermore, these analysts note that German foreign policy, while pursuing its own aims, objectives and interests, has often (at least since 1945) sought external models for its political behaviour and diplomatic action. For example, Bonn embraced Washington's cold war crusade perhaps more firmly than any other ally and consequently remained opposed to détente for much longer than other NATO countries (the Hallstein doctrine tended to paralyse German diplomacy). And yet, after conversion to *Ostpolitik*, which was of course originally developed in Washington and Paris, the new approach was pursued with unparalleled consistency. This relative quest for an external form of leadership also reflected the limits of internal sovereignty. Even today, Germany constantly denies trying to pursue a *Sonderweg* or special path. But is there, in 1991, a dominant 'external' approach to foreign policy which might take Germany along with it? Here again, the return of sovereignty, added to economic muscle and the parallel decline of the great powers, changes the rules of the game and makes predictions hazardous.

Nevertheless, when faced with these two sets of alternatives, and without trying to estimate the potential permanence of the first approach or the reality (in terms of democratic progress and integration) of the second, there are three features of today's world which are likely to be of influence.

The first concerns the permanence of German attitudes in a rapidly changing situation. The unification process revealed an astonishing loss of memory in relation to the categoric assertions which had recently been made about the German nation. From a majority view which considered that German unity was not a tangible aim, at least not immediately, there was a shift, within a matter of weeks, to a consensus position which saw unity as a constitutional requirement which needed to be satisfied as soon as possible and which was in the first instance a purely German affair. This development would not in itself have surprised French observers (by no means strangers to a highly unitary concept of the nation) had it not been for the fact that, for decades, the French had been accused by their German interlocutors of judging Germany through Jacobin eyes. One is forced to conclude that the official line on the predictability of German foreign policy in fact conceals a strong tendency towards change. Or rather, since Germany has not yet discovered, and above all not experienced for any reasonable length of time, what one might call a definitive political framework, variations and U-turns seem almost inevitable.

The second point concerns the reassuring statements to the effect that the move from a state of sixty million to one of eighty million people will be of no consequence – that it amounts to no more than adding the equivalent of a *Land* like Hesse. These statements inevitably give rise to scepticism and incredulity. The acceptance of a general low profile approach, which can be explained by the heritage of the war, has in fact led to a mixture of under-estimation and dissimulation of German national objectives and interests, interests which, when necessary, are firmly and legitimately defended. Moreover, these emollient reassurances take no account of the long-term consequences of the integration into German political life and particularly into foreign policy, of the sensitivities represented by the population of the former GDR. While it would be over-simplistic to imagine that what will happen will be the superimposition of a 'Prussian mentality' on foreign policy, nevertheless, opinion polls and election results show that the Eastern populations seem willing to abandon themselves totally to market forces, revealing a strong overall conservative thrust and a relative ignorance of the workings of European integration.

Thirdly, given that Germany today has less need than previously to pursue the roundabout route of alliances in order to identify and defend her interests, the response to the old question about the way she will choose to insert herself into the network of foreign relations depends as much on the attitude of her partners as it does on the definition of her own interests.

SECURITY POLICY

In the case of contemporary Germany, it is perhaps more essential than in the case of other countries to stress the distinction between security and defence. Defence is only one part of security, which also embraces disarmament and a range of general political problems covering economics, ecology, human rights and the defence of democracy.

The legacy of NATO

At the defence level, the last forty years have witnessed an unshakeable attachment to NATO with the Federal Republic providing the lion's share of the conventional ground force contribution to the Alliance's integrated command. The FRG's geographical position made it from the outset an indispensable element in any military organisation facing up to the threat from the East. Under the Christian democrat Chancellor Adenauer (and in the teeth of opposition from the social democrats who opposed remilitarisation) the Federal Republic, which was both the principal stake in and the main potential victim of any confrontation, agreed to become the cornerstone of the Alliance's continental defences. But, in accordance with a classic device of German foreign policy, the Chancellor, in exchange for his efforts to sell rearmament and NATO integration to the German electorate, obtained recognition of Germany's status as a military ally – the first step on the long road to sovereignty. The FRG also obtained a certain military security to which she contributed less in terms of percentage of GDP than countries like France and Great Britain. The 1960s and 1970s saw relative calm and stability.

The 1980s were marked by the debate over the so-called Euromissiles. This set the Christian democrats, who supported the 'twin-track' NATO policy of deploying Pershing 2 missiles and simultaneously opening disarmament talks, against the vast movement of opinion which rejected any new deployments on German territory (rightly perceived as the most militarised in the world). This debate concerned ways and means of attaining an objective which public opinion saw as primordial: the preservation of peace and security in a territory whose population was paralysed by its own cultural representations of war or even of military conflict. Every state justifies its military expenditure by the need for security, and all states deny any aggressive intentions. But in Germany's case, the problem goes deeper than this: the refusal of war and a certain disdain for military power are part and parcel of the legacy of the first half of the twentieth century. In Germany the quest for security is as compelling as it is complex. It is a blend of the most powerful experiences and memories of destruction – not just physical destruction, but also social, economic and moral. The concrete experiences of the older generations, who are understandably nervous about the risk of prejudicing their regained peace and prosperity, are superimposed upon the yearning for peace of the succeeding generations, who have been educated, at least in West Germany, to criticise and reject war and militarism. This mix of bequeathed guilt and prized economic prosperity has always made the acceptance of defence constraints a sensitive issue. Nevertheless those constraints were, until recently, legitimised by the reality of the threat and concretised by national division. The dismantling of confrontation has thrown everything out of kilter, including the psychological and social dimensions. The disarmament process undertaken between the Western powers and a Warsaw Pact effectively reduced to a disintegrating Soviet Union has radically changed perceptions in the Federal Republic.

In military terms, the 'front' has shifted from the centre of Germany to a point more than six hundred kilometres to the East, turning Poland, in effect, into that dreaded 'buffer zone' which Germany herself recently constituted. Of course, the 380 000 Soviet troops will be progressively withdrawn over a four year period. But confidence-building measures and reductions in force levels have considerably diminished the prospect of a surprise attack. Although the '2 + 4' treaty signed on 12 September 1990 in Moscow[3] allows for united German troops to be stationed on the territory of the former GDR once Soviet troops have left, it also stipulates that no foreign troops, no nuclear weapons or their delivery systems (including dual capability systems) can be stationed on that territory. A further clause prohibits any NATO manœuvres on the territory of the former GDR without the consent of the German government. This stipulation, which Great Britain had resisted, is indicative of the new clout wielded by Germany. By asserting full sovereignty over all her territory, she has signalled not only her right to belong to (and presumably potentially to withdraw from) an alliance, but also the means whereby she intends to organise her territorial defence.

The pursuit of the disarmament process on the other hand allows for force reductions in the *Bundeswehr* and thus offers a solution for the political and military problems otherwise brewing as a result of the forthcoming demographic downturn. Above all, therefore, what is at issue is the cashing in of the 'peace dividend' at the same time as guarantees are provided for just sufficient security to ensure that any future tension should not jeopardise the most urgent task of all: the completion of German unity. There is consequently no need today to call into question the structures and mechanisms (including those of NATO) which have served so well in the past. At the same time, nobody has failed to notice that those structures and mechanisms themselves have far less credibility than was formerly the case.

What use are NATO's nuclear systems?
In the context of NATO's military strategy, nuclear weapons constituted a major element in the doctrine of 'flexible response'. On this point, the FRG found itself split between two contradictory desires. First, a desire for the greatest possible certainty that the United States would have recourse to the threat and even to the use of nuclear weapons, which eventually led to the demand that the Soviet arsenal should be countered by the deployment in Europe and above all in Germany, of new American weapons. But secondly, and in parallel, the hope that these nuclear weapons would not in any way turn German territory into a 'special case', either in terms of peace-time stationing or in terms of deployment or use in the event of a crisis or war. To this traditional dilemma, recent events have now added an even more compelling question mark where nuclear weapons are concerned. Whatever the technical problems, the START negotiations are almost certain to bring about 50 per cent reductions in the superpower central systems by the end of the decade. In theory, this development does not affect NATO's nuclear guarantee. But at the same time, there is almost certainly going to be a drastic decrease, if not an actual elimination of all ground-based tactical nuclear systems. Europe, it seems, will only agree to accept air-based systems, including the new TASMs (Tactical Air-to-Surface Missile), whose deployment would give rise to intense debates in Germany. This in turn could not fail to draw attention to the continued existence of the gravity bombs which have recently been rather ignored by protest movements. Such a debate would also pose the question of the stationing of these weapons. It is scarcely conceivable that they would only be deployed in the UK and Turkey. Yet if they were also to be stationed in Germany, what political justification could be found to pacify a public opinion acutely conscious of the uninterrupted disintegration of the Soviet Union and of the consequent anachronism of NATO's traditional strategy, an opinion, moreover, which believes that the pursuit of classical disarmament will remove the need for any new nuclear deployments?

Current developments in arms reductions seem bound to lead to the revival of 'classical' strategic doctrine and the re-allocation to strategic systems of the role they played in the late 1950s: the defence of national territory against a similar threat. We will then have witnessed over a period of twenty-five years a ruinous arms race (which the United States may well prove to have 'won') which will have forced the adversaries to return to the crude reality of 'mutual assured destruction' based on reduced deterrent arsenals designated as 'minimal' or 'reasonable'.

Even more than the disarmament process, the changing pattern of risks and threats in Europe has shifted German perceptions of security and national defence. The classical dichotomy between nuclear and conventional forces was mirrored by the *de facto* dichotomy between national decisions on nuclear weapons (at least on strategic systems) and integrated decisions on conventional forces. This was never made explicit, but the firing of a nuclear weapon for any reason other than national survival remains to this day unthinkable. This is not a question of national egotism but has to do with the specificity of nuclear weapons which demand unity and centrality in the decision over use, which carries with it the responsibility for the risk of reprisal. The stakes are simply so high that it is inconceivable that they could come into play at any level other than that of the nation.

Moreover, reductions in tactical nuclear systems actually reinforce the national role of strategic systems. Until recently, the overlapping and redundant arsenals of tactical weapons in Europe made it just possible to imagine that the United States might decide on 'limited' use. But in the present and especially the future context of reduced tactical systems, the nuclear powers find themselves not only face to face but at the same time with their backs firmly to the wall. The consequence is that each nation has to invent a nuclear doctrine which, while not exactly new, nevertheless has to adapt to a situation which has already destroyed many illusions. Thus the NATO summit in July 1990 came up with the notion of 'last resort', which pushes back a bit further the use of nuclear weapons. This was presented as progress because its stated aim was to prevent a catastrophe. But it could equally be interpreted as a form of nuclear disengagement, which is logical once the withdrawal of land-based tactical nuclear systems from central Europe reduces the risks for German security.

The risks presented by a strong nuclear power are currently being replaced by a whole range of new threats: more limited and multifarious and for the most part situated beyond the frontiers of Europe (West and Central). In the face of these new risks, which stem from the decomposition of the Soviet empire on the one hand and from unequal economic development on the other, Germany's attitude at the present time is exceedingly cautious. This is first and foremost because the main objective, national unity as fast as possible, had to be made a social and economic success. Yet the atmosphere of international détente and the social and political enthusiasm of the Eastern countries cannot much longer conceal the scale of the difficulties facing them. German leaders, and above all Helmut Kohl, had attempted to press unity through as fast as possible while international tension was at its lowest ebb. But the Gulf War demonstrated the vulnerability of Eurocentric planning to 'out-of-area' problems.

Security and the question of ethnic minorities

These national, ethnic and economic contradictions, difficulties and rivalries could give rise to confrontation in Europe itself, especially in the form of agitation from ethnic minorities. In this respect, Germany will be doubly affected: as the major power of the general zone at the heart of the problems; and as the protector, *volens nolens*, of the German minorities. The biggest contingent of ethnic Germans undoubtedly comprises those known as the 'Volga Germans'. These are the descendants of the peasants of the Palatinate, of Hesse, of Baden and of Wurtemberg who were brought to Russia under Catherine the Great in the eighteenth century. They gradually acquired land around the lower Volga and in 1924 created the autonomous socialist Republic of Volga, whence they were expelled by Stalin in 1941. In October 1989, a committee of the Nationalities Soviet proposed giving them back these former lands, but this gave rise to massive local resistance. In 1987, 15 000 Volga Germans sought permission to return to the Volga, a number which rose to 50 000 in 1988, to 107 000 in 1989 and estimates went as high as 150 000 in 1990. But faced with the reticence of the local population to accept them, a preference is now being expressed for a return to eastern Prussia around the area of Kaliningrad. This has major consequences for regional balance because a large-scale return of ethnic Germans to a part of the former east Prussia would reopen the question of Poland's eastern borders.

In Poland itself, the German minority in Silesia (estimated at 100 000 by Warsaw and 1000 000 by Bonn) receives, through its cultural associations, a substantial share of German aid to Poland, some of which does not even transit through Warsaw. This is giving rise to some minor tension with 'fellow-Poles' who do not enjoy the benefits of such generosity. If one adds to the picture the often strained relations between the inhabitants of the former GDR and Polish entrepreneurs who are inevitably making increasing incursions on to the 'patch' of their western neighbour, one can easily sense the seriousness of the situation. Dr Kohl linked the ratification of the treaty on the Oder-Neisse line to provisions for safeguarding the rights of the German minority in Poland. In Czechoslovakia, the German minority which was put at 3.5 million in 1939, now numbers fewer than 150 000. It poses no real problem. But in Rumania, the German minority of around 100 000 people, which in fact forms a majority of the population of towns like Sibiu (Hermannstadt) and Brasov (Kronstadt) and of areas around Timisoara (Temesburg), hopes to be allowed to settle in Germany. They remain of course at the mercy of a deteriorating social and political situation or even of a military confrontation between Hungary and Rumania.

This is not to conjur up catastrophe scenarios involving persecution of minorities or leading inevitably to operations similar to that used over the Sudetenland. But it does suggest that the current official German line might come unstuck in perfectly understandable and foreseeable circumstances involving ethnic Germans (*Volksdeutsch*).

It would be even simpler to imagine other 'internal' risks in Europe involving Turkish minorities in Greece or in Bulgaria or the Kosovo business. What would Germany's attitude be in these situations? Already, within the CSCE (Conference on Security and Cooperation in Europe) process, Germany has paid great attention to the protection of the rights of minorities, and the decision to open a Centre for Conflict Prevention in Vienna is proof of a desire to deal with these local difficulties without having recourse to military action. The German preference leans heavily towards preventive, peaceful, economic and social solutions to these problems. For decades, the FRG has used these means to alleviate the situation of Germans throughout eastern Europe, above all in Rumania where the government used to remark cynically that Germans were the country's biggest export. But a sovereign Germany with great power status would be unlikely to wish to continue to indulge in these sorts of trade-offs. Beyond the issue of security structures, it is essential to anticipate the situations in which violent confrontations would make it difficult for Germans and other Europeans to remain on the touch-line.

It is therefore necessary to face up to a whole range of threats which currently fall totally outside NATO's remit. If they actually led to confrontation, it would be undesirable and indeed unthinkable to attempt to solve them by the intervention of the great powers. Germany, which has an understandable need to preserve her defence and security structures during the period of economic integration which we are now entering, is happy to envisage a NATO force capable of forward projection into eastern Europe. Some of the eastern countries, now free of the constraints of the Warsaw Pact, are not ill-disposed towards an American presence which might counterbalance potential leadership by a *European* state, nor towards the elaboration of a system of collective security. Current plans for military hardware in the future all stress polyvalence and mobility.

The relationship between the different missions which might await the Europeans and the military forces, under both national and alliance control, which are available to them, urgently needs redefinition. NATO is already thinking hard about this and considering the constitution of multi-national units. Cooperation with former members of the Warsaw Pact is also being examined. These new structures could rule out a purely *European* capability for the management of European crises unless agreement is reached rapidly on the breakdown of responsibilities.

Germany's future military means
The future German army will number 370 000 men all told, involving a reduction from 450 000 to 320 000 for the *Bundeswehr* and from 100 000 to 50 000 for the former East German army (NVA). The 50 000 troops remaining from the NVA will be progressively phased into the *Bundeswehr* between now and 1994. Hardware will also be substantially reduced:

Tanks	7200 to 4200
Light armour	8300 to 2800
Artillery	4700 to 2300
Aircraft	1200 to 700
Helicopters	400 to 300

Military service will be reduced from fifteen months to twelve months and the alternative civil service from twenty months to fifteen.

The question of allied troops stationed in Germany poses numerous problems. The biggest question is obviously the size of American withdrawals. Although this will eventually have to have congressional approval, speculation in the autumn of 1990 involved figures of 50 000 to 70 000 troops for the near future. Sizeable troop levels were then sent to the Gulf and nobody expects them to return to Germany. The pattern is likely to be the same for American forces in general. Whatever the eventual outcome of NATO's strategic review, it will have to amount to much more than mere redeployment of a constantly diminishing contingent of American troops. British troop levels in Germany are also to be cut by more than half over the next five years. The Canadian contingent of 8000 men is also being reduced in 1991, thus eventually posing the political issue of a North American presence which would be limited to that of the United States.

As for Franco-German military cooperation, it reached a crossroads towards the end of 1990. The joint communiqué following the Franco-German summit in Munich in September 1990 stated that 'the Federal Republic thanked France for the solidarity she had demonstrated in preserving German liberty over the previous forty years, in particular through the stationing of French troops. The Federal Chancellor stressed that French soldiers would remain welcome in Germany. The French government informed the German government of its intention to reduce French troop levels by half over the next two years. The Franco-German brigade and the French troops in Berlin would not be affected by these developments'. In answer to journalists' questions, President Mitterrand added: 'The aim is to withdraw all French troops stationed in Germany'.

French troops have to be withdrawn for three reasons. First, budgetary imperatives in Paris. Second, the health of the local German economy. Third, the evaporation of their military function. French troops in Germany traditionally played a dual role: as an expression of French solidarity with the Federal Republic; and as a test of the intentions of any agressor who, in confronting them, would thereby come face to face with the totality of French military might, including the strategic nuclear dimension. In the new context of a rapidly evolving security situation in Europe, these functions now have to be revised. On 4 October 1990, President Mitterrand told a group of German journalists: 'I have always believed that once Europe succeeded in developing a sense of political unity, it would then immediately need unity in security policy. It is difficult to reverse things. They have a way of following their natural course. I continue to believe that the prospect of a European defence, involving the Europeans themselves (but without denying alliances or friendships, which remain crucial), is now a matter of great urgency.'

Current arrangements for Germany's defence and security can therefore only be transitory, fashioned by the lack of clarity about future developments. Yet while France and the other European countries might now expect to enjoy a period of military respite, the requirements of the current unstable situation demand of Germany both imagination and creativity. As with the Soviet Union, although for different reasons, Germany has to act and to construct rapidly. Yet it would be extremely dangerous for the partners of these two countries not to show a similar measure of rapid imagination and creativity. In coming years they could well find themselves confronted with a far less malleable situation. The arguments of those who insist that it is 'urgent to wait and see' have both justification and legitimacy given the fluidity of the present. But they nevertheless need to come to terms immediately with the consequences of the German '*Blitzfried*'*. All of this must be set in the context of trans-European evolutions. What is Germany's attitude towards that process?

GERMANY'S EUROPEAN POLICY OR GERMANY AND EUROPE

Europe played an important mediating role for Germany, facilitating her reinsertion into the world of international relations. Yet the 'European

---

* 'Lightning peace', a play on *Blitzkrieg* (translator's note).

myth' no longer has the same power of representation or promise within Germany as it did in the 1960s. Moreover, with unification came fears from without that Germany would turn away from the European project.

Some felt that she would see herself, if not as self-sufficient, at least as now capable of transferring directly to the world stage the requirements of her internationalisation. Why, they asked, should Germany reinforce Europe when her strength allowed her to play an increasing world role? Does the European framework offer her anything special in the defence and security field?

In reality, while these fears that unification would give rise to an outpouring of nationalism were often voiced outside Germany, within the country each successive month saw, on the contrary, both a growing concern about the cost of reconstruction and a reassertion of German attachment to Europe. A poll conducted for the EC showed that while three out of four Germans favoured unification, such support became a minority if unity meant leaving NATO, while only one German in five was prepared to relinquish membership of the EC in exchange for national unity.[4] As for the former GDR, massive support for European unity (over 80 per cent) must also be seen as rejection of the former regime. The German public also perceives the role in the unification process of her major international partners in very different ways. The Soviets are seen to have given (or abandoned) a great deal – less, it is felt, out of faith in *perestroika* and democracy, and more as a result of economic ruin and hope of German financial assistance. American support is seen as decisive as compared with the foot-dragging of the other European governments.

The European Commission in general and particularly its president Jacques Delors demonstrated great understanding. Many European leaders, on the other hand, along with a not inconsiderable number of West Germans, deplored the speed of unification. There is reason to believe that if Chancellor Kohl had sought to coordinate unification in consultation with the Europeans, their main contribution would have been to prevent it from happening. On the other hand, the various institutional bodies of the EC were overtly supportive. Yet, the costs to the Community of unification have been estimated at two thousand million ecus for 1991 and 1992, as against an expected tax revenue of one thousand five hundred million. The Federal Republic, which was the main contributor to the community budget until 1990, will therefore now be able to benefit from its participation in the different funds. By the same token, the main contribution to unification for the other European countries is likely to be through community finances. In short, neither politically nor financially is the community process likely to

TABLE 5.1 *German Trade 1988–89*
(billions of DM)

	Exports		Imports	
	1988–89		1988–89	
France	71	84	53	60
Britain	53	60	30	34
Italy	52	60	40	35
Holland	50	54	45	52
USA	46	46	29	38
Belg/Lux	42	46	31	35
Switzerland	34	38	20	21
Austria	31	35	19	21
Spain	17	21	9	10
Sweden	17	18	11	12
Japan	13	15	28	32
Denmark	11	12	8	9

be harmed by unification. As for Germany's economic interests, measured in terms of trade, Europe plays an increasingly important role.

The interests of the foremost trading power in the world are therefore massively directed at Europe. The USA accounts for no more than 10 per cent of the German market, the same as the developing countries. Before unity, the East accounted for 5 per cent of German trade although this is now bound to increase rapidly as the former COMECON countries turn to the West. Furthermore, Germany will honour whatever commitments she has made to the Soviet Union, whose economy is in tatters. Far from Germany dropping Europe in favour of unification, it is more realistic to imagine that she will make Europe her main priority. Those who, today, are nervous about negotiating Europe's new structures with a united Germany might care to reflect on the far greater influence which she will eventually wield when fully in control of all her assets.

If one accepts that German unification is not the end of the European process, then the question arises of what contribution Germany might make to collective defence and security systems. The problem is that there are two possible answers to the question. The first – which is essentially an Anglo-Saxon, if not American approach – involves extrapolating from the existing situation (troop levels, equipment, institutions) and assessing possible transformations and developments. It reflects the traditional caution of British diplomacy, always preferring step by step pragmatism to the visionary approach or the grand statement of intent. But it also corresponds to a certain German desire, in a period of rapid transition, neither to lose hold on reality nor to awaken unnecessary fears. The second approach, on the contrary, begins with the ultimate political objective, the prospect of political union. This dimension is all the more important in defence and security matters in that these, unlike social or economic matters, cannot function without a central authority. Or, to put it more precisely, strategic prospects depend more on the nature of political structures than on available forces or matériel. Italy, for example, boasts a super-abundance of military hardware and forces, but these are rendered relatively ineffectual as a result of the absence of any real national decision-making centre. On the other hand, a clearly expressed national will – particularly with nuclear backing – can exercise a certain influence even if the material support is not at full strength. Moreover, different military objectives require differing degrees of willpower or political unity.

While France officially presses for progress towards political union, the consequences of such a course in terms of sovereignty – issues of control and use of different types of weapons systems – are swept under the carpet, in large measure because everybody is afraid of facing up to them. The poverty of the various schemes for a new European security architecture stem from this dilemma. And there is no reason to believe that the notion of subsidiarity, the fudge which is often used to circumvent this issue, has any meaning in defence terms. Hence the refusal to strike compromises, which are merely perceived as plastering over the cracks and take no account of current transformations, not only in the position of the 'front', but also in the balance of forces in Europe.

The evolution of defence and security institutions will thus be the cardinal feature of this new power geography and of the different political objectives informing it. The maintenance of a dominant influence for the USA by means of the Atlantic alliance, a reorganised NATO and a parliamentary structure for the North Atlantic Assembly; a pan-European system offering a major role to the USSR by means of the permanent or the *ad hoc* structures of CSCE; a new division of labour on foreign and defence policy between WEU, the European Council and the Commission; but also within these different structures, which are not mutually exclusive, assertions of national, bilateral or multilateral interests. The three main areas of concern will remain the Russian empire, the fissiparous Eastern countries, and the 'South', including both the Mediterranean and the Middle East. In this context, Germany will shortly have to face up to at least two major issues: what to do about nuclear weapons and what to do about the Soviet Union.

By the end of the century, the British and the French nuclear arsenals will each represent about one tenth of the size of the superpower arsenals. The deterrent value of strategic nuclear forces in Europe will not be affected. Their relative strength will have grown, but not to the point at which they will become automatic candidates for inclusion in future arms reductions talks. On the other hand, the pursuit of disarmament processes will almost certainly highlight another issue, proliferation. This is already a major problem where missiles are concerned and while access to nuclear warheads remains very difficult for non-nuclear powers, chemical and biological warheads are much easier to come by. Finally, it is impossible to foresee the consequences of the breakup of the Soviet empire in terms of the dispersion of political and military power between the republics. The situation is therefore likely to remain as follows. There would be two fairly autonomous nuclear powers in Europe which would remain relatively 'weak' in comparison to the one 'strong' nuclear power which they would nevertheless continue to be able to deter. For these powers, however, a new question now arises: how do they, as relatively 'strong' nations, deter 'weaker' ones, non-nuclear but armed with missile-borne weapons of mass destruction. This issue will have bearing on the choice of new systems to develop and will argue for airborne and particularly carrier-borne nuclear systems and for anti-missile systems to be shifted from the central front to the 'South'.

Within this context, a major power like Germany would have to make do with *de facto* deterrence. Germany would have renounced nuclear weapons but would continue to be protected by them through 'territorial contiguity' – an impossible French concept now being assessed by the whole of Europe. But this scenario is based on a hypothetical situation in which European solidarity had developed to such a extent that a sovereign Germany, in an international environment characterised by the proliferation of weapons of mass destruction, nuclear and otherwise, and in which Atlantic security had loosened, would opt *not* to develop its own minimal deterrence.

The full effects of Germany's return to sovereignty remain to be seen first and foremost because everything has happened so quickly. Clearly, German leaders have not had time to work out their own ideas. In the nuclear realm, the country for the first time has the possibility of sovereign choice. The question does not arise immediately because Germany has repeatedly committed itself to the non-proliferation process. Nor is it simply a question of what attitude will be adopted when the non-proliferation treaty (NPT) is reviewed in 1995. The more significant fact is that, in order to become a nuclear power, certain technical and political conditions have to met, which Germany did not meet when it signed the treaty in 1969. The organisation of nuclear deterrence demands that the state in question exercises sovereignty over a coherent national territory. The division of Germany together with West German concern about nuclear strikes in East Germany highlighted the incoherence which would have attended any claims Bonn might have made in the past with respect to nuclear weapons. However, those who opposed Germany's signing of the NPT were formulating objections for the future, and drew attention in particular to the possibility of some future need to participate in a European deterrent. Today, the 'territorial' conditions for access to nuclear status are almost complete, and the absorption of the eastern *Länder* fulfils yet another condition: the unicity of political decision.

Germany was a signatory to the non-proliferation treaty, reiterated her commitment to it in the context of the unification treaty, and repeated that commitment before the general assembly of the United Nations. But if the above scenario of a return to 'all or nothing' deterrence were confirmed, and were accompanied by a reduced American commitment to Europe, this could lead Germany to have to choose between two contradictory attitudes. The first attitude would be to demand access to 'deterrence' or 'nuclear protection', perhaps not alone, but via some new European security structure. Is it conceivable that a fully sovereign Germany could accept *de facto* inferiority with respect to the UK and France in this vital area? While an expert like Egon Bahr might accept the notion that French and British nuclear weapons 'counterbalance' Soviet weapons in Western Europe, other German leaders such as Alfred Dregger seem more demanding. What would France's position be if, in the event of an increase in nuclear decision-centres in the northern hemisphere, Germany decided that her security required the possession of a minimal nuclear deterrent? The second attitude would be to exert pressure to accelerate nuclear disarmament by insisting that arsenals other than those of the superpowers be included. Although there is currently nothing in the statements of Germany's leaders which presages such pressure, the fact remains that the denuclearisation of Europe has much greater political support in Germany than minimal deterrence.

The other side of the nuclear coin is this strong desire in Germany for denuclearisation. Just as nuclear weapons were to some extent predicated upon East-West conflict, so the fading of that confrontation reduces the legitimacy of such weapons on Germany's borders, not only in the eyes of the public, but also in those of various German leaders. In this regard, cooperation with the former adversary, the USSR, is both a credible and an attractive alternative. There is already a long history of such strategic understanding between the German and the Russian/Soviet governments. After the death in 1761 of the Russian Empress Elisabeth, who was allied to Austria against Prussia, her successor Peter III, an admirer of Frederick the Great, immediately reversed Russian diplomacy by signing an alliance with Prussia. This was subsequently replaced by effective neutrality under Catherine the Great. Half a century later, in 1812, the Prussian general von Yorck and the Russian general Diebitsch (who had been born in Silesia and was a former Prussian army officer) signed the Tauroggen agreement according to which the Russian army and Prussian units in Napoleon's Grand Army would observe reciprocal neutrality. This agreement can be seen as the origin of the Holy Alliance.

In 1887, under Bismarck, the German Reich concluded a treaty of neutrality with Russia aimed at preventing a Franco-Russian alliance. This treaty was not renewed by Bismarck's successor Caprivi, and Russia was thereby pushed into an alliance with France. In 1922 at Rapallo, Germany and Russia mutually renounced all reparation or debt payments and resumed their economic and diplomatic activity. The German government was searching for greater margin of manœuvre in foreign policy and hoping to prevent a Franco-British agreement with the Soviets. When Germany joined the League of Nations in 1926, she laid down one condition: that she would not participate in any future collective sanctions against the USSR. On Soviet insistence, the Germans went even further and the Treaty of Berlin in 1926 guaranteed reciprocal neutrality in the event of either country's being attacked by a third. One of Hitler's first acts on taking power in 1933 was to extend that treaty. The Molotov-Von Rippentrop treaty of 1939 involved not only a guarantee of mutual non-aggression, but also economic assistance, the establishment of permanent consultation and above all the secret establishment of spheres of influence in central and eastern Europe.

On 9 November 1990, Messrs Kohl and Gorbachev (the latter having not so long previously reminded the former of Joseph Goebbels) signed in Bonn the 'Treaty between the German Federal Republic and the Union of Soviet Socialist Republics on relations of good-neighbourliness, partnership and cooperation'. Article 3 of this treaty is highly significant:

> The FRG and the USSR restate that they will refrain from the threat of the use of force or from any recourse to force directed against the territorial integrity of the other party, or which would be in any other way incompatible with the aims or principles of the United Nations Charter or the Final Act of the CSCE.

> They will settle their differences exclusively through peaceful means and will never use any of their arms, except in individual or collective self-defence. Under no circumstances will they ever use armed force first, either against each other or against any third country. They request all other states to join them in this commitment to the refusal of attack. If one of the two parties is attacked, the other party will not supply the aggressor with either military or any other form of assistance and will take all necessary measures to settle the conflict through application of the principles and procedures of the UN and of other collective security structures.

The sentences about non-recourse to the threat of force were instantly perceived in France as undermining deterrence. The Germans insist that they are in strict conformity with NATO and United Nations commitments. But the commitment to abstention in the event of third-party aggression seems to be so extensive that countries considering an alliance with Germany might have to think twice. What would Germany's attitude be in the event that Turkey (a NATO member) intervened to protect its minorities in a hypothetical explosion in the Soviet Muslim republics? Would there be different reactions from the Western nations in the event of trouble in the Baltic states? Who would define the word 'attack' – the security council, of which the USSR is a member?

Bonn justifies its commitment as a necessary form of support for Gorbachev in order to prevent any break-up of the union, whose consequences would indeed be highly unpredictable. But France, when faced with the same Soviet requests, refused. There are many differences discernible in Western policies towards the East. But if eastern Europe has changed for everybody, it remains absolutely central to German preoccupations. This opening up of German diplomacy is revealing, both of a conception of future security which instinctively looks to reciprocal agreements and of Germany's aptitude for situating herself within a pan-European framework – in particular by concluding immediate and far-reaching relations with the Soviet Union. There is greater urgency for both these states than for other European states and urgency facilitates imagination. There is no doubt that agreements in the East, which the western nations would prefer to forget about, will be given a new historical content.

So is a European defence policy a German objective? If the question is put in this simplistic way, the reply, at any rate in the short and medium term, must be negative. But in fact the same would be true for all the great sovereign states of Europe. Nothing can yet be brought into focus: neither the actors involved, nor the space to be covered, nor the means necessary to achieve the aim. We referred earlier to the necessary political conditions for any significant progress towards political union. The recent Kohl-Mitterrand proposals on upgrading the role of the European Council in that process gave rise to passionate reactions which are a measure of the complexity of the institutional problem. At the same time, it would certainly be a mistake to overestimate long-term German confidence in a 'militarily defunct' NATO. Many other structures, particularly conventional ones, can come into being without constituting the collapse of the alliance. The Germans, for instance, often speak of 'multinational forces', but probably do not envisage anything very grand or very tightly structured. The idea is essentially to redeploy a substantially reduced volume of troops along certain priority axes in central Europe. One in the north with the British, one in the south with the remaining Americans, while the French would retain a reservist role. 'Multinational integration' would simply involve a few major command units whose permanent establishment would permit enhanced interoperability in time of crisis.

Franco-German conventional cooperation which is, of necessity, going to be re-thought, and will almost certainly be reduced in the first instance, might eventually, paradoxically, be reinforced. The reciprocal stationing of national units on each other's territory could give the Paris-Bonn defence axis a new lease of life and above all underscore its exemplary function in political terms.

CONCLUSION

German foreign policy, and particularly its defence and security components, is in search of its identity. It has changed both its means and its capacities and has, above all, regained its sovereignty. It has not yet defined its objectives or even its direction. No longer subjected to the same political constraints, but rather to those of geography (and its consequences), this policy-in-the-making will almost inevitably re-engage with well-trodden historical paths. Germany's partners would be wrong however to assume that they will lead to the same destinations. The strength not only of economic but also of human relations which binds Germany to all its European neighbours and to its North-American cousins has galvanised a collective political feeling of an inevitable shared destiny. Although in defence and sometimes even in security policy, alliances and agreements prove to be fragile, at the end of the day the similarity of risk if not of threat which hangs over Germany and her neighbours allows us to conclude that this community of destiny will be extended to a future common foreign policy. It has been said in France that, faced with the events of 1989, we lost the battle of Germany. We must now win the battle of Europe.

NOTES

1. On 12 September 1990, during the signing ceremony for the 2 + 4 treaty, Mr Baker stressed that 'A year ago, the division of Europe and of Germany seemed to be a permanent fact. It is the new thinking in Moscow which has offered a new vision of Soviet interests which are themselves compatible with constructive international action'.
2. K. J. Muller, 'Les deux tentations de la politique extérieure allemande de Bismarck à nos jours', *Revue de l'IHTP*, Autumn 1990.
3. This treaty was signed by the two German states and the four powers which had exercised tutelage over Germany since 1945.
4. Eurobarometer no. 33, June 1990.

6 British Security Policy: Between the Special Relationship and European Cooperation

Christoph Bluth

British security policy in the post-war period has been marked by the principal role Britain has played in European security within the NATO Alliance and by the special relationship with the United States. As we witness the process of German reunification and a fundamental shift in the European security landscape, this chapter will seek to define the general parameters which have determined British security policy and to see how Britain's role in the emerging European security architecture can be expected to change in future.

BRITAIN'S SPECIAL RELATIONSHIP WITH THE US AND THE INDEPENDENT NUCLEAR DETERRENT

The special relationship between Britain and the United States derives from a multiplicity of cultural and political relations and commonalities of interest. But the special relationship has been most emphasised by the British government in the realm of security cooperation with the United States. For the first three decades in NATO the primary focus of the special relationship was a degree of sharing of nuclear weapons technology with Britain which was in marked contrast to the relationship between the United States and its other Allies in this sphere. British-American cooperation with regard to nuclear weapons dates back to the war. The theoretical breakthroughs which established the feasibility of an atomic fission bomb were made in Britain. Eventually Britain participated in the Manhattan project to produce the atomic bomb. After the war, Britain was determined to acquire atomic weapons as it appeared inconceivable for a Great Power not to possess such a weapon. For this purpose, it was vital for Britain that the cooperation with the United States should continue. However, the McMahon Act of 1946 which prohibited the dissemination of information about atomic weapons to any foreign country made it theoretically impossible for US Presidents to engage in such cooperation. Nevertheless, Britain continued successfully with her atomic bomb project, and a top priority in British-American relations during the following decade became the modification of the McMahon Act to allow greater sharing of American technology. Britain was clearly seeking an exclusive relationship with the United States since this rationale was not applicable to either West Germany or France. The Sandys White Paper of 1957 which defined the direction of Britain's post-Suez security policy marked a significant shift towards nuclear deterrence. On the declaratory level, the need for an independent British deterrent (the 'standing alone' hypothesis) was emphasised. The actual policy pursued, however, was directed at ever closer cooperation with and technological dependence on the United States, proceeding from the realisation that Britain would be unable to face the Soviet Union alone. The British approach to targeting was based on the premise that operations would be carried out in conjunction with the United States; the abandonment of Britain's own ballistic missile project, *Blue Streak*, constituted a clear decision to move towards even greater reliance on technological cooperation with the US.

The British response to the dilemma of extended deterrence was paradoxical. On the one hand, it took the one route which could secure nuclear deterrence on behalf of British security interests, and which at the same time resolved the problem of nuclear control, namely that of developing its own nuclear force. On the other hand, it moved in the opposite direction, by seeking to bind the United States closer to itself and at the same time making itself more dependent on the United States. The connection between the two objectives, strengthening the British nuclear deterrent, and developing the special relationship with the United States was thus highly paradoxical, since one was the *means* to promote the other, but the issue as to which was the end and which was the means became confused, and the emphasis frequently shifted from one to the other. Many of the articulated goals with regard to the special relationship related to gaining access to US technology, cooperation in targeting and exercising influence on US security policy. 'Means' and 'ends' were thus intertwined in a contradictory manner. It is important to emphasise that British policy was directed at solving both the problem of nuclear control by way of direct access to nuclear weapons and the problem of nuclear participation in strategic planning, albeit in a manner which gave Britain a privileged status with respect to other European Alliance partners. Macmillan was of course aware of the adverse effects of this policy on his objectives concerning British relations with Europe, and with France and Germany in particular, but this was subordinated to the preservation of some form of British nuclear deterrent and the special relationship with the United States. This approach has been described as 'independence in concert'.[1]

The whole question of the future of Britain's 'independent nuclear deterrent' became enmeshed with the debate about nuclear sharing. As the V-bomber force had become vulnerable to Soviet air defence, Britain embarked on a programme to develop its own nuclear ballistic missile (*Blue Streak*) which was to become the principal platform for its strategic nuclear weapons. In April 1960 Britain decided to scrap the programme, since it was proving too costly and there were considerable technical difficulties. As a liquid fuelled missile with slow reaction time, the technology of the missile design (based on the US Atlas InterContinental Ballistic Missile (ICBM)) was now considered obsolete.[2] The US Administration was willing to sell Britain either *Polaris* or the air-to-surface missile *Skybolt* which was then in development. The British Government decided to go for *Skybolt* as a means of prolonging the life of the V-bomber force.[3] The failure of *Blue Streak* and the *Skybolt* decision allowed the Labour Party to raise the whole issue of Britain's 'independent deterrent' (or 'dependent deterrent' as Labour Party spokesmen called it). The controversy, which was also carried out within the Conservative Party itself, ranged across the wider political issues of the early 1960s such as Britain's role in Europe and the possibility of British participation in a European nuclear deterrent. Such a force would have constituted an important form of burdensharing and would have reinforced the European pillar of the Alliance. Britain's contribution on the basis of her own nuclear weapons programme and aircraft industry would have been the centrepiece of a new European defence community. Such a development would have conformed with the other long-term political trends as manifested by Britain's endeavours to become a member of the EEC. It would also have solved the 'problem' of German nuclear ambitions.[4] Already, there were occasional hints that if Britain became a member of the EEC, a common nuclear deterrent based on Anglo-French nuclear cooperation might be on the agenda.

The various schemes for a European deterrent, a NATO nuclear force (such as advocated by Alastair Buchan) or a nuclear force in the framework of the Western European Union (WEU) were not acceptable to the Macmillan government. Andrew Pierre has correctly discerned that the two major strands of British foreign policy (seeking closer integration with Europe through the EEC; and the pursuit of an exclusive relationship with the United States in nuclear weapons technology) ran completely counter to each other. The attempt to integrate British policy on nuclear defence with its European policy was therefore never made.[5]

Nevertheless, it is worth pointing out that there was, in the early 1960s, a 'Gaullist' tendency in the Conservative Party. Peter Thorneycroft, who became Minister of Defence in 1962, and Minister of Aviation Julian Amery in particular believed that Britain should become less dependent on the United States and increase its collaboration with Europe and especially with France. Thorneycroft and Amery indicated to their French counterparts their personal preference for future nuclear cooperation. There are indications that there was some interest on the French side in assistance from Britain for the French nuclear programme, which was beset with financial and technical difficulties. Apart from possible access to American technology by this route, France would also acquire a cheap source of enriched uranium, as Britain was experiencing a surplus of fissile materials.[6]

Interestingly enough, on the American side there had also been some thinking about Anglo-French nuclear cooperation as a means of sharing American technology with France. But when the decision was made not to cooperate with France, the idea was discarded and it was clear that the nuclear agreements between the United States and the United Kingdom did not allow sharing the technology with France. Macmillan put a high priority on preserving nuclear cooperation with the United States. When de Gaulle broached the subject at a meeting with Macmillan at Rambouillet, in December 1962, Macmillan's reply was non-committal.[7] Thus Britain once again made a choice in favour of the special relationship with the United States and the preservation of its nuclear deterrent over European cooperation.

With the 'independence' of Britain's nuclear deterrent under challenge at home, it was a great embarrassment to the Macmillan government that the *Skybolt* project also ran into technical trouble, and on 7 November 1962 the Kennedy administration finally decided to cancel it. Although, at various stages in the development of the missile, there had been warnings to Britain that there were difficulties and that the possibility could not be excluded that deployment would have to be abandoned after all, the American administration neglected to give Britain advance notice of the decision and Thorneycroft issued reassurances in the House of Commons as late as 2 November 1962 with regard to *Skybolt*. Britain therefore reacted with great surprise and dismay to the cancellation announcement. The whole *Skybolt* issue became a major crisis in Anglo-American relations. The British feared that the Americans were inclined to push them out of the nuclear club altogether. After the cancellation of *Skybolt*, the only system the British would now accept was the *Polaris*. The deal was hammered out between Macmillan and Kennedy at a meeting in Nassau on 18–21 December 1962. The agreement specified that the British Polaris force 'would be made available for inclusion in a NATO multilateral nuclear force'.[8]

In the autumn of 1964 Harold Wilson became prime minister with a commitment to 'renegotiate' the Nassau Agreement. In the end his government went ahead with building four of the five projected Polaris submarines, after he and his Defence Secretary, Denis Healey, had come to the conclusion that the Polaris deal was a very cost-effective way for Britain to remain in the nuclear business and maintain its influence as a world power.[9] However, it soon became apparent that Britain would no longer be able to continue in its global role given the severe problems of the British economy. The progressive withdrawal from East of Suez, which had become inevitable, resulted in a fundamental re-orientation of British defence policy. Indicative of the trend was the decision to phase out the British aircraft carrier programme which would have been crucial to global power projection. A supplementary White Paper on Defence in July 1967 went considerably further: it called for the complete withdrawal of British forces from East of Suez by the mid-1970s. In May 1967 Britain made its second application for membership of the EEC (which was vetoed by France).

The Nassau agreement had secured the independent nuclear deterrent for the time being. Yet the mid-1960s saw an increasing convergence of interest between Britain and the other European Allies *vis-à-vis* the United States. The strategy of flexible response proposed by the United States in 1962 led to mixed reactions in Europe. The Germans in particular were opposed to any diminution in the American willingness to use nuclear weapons, whereas the British were reluctant to provide the level of conventional forces that McNamara's concept demanded. Denis Healey saw himself very much as a bridge between the United States and Europe (especially Germany) in the area of nuclear strategy. In developing the compromise formula accepted by NATO in 1967 and the work of the nuclear planning group which followed, the British were for the first time closely cooperating with the other European allies (except France). The Eurogroup, founded by Denis Healey, served as a forum to discuss defence issues at a European level and was designed to appease American demands for greater burdensharing.

The French withdrawal from the military structure of NATO in 1966 considerably reduced the depth of the territory to be defended (given the small breadth of the Federal Republic, and given that French territory was now no longer available). It created a host of other problems, such as those regarding supply and communications lines. The United States was preoccupied with Vietnam, and Alliance problems were therefore accorded a much lower priority. A perception of some relaxation in tensions between East and West and thus a reduction in the Soviet threat made the rationale for the existence of NATO appear less convincing than hitherto. Paradoxically, the 'shift to Europe' in 1968 coincided with the withdrawal not only of British forces from East of Suez, but also of a full brigade from the British Army of the Rhine (BAOR).

As far as the fundamental questions of NATO strategy for the defence of Europe were concerned, Defence Secretary Denis Healey was a firm supporter of the American strategy of flexible response. However, he was extremely critical of wishful thinking with regard to what could be done with conventional forces. Here, as we have pointed out, Healey shared many of the concerns of the German opponents of flexible response. In his view, the emphasis should not be on war-fighting, but on nuclear deterrence. He considered the threat of an early use of tactical nuclear weapons to be a likely requirement for a successful deterrence strategy. Healey feared that if doubt were cast on the American commitment to the strategy of nuclear deterrence in Europe, this would feed the pressures in European nations to acquire independent nuclear deterrents (rather than inducing them to build up their conventional forces).[10]

Although Healey argued strongly that there was no realistic hope of NATO increasing conventional forces to levels which would enable it to counter a Soviet attack on a purely conventional level, thus by implication rejecting the American notion of significantly raising the nuclear threshold, his views were in accordance with the basic idea of flexible response. At that time, he saw tactical nuclear weapons as a counter to the 'middle range' of aggression and, in the event that deterrence should fail, they would, he believed, open up the possibility of holding out against the forces of the aggressor long enough for attempts to end the conflict on a diplomatic level before escalating to the strategic level. This contradicted McNamara's original concept of flexible response, which was designed to force the enemy to make the decision to use nuclear weapons first, with all the associated risks. Healey's views at the time, however, were much closer to, for example, German views and to those that were actually adopted by NATO.

British emphasis on the 'special relationship' with the United States was strongly bound up with the development of British strategic nuclear forces. Once this strategic relationship was secure, and once the dream of a 'special relationship' with the United States on a global scale was finally abandoned, it became clear that as far as the problems within the Western Alliance were concerned, Britain's interests lay with the other European members of the Alliance, and particularly with Germany.

THE BRITISH APPROACH TO ARMS CONTROL

If the possession of nuclear weapons confers Great Power status, or at least greater political influence, particularly in the area of security policy, one aspect of this involves participation in disarmament negotiations or arms control. British interest in disarmament/arms control was motivated by the desire to maintain the greatest possible degree of influence in world affairs, as well as by the need to ensure that British security interests were maintained.

By the mid-1950s Britain had come to consider a deliberate Soviet invasion of Western Europe as unlikely.[11] Britain's interests seemed to be best served by mutual acceptance of the status quo. Britain was therefore very interested in pursuing diplomatic means for reducing East-West tension and the risk of military confrontation in Central Europe – by arms control measures, for instance, and confidence building schemes for military disengagement. An important constraint on British policy was that of resources – a relaxation in the East-West confrontation would allow a reduction in British commitments. This approach led to disagreements with Britain's allies; in particular these aspects of British security policy ran completely counter to West German policy and were treated by Chancellor Adenauer (and at times the US Secretary of State, John Foster Dulles) with considerable suspicion. In particular, the Germans frequently suspected that the British were seeking reasons to withdraw from their European defence commitments.

Britain was also involved with the United States in negotiating the Partial Test Ban Treaty (PTB). For Britain, there was an interaction of mixed objectives since a test ban did restrain Britain's efforts to develop its independent nuclear deterrent. By the time the PTB Treaty was signed in 1963, however, Britain had completed an important series of tests, and in any case underground testing would still allow her to proceed with the development of nuclear warheads, even though it further increased her reliance on cooperation with the United States. On this issue, again, the UK fell foul of a major European partner, in this case France, which saw the PTB as a device to exclude her from the nuclear club.

ARMS CONTROL IN THE THATCHER/REAGAN ERA

The endeavour to revitalise the 'special relationship' with the United States played a central role in British foreign policy in the Thatcher/Reagan era. This was accompanied by a special personal relationship between

Prime Minister Thatcher and President Reagan, who shared a fundamentally similar view of the world. The structural difficulties in transatlantic relations during the Reagan period nevertheless also affected Britain and despite the prime minister's personal inclinations, Britain developed closer relationships with Europe.

The ideological commonalities between the Thatcher government and the Reagan administration were most obvious in the area of East-West relations. Margaret Thatcher had already distinguished herself during her time as Leader of the Opposition as a stern critic of the Soviet Union. Her natural instinct to take a strong line against the Soviet Union bore some resemblance to that of President Reagan. As she came to power during the decline of détente, this tendency found expression in strong condemnation of the Soviet invasion of Afghanistan (including support for a boycott of the Moscow 1980 Olympics which resulted in a row with the British Olympic Committee), support for the 'dual-track' decision to deploy Intermediate-Range Nuclear Missiles and the declared willingness to station cruise missiles in Britain, and later strongly worded statements about the crisis in Poland. None the less, despite some changes in emphasis, Britain continued to take a line closer to that of Europe than to that of the United States on issues such as détente and arms control. While it was recognised that East-West relations were at a low point, détente, the continuation of the Conference on Security and Cooperation in Europe process and arms control were still seen as desirable objectives. This was in stark contrast to the views of the Reagan administration, which opposed the very idea of détente and was strongly influenced by people who objected to arms control agreements as a matter of principle.

Despite British insistence on the reality of the Soviet threat, and on the need to maintain an adequate defence posture (which for Britain included nuclear weapons), and despite Britain's joining in the condemnation of the invasion of Afghanistan and of Soviet pressure on Poland over Solidarity, perceptions in London of the security environment were markedly different from those in Washington. Thus British officials and defence experts generally discounted American claims of ICBM vulnerability ('the window of vulnerability') in view of the invulnerable second strike force of Submarine Launched Ballistic Missiles (SLBMs), and placed greater emphasis on deterrence and the ability to inflict unacceptable damage on the Soviet Union, rather than on war-fighting capabilities. There was no sense in London of the imminent threat to deterrence stability which was projected by the US administration and its supporters in Washington. Nor was the British government particularly keen to have its trading interests damaged by the deterioration in East-West relations.

These fundamental differences in perception and implied policy preferences were usually obscured by Britain's public position, which sought to maintain the spirit of the special relationship with the United States and to avoid adding to the negative sentiment about US foreign policy developing in broad sections of the British population. Nevertheless they were starkly revealed by the announcement of the Strategic Defence Initiative (SDI) in March 1983. The rationale for SDI was couched in language which strongly questioned the morality of continued nuclear deterrence and thus the entire basis of NATO defence policy. Having just withstood phenomenal political pressures with regard to Intermediate Nuclear Forces (INF), European governments including the British were not keen to have another major defence controversy. Furthermore, Britain had always been sensitive to the potential of Soviet Ballistic Missile Defence (BMD) in downgrading the effectiveness of Britain's independent nuclear deterrent, a spectre that might raise its head again if the limitations of the Anti-Ballistic Missile (ABM) Treaty were discarded. The position eventually adopted by the prime minister on SDI, while giving qualified political support to the project, saw its role as being substantially different from that envisaged by President Reagan. In Thatcher's view, the goal of SDI should have been to *enhance* deterrence, not do away with it. The West should state clearly that it was not seeking military superiority (eg. a first-strike capability). SDI-related research should be conducted within the confines of the narrow interpretation of the ABM Treaty; if it came to development and deployment of any systems this should be subject to negotiations with the Soviet Union. Similarly qualified support for SDI was expressed in a speech by the then Foreign Secretary, Sir Geoffrey Howe, in March 1985; because of its tone it was interpreted as being more hostile to SDI.[12]

Changes in Soviet arms control policy with the succession to power of Mikhail Gorbachev resulted in a much more flexible approach which suddenly conferred credibility on even more sweeping proposals than those already advocated by the Reagan Administration in the previous INF and Strategic Arms Reduction Talks (START) negotiations. This became dramatically apparent at the Reykjavik summit in October 1986. Despite its failure because of Gorbachev's insistence on a link between restraints on SDI and an INF agreement, both leaders agreed in principle to the desirability of a zero option with regard to INF and deep cuts in strategic ballistic missiles, with the eventual objective of their total elimination.

The British government, like other European governments, responded to the Reykjavik proposals with considerable (if publicly restrained) alarm. From the British perspective, the purpose of arms control was to legitimise nuclear deterrence and provide it with a degree of stability, not to eliminate nuclear weapons. The Reykjavik proposals threatened to undermine both extended deterrence and the legitimacy of the British independent deterrent.

One of the positive aspects of Reykjavik for the British appeared to be that Gorbachev did not insist that British and French nuclear systems should be included in a Soviet/American INF agreement. But it was also clear that if the obstacle which SDI posed to deep cuts in strategic arsenals were overcome, then the British nuclear force would become an issue, particularly after its modernisation. The British government has already engaged in a pre-emptive unilateral arms control initiative by restricting the Trident D-5 missiles to eight warheads. Even so, the Trident 2 submarine may eventually carry a total of 512 warheads, as opposed to an estimated maximum of 192 Polaris-Chevaline warheads. This still represents a substantial increase in firepower, range, and penetrability. The British accept in principle that at some stage their arsenal will have to be put on the negotiating table, but all that is being said so far is that this can only happen after substantial reductions in superpower strategic weapons have already been achieved. This is virtually identical to the French position. During Prime Minister Thatcher's visit to Moscow in 1987 she forthrightly took issue with Gorbachev's vision of a nuclear-free world and stressed the need to maintain nuclear weapons for deterrence. British government statements clearly voiced concerns about European denuclearisation while a large imbalance of conventional forces remained, and Thatcher's response to an impending INF deal in 1987 was that denuclearisation in Europe had gone far enough.

The debate on short-range nuclear force (SNF) modernisation within NATO also proved very divisive, with the potential of becoming another 'INF'. The SNF debate was an interesting example of internal Alliance politics, with Britain attempting to serve once again as a bridge between Washington and Europe, and West Germany showing an unusual assertiveness which caused not a little exasperation in London as the FRG was accused of reneging on compromises previously agreed to by NATO. The explanation lies in the consequences of the INF controversy, which led to a decisive shift in public attitudes towards a nuclear defence policy in West Germany, a shift so permanent that no German politician can afford to ignore it. One of the surprising features of the recent debate was that the pressure to move towards a 'third zero' (i.e. mutual elimination of all battlefield nuclear weapons) came not merely from the social democrats and the Greens, but even from within the conservative CDU/CSU. The president of the party caucus Alfred Dregger advanced the notion of the 'singularisation' of West Germany on the basis that most of the theatre nuclear weapons were based in Germany, thus making West Germany a unique target for Soviet attack, and furthermore in case of conflict these weapons would be detonated on German soil (East or West). This debate received additional impetus by a report commissioned by the US government and written by Fred Iklé and Alfred Wohlstetter on 'discriminate deterrence' which emphasised the military ('war-fighting') function of theatre nuclear weapons and explicitly argued against assigning them the function of 'coupling' to the US strategic arsenal, thus denying a central tenet of NATO nuclear doctrine and, despite the unofficial nature of the report, causing considerable alarm, especially among the conservatives in Germany.[13]

The recent changes in Eastern Europe, the virtual collapse of the Warsaw Treaty Organisation (WTO) as a military organisation, the impending withdrawal of Soviet forces from Eastern Europe and the reunification of Germany have fundamentally altered the security environment in which the SNF debate takes place. The military rationale for SNF, which was already tenuous, has now collapsed. Despite this, the British government continued to push for SNF modernisation until May 1990 when President Bush announced the cancellation of the Follow-On to Lance programme and any modernisation of nuclear artillery shells based in Europe. In terms of Alliance politics, this was seen as a clear shift from the British view to the German perspective.[14] British insistence on proceeding with SNF modernisation was not based on any clear rationale for SNF in the context of flexible response, but on the perception of the need to halt the process of 'denuclearisation' in the European theatre. The only remaining SNF modernisation programme that still has support in the Alliance and is being supported particularly strongly by the British is the stand-off Tactical Air-to-Surface Missile (TASM). In the forthcoming negotiations on SNF, the preservation of an option to deploy TASM will thus be one of the key objectives along with drastic reductions in nuclear artillery shells. This issue may well see the British aligned with the French in opposition to the Germans.

BRITISH ATTITUDES TO WEST EUROPEAN SECURITY COLLABORATION

In the early 1980s there was much renewed interest in West European security collaboration. There were a number of reasons for this. One important source of pressure lay in the divergence between European and American views on strategic and arms control issues and on the conduct of East-West relations. This divergence was brought into particularly sharp focus as a result of the Carter administration's maladroit handling of the enhanced radiation warhead (Neutron bomb) issue and, during the early 1980s, by the excessively alarmist view of the strategic environment on the part of the Reagan administration and its hostility to détente and arms control. The existence of perceived differences of view and political interests was a major incentive for a stronger and more united assertion of Europe's responsibilities for its own defence. This factor was complemented by the emergence within important sections of opinion in the United States of doubts about the wisdom of American commitments to the defence of Europe, accompanied by the attempt of the 1984 Nunn amendment to push Europe to assume a greater share of the burden for its own defence. The obvious advantages of joint European arms production also provided a powerful push in the direction of greater West European security collaboration. Particularly significant were developments in Franco-German relations. President Mitterrand initiated a new policy towards Germany, involving considerably expanded military cooperation as a result of concerns over the rise of anti-nuclear and 'neutralist' sentiment in West Germany. Apart from setting up inter-ministerial mechanisms for direct *bilateral* cooperation, the French also initiated the revitalisation of the Western European Union (WEU) as a vehicle for the expansion of their defence cooperation with West Germany, and sought to include other European nations. The first real test for this emphasis on developing European responses to American initiatives in security policy came in March 1985 when Caspar Weinberger issued his letter inviting participation in SDI research.

Attempts to arrive at a coordinated European response to the American invitation failed lamentably. At the time the focus of disagreement appeared to be between Britain and France. Britain had taken a supportive stand for SDI as a research programme, and intended to accept the invitation to participate. It also rejected the WEU as the appropriate forum to discuss and coordinate the political and strategic aspects of SDI as they would affect Europe, and would only agree to the WEU dealing with the practical aspects involved in the negotiation of research contracts. The French, who rejected SDI on technological and strategic grounds, saw the American invitation of European participation as a political ploy to obtain European support for SDI, and thus opposed such participation. A coordinated European response therefore became impossible. The West German government had already expressed its qualified support for SDI, and its interest in participation in research.[15]

The Reykjavik Summit in October 1986 was another occasion where American policy initiatives were perceived to endanger European security interests. This time the WEU functioned successfully as a forum to co-ordinate a European response, which found its expression in the Platform on European Security Interests of October 1987. The WEU also served to co-ordinate European participation in the naval operations in the Gulf during the 'tanker war' of 1987 to safeguard Western interests.

For the British, involvement in the WEU has been important in order to contain the predominance of the Franco-German axis in defence collaboration. The United Kingdom has valued the WEU as a high-level discussion forum, but has staunchly resisted any changes in the WEU which might give the appearance that it would encroach on the functions of NATO. In the new security environment, the significance of European defence cooperation will increase as responsibility for security in Europe shifts away from the United States. While at present any pressures to dismantle NATO are being resisted, the fact must be faced that the threat of a large-scale military invasion by the Soviet Union and its allies has been NATO's primary *raison d'être* and the source of political cohesion. If the Soviet threat continues to recede, then the relevance of NATO as a military alliance will also largely disappear. The notion of transforming NATO into a political alliance is a rather dubious one. What will be required in future will not be a Western alliance (the whole concept presupposes East-West conflict) but rather a collective security regime that encompasses the whole of Europe. The WEU has emerged as one possible candidate to serve as the institutional basis for a new European security council, although both the USSR and Germany favour the CSCE framework to construct a new pan-European security order. The WEU, however, is the most likely institutional basis for Western European cooperation in security policy which will substantially increase in importance in future.[16] In this context it is interesting to note that Britain's contribution to this debate so far has been to disparage the CSCE as a framework for European security cooperation and to emphasise the continued need for NATO. The domestic political debate about Britain's relations with Europe which has proved very divisive in the Conservative party has centred on economic rather than security issues. The November 1990 change in government will most likely result in a more active British role in European security cooperation. An alternative leadership of the Conservative party will probably result in more emphasis on the established modes of European cooperation, whereas a Labour government would take a greater interest in the development of alternative collective security structures in Europe such as are being advocated, among others, by the German Foreign Ministry under Hans-Dietrich Genscher. In any event, Britain is likely to adapt to changing circumstances and play a major part in any new development in West European security cooperation in the future.

THE PARAMETERS OF FUTURE BRITISH SECURITY POLICY

In 1989, the collapse of communist regimes in Eastern Europe and, most of all, the collapse of the Berlin Wall, which led rapidly to a united Germany and the complete dismantling of the Central Front, has had profound implications for British security policy. The external security environment which Britain faces in the 1990s is therefore likely to be characterised by a sharply reduced threat in Central Europe and, concomitantly, a reduced American military presence. Indeed, it is not clear what the configuration of security alignments is going to be. The NATO Alliance may continue for an indefinite period but is likely to lose any significant function in the next few years. As a result, British security policy is confronted with a number of fundamental issues.

The first consists simply of the redefinition of Britain's defence needs on the basis of the new threat environment. The collapse of the Warsaw Pact still leaves the Soviet Union as the major military power on the continent of Europe, both in terms of its nuclear arsenal and its conventional force posture. But it is now surrounded by a number of states which, in the event of a war against Western Europe, would at best be neutral and most likely hostile to the USSR. These changes and the conventional force reductions already undertaken as a result of President Gorbachev's announcement to the United Nations in December 1988 have invalidated the fundamental threat scenario around which NATO's force planning has been built. The notion of a sudden large-scale invasion of Western Europe by Soviet forces is now largely accepted as improbable to the point that it does not form a valid planning assumption.[17] British defence policy, in common with Western defence policy in general, still does assume a residual Soviet threat. The process of democratisation in the Soviet Union is still fragile. On the one hand there is the possibility of a right-wing backlash or even a military coup which, while unlikely to result in a war with the West, could lead to a resumption of more hostile relations. More likely is the continued disintegration of the Soviet Union which could be more or less chaotic and result in internal conflicts that could spill over into Eastern Europe and destabilise the entire region. Nevertheless, if present trends continue, then the domestic political pressures will force substantial reductions in military expenditures. The cuts announced in July 1990 by the Secretary of State for Defence, Tom King, amount to an 18 per cent reduction in manpower by the mid-1990s and a reduction in the number of frigates and destroyers by ten and submarines by eleven.[18] The debate about a fundamental restructuring of the British force posture and the future direction of British defence policy is already well under way.

The second issue lies in the role of Britain in the emerging European security architecture. The united Germany will without question be the major power in Central Europe. With the end of military confrontation, Germany will no longer be reliant to the same degree on the NATO Alliance, including Britain, for military security against an imminent threat at its Eastern border. With reunification, Germany no longer needs the Alliance to promote its central foreign policy objectives. German unity also means that Germany has finally regained much of the sovereignty lost as a result of the World War II. None of this implies that Germany will leave the Alliance, or the European Community. It simply means that power relationships on the continent of Europe have undergone a fundamental shift. They are no longer determined, to the extent that they were before, by the parameters of military security, but much more by economic realities.

It has been taken for granted that a stable European order is only possible with a substantial American presence. There appears to be general agreement that the American security guarantee will continue to be required even if the current changes in progress are fully implemented. Nevertheless, it is undoubtedly the case that in future European security will depend less on the American security guarantee and more on the emerging structure of relationships within Europe itself, in particular in terms of their economic dimension. Britain's special strategic role based on her position as one of the Allied powers after the war and special relationship with the United States will therefore substantially decline in significance, even though Britain will deploy the Trident D-5 system and thus retain a strategic nuclear deterrent. Within the next ten years, however, if the superpowers continue the process of strategic arms reductions, the role of British strategic systems in defence and arms control policy will have to be substantially reviewed. The envisaged partial withdrawal of British troops from German territory (the BAOR is to be halved over five years), which will probably be followed by large-scale withdrawals of American troops in the aftermath of a Conventional Forces in Europe (CFE) agreement is the most visible manifestation of this trend. Unlike British troop withdrawals in the past, the present cuts will not meet with German opposition; quite to the contrary. It appears that as Allied Forces stationed in Germany are being reduced, they may have to be integrated more closely into a multinational force, as the maintenance of national corps may no longer be credible.

Nevertheless, Britain still has a significant role to play, but her only hope of doing so lies within a framework of European integration. Indeed, the only way in which Britain can hope to deal successfully with the fears of German dominance in Europe which came to the surface in mid-1990, resulting in the spectacular resignation of Trade and Industry Secretary Nicholas Ridley, is by binding Germany firmly into the institutional framework of the community. Unfortunately, the Thatcher government's attitude to European integration did not make for a very constructive policy in this direction. The consequence of recent policies is that Britain was unable to exercise much influence on future developments. If the British government were to abandon its tendency to pursue the perpetuation of the status quo and were to become engaged in a constructive process of building a new security structure for the whole of Europe, instead of effectively leaving it to the Russians and the Germans, the entire process would benefit enormously, while Britain would be in a good position to safeguard her own interests.

The fundamental tensions in British security policy between the special relationship with the United States and European defence cooperation, between a residual global role and the commitment to the defence of Europe, appeared to be resolved by the end of the 1960s whereby cooperation with the United States secured Britain's independent nuclear deterrent, while the fundamental orientation of British security policy was redirected towards Europe. This resolution endured through the Thatcher era. The fundamental changes in East-West relations at the end of the 1980s, however, have opened up many of the old questions. After struggling for decades to adapt to the post-war international environment, Britain now once again is faced with fundamental choices about her future role.

NOTES

1. This concept has been developed in Martin S. Navias, *The Sandys White Paper of 1957 and the move to the British New Look: an analysis of nuclear weapons, conventional forces and strategic planning 1955–57*, unpublished PhD Thesis, London, King's College, 1989, Ch. 4.
2. Oral History Conference, *Nuclear Planning and British-German Relations 1966–1970*, King's College London, 12 April 1989, Transcript of Proceedings. See also A. J. P. Groom, *British Thinking About Nuclear Weapons* (London: Frances Pinter, 1974), Ch. 29.
3. See Groom, op. cit., for more details on this decision.
4. See, on this, Andrew Pierre, *Nuclear Politics* (London: Oxford University Press, 1972), p. 218.
5. For example, Britain could have *attempted* to use Anglo-French nuclear collaboration as a ticket to enter the EEC. Whether de Gaulle would have agreed to this is another question.
6. See Pierre, op. cit., p. 222.

7. Pierre, op. cit., p. 223. Apparently, this was not quite how it looked from the French perspective. Both at the meeting at the Château de Champs in June 1962 and at Rambouillet in December 1962 when Macmillan explained the problems of *Skybolt*, the French believed that Britain had shown itself favourably disposed towards Anglo-French nuclear cooperation. The French Ambassador to London, de Courcel, who was present at the meeting in Champs, claimed later that Macmillan did make a direct offer of Franco-British nuclear collaboration in return for French support of Britain's entry into the EEC. See Alistair Horne, *Macmillan* 1957–1986 (London: Macmillan, 1989), p. 328.
8. The relevant paragraphs of the agreement are quoted in David N. Schwartz, *NATO's Nuclear Dilemmas* (Washington: Brookings Institution, 1983), p. 103 ff.
9. Denis Healey, *The Time of My Life* (London: Michael Joseph, 1989), pp. 301–4.
10. Denis Healey, 'NATO, Britain and Soviet Military Policy', *Orbis*, xiii (Spring 1969) 1: 48–58, p. 51.
11. For an exposition of the more sanguine British assessments of the likelihood of a Soviet attack on Western Europe, as compared with the American views (which rated the risk of war more highly and thus demanded a higher level of defence preparations) see DEFE 7/677, Sir O. Franks, no. 822 to Foreign Office, 3 August 1952. This reference is discussed in Ian Clark and Nicholas J. Wheeler, *The British Origins of Nuclear Strategy 1945–1955* (Oxford: Oxford University Press, 1989), p. 174 ff.
12. Reprinted in *Journal of the RUSI* vol. 130 (March 1985) 2: 3–8.
13. Helga Haftendorn, 'Transatlantische Dissonanzen. Der Bericht ber "Selektive Abschreckung" und die Strategiediskussion in den USA', *Europa-Archiv*, Folge 8, pp. 213–22. See also the article by Egon Bahr, '60 Millionen wiegen schwerer', *Der Spiegel*, 29 February 1988, p. 30.
14. The issue created some embarrassment for the British government because it publicly insisted on the need to modernise Lance missiles right up to the time when President Bush announced his decision. For a discussion of the SNF issue, see Karl-Heinz Kamp, 'Die Modernisierung der nuklearen Kurzstreckenwaffen in Europa', *Europa-Archiv*, vol. 43 (1988) 10: 269–76.
15. For more detailed discussion of the response of the European Allies to SDI, see Trevor Taylor, 'Britain's response to the Strategic Defence Initiative', *International Affairs*, 62 (Spring 1986) 2: 217–30; John Fenske, '*France and the Strategic Defence Initiative: speeding up or putting on the brakes?*', ibid., 231–46; Christoph Bluth, '*SDI: the challenge to West Germany*', ibid. 247–64.
16. See Ian Gambles, *Prospects for West European Security Co-operation*, Adelphi Papers 244 (London: IISS, 1989), pp. 28–33.
17. For more detail, see Christoph Bluth, *New Thinking in Soviet Military Policy* (London: Pinter Publishers, 1990).
18. *Financial Times*, 26 July 1990.

Part Three
Politics and Political Culture: National Sovereignty or Supranationality?

7 The Two Souls of Marianne: National Sovereignty versus Supranationality in Europe

Rainer Riemenschneider

PROLOGUE

Time and place of the action: Parknasilla, a small coastal town in Ireland, on the weekend of 19–20 May 1990.

Dramatis personae: The foreign ministers of the twelve EC states as the chorus. Foreign minister Roland Dumas and Jacques Delors, President of the EC Commission, as protagonists.

Chorus: 'We, the foreign ministers of the venerable states of the European Community, hereby solemnly, emphatically (and once again) declare that we are unanimously in favour of the strengthening of the institutions of our community; that we will studiously avoid agreeing on or even announcing concrete steps towards achieving this; and that while we all have the greatest respect for the European Parliament, we will nevertheless ensure that it has only a hint of legislative power. From now on, but not necessarily for ever after. Amen.'

Roland Dumas (stepping forward from the chorus): 'I, Roland Dumas, head of the French diplomatic service, hereby make it known that no country is willing to hand over even an ounce of its right of sovereignty in internal and security matters to the lady Europe.'

Jacques Delors (stepping in from the side): 'Don't despair, Europe my love! You can be sure that these gentlemen will submissively lay at your feet by night what they vehemently deny you by day. Just go on dreaming your federalist dream – one day, it will become a reality, trust me.'[1]

On a screen above Dumas and Delors appears the portrait of Marianne with a star-spangled blue headband and wrapped in a flowing red, white and blue robe; from the loudspeaker sounds a melodious woman's voice reciting from Goethe's Faust: 'Two souls live in my heart . . . ' The voice dies down, the stage lights up.

INTRODUCTION

It is not easy for Marianne, for indeed, two souls do live in her heart. One is directed at the preservation of national independence, at the assertion of France's position in the international power hierarchy, at the painstaking preservation of national sovereignty. The other soul strives for a European mission for France, for the genuine construction of Europe, for integration leading to political union. This dualist conception of French foreign policy was manifestly expressed in the juxtaposition of the Tricolore and the European flag during President Mitterrand's press conference, rich in tradition, at the Elysée palace on 13 May 1989. As von Krosigk has suggested, it was no coincidence that both themes – the position of France in the world's power hierarchy and the building of Europe – were in the foreground of his foreign policy declarations. The two flags were shown in exactly the same way again in a television interview with President Mitterrand, broadcast on 25 May 1990. Once again, the discussion was about the same foreign policy themes, although on this occasion the European perspective dominated by virtue of its topicality. Given the imminent unification of the two German states, Mitterrand spoke out in favour of an acceleration of European political union.

'Union politique européenne' – what does this mean? Is it, given the dualism of France's foreign policy, more than a non-committal vision of the future? Is it intended to provide a replay of the Euro-euphoria in France which was stage-managed by the media after the acts of unity and the single market project were announced, but which has recently died away? Does the 'political union of Europe' stand solely for a somewhat forced, but otherwise rather traditional pragmatic cooperation between states; or does it suggest a more extensive integration, at the institutional level, leading to a European Federation? In other words how relevant are the two European political concepts – national sovereignty and supranationality – in France today?

It would be presumptuous to seek comprehensive answers to these questions or even a complete overview. I shall therefore restrict my remarks to a few key issues: the attitude to Europe of the French population and of the political parties; debates about Europe among intellectuals; and the Europe of the regions. Finally I shall attempt to strike some sort of balance. To begin with we must take a look at post-war history.

MONNET AND DE GAULLE: THE RELEVANCE OF THE CONTRADICTORY EUROPEAN HERITAGE

France has produced probably the highest profile representatives of both conceptions of European politics: Jean Monnet and Charles de Gaulle. Nobody would dispute the outstanding historical importance of these two vastly different personalities. Monnet as the ingenious organiser and discreetly effective planner, the originator of the French economic plan and the inspiration for the European Coal and Steel Community (ECSC) which went down in history as the 'Schuman plan'. Jean Lacouture calls him 'The Godfather and augur of European integration'.[2] Since he succeeded in this way in taking the first decisive steps towards a Europe which would grow together, the title of 'Father of Europe' befits him. The name Monnet stands for the future supranational development of Europe. Following the example of the USA, he wanted to build the 'United States of Europe'. Basic cornerstones of this building were the axiom of Franco-German reconciliation as a prerequisite for a new beginning in Europe, as well as trying to enlist a contribution to Europe from Great Britain. He was successful with Franco-German understanding, which was forward-looking and showed the way for all French foreign policy since World War II. Monnet had no luck, however, in enlisting support from Britain. This attempt was defeated above all by Britain's refusal to choose between the Commonwealth and a then rather vague European project. And when the British did eventually knock at the gates of the EEC, their entry was blocked by the opposite of Monnet, General de Gaulle.

The founder and first president of the Fifth Republic was against Britain's joining the EEC principally because he saw in her a Trojan horse for American influence in Europe.[3] As Grosser has written, for a long time this was one of the paradoxes of French life: that a widespread, politically and ideologically informed anti-Americanism went alongside a general Americanisation of the culture and daily life of the French. This anti-American feeling was to be found in all political camps. The communist left, in particular, but by no means exclusively, were conditioned by it. Jean-Pierre Chevènement, one of the founders of the left-wing socialist faction, CERES (Centre d'études, de recherches et d'éducation socialistes) and former defence minister, spoke out against the United States of Europe, because he felt it would become the Europe of the United States.[4] Krosigk quotes General de Gaulle as referring to Monnet, with his own unique brusque arrogance and biting irony, as a 'great American'. The public appearances in which the General snubbed the supranational engagements of the Fourth Republic were some of the masterpieces of Gaullist rhetoric, because of their destructive edge, and their vision of a 'Europe from the Atlantic to the Urals', informed as it was by the maxims of a Europe of individual states clutching their sacrosanct sovereignty. For de Gaulle, these states would at most be bound together loosely in the form of a confederation.

During the eventful decade of the General's presidency, France experienced a revived exaltation of national greatness and overt pretensions to world power. In this situation Europe had to take a back seat. Yet research has suggested that, despite his emphasis on the national principle, de Gaulle was never anti-European.[5] The best biography written on de Gaulle, that by Jean Lacouture, describes him as an 'unhappy European' because he did not succeed in convincing his partners of the excellence of his 'superb project' to build a European Europe independent of the USA, which would confederate the national states of the old continent around a central magnet, to be situated in Paris, and whose mechanism would be operated by de Gaulle himself. Europe would be an extended France, a 'spatial prolongation'. Lacouture quotes the apt comment of Macmillan in 1961: 'De Gaulle talks Europe and he means France'.

At that time, the European Community was hardly being promoted in any practical ways by de Gaulle. Indeed, France put the infant community through the mill. Nevertheless de Gaulle never revoked the contractual obligations with which earlier governments had bound France to Europe. In honouring the European Coal and Steel Community and the Treaty of Rome, he ensured an admittedly minimal but nonetheless clear continuity of European policy from the Fourth to the Fifth Republic. From this point of view there is a deeper solidarity between Monnet and de Gaulle than appears at first sight. It was not de Gaulle who signed these unpopular European agreements, yet the Fourth Republic would probably not have been in a position to implement them. Raymond Aron has referred to this in Hegelian terms as a 'Ruse de la Raison'.

If one ponders the vitality of this double heritage in France's political and cultural life, the relevance of these two personalities is a clue. 1990 is the 100th anniversary of de Gaulle's birth. With their own unique ability to organise centenary celebrations, the French commemorated their great statesman in various functions throughout the year. Certainly de Gaulle will be remembered as a 'great European' who aimed to establish Europe as a power in its own right between the two superpowers, but most of all he will stand as a symbol for the national identity and culture of the French. This, at any rate, is how he is remembered by Régis Debray, the former comrade in arms of Che Guevara, who from 1967 to 1970 was imprisoned in Bolivia, after which he became an adviser to Allende in Chile and, since 1975, to

Mitterrand. Debray is now a member of the Conseil d'Etat. For many French people who feel uncertain in times of far-reaching socio-economic and cultural changes, national self-assurance has become a necessity.

Jean Monnet was given many honours in his lifetime. After a difficult period, which was finally ended after the resignation of de Gaulle and the demise of President Pompidou, he was demonstratively embraced by President Giscard d'Estaing at the start of 1975, when the formation of the European Council was agreed. When Monnet died in 1979 at the age of 90, just a few months before the first direct elections to the European Parliament, the French President and the West German Chancellor stood side by side at the grave of this last 'father of Europe'.[6] On Mitterrand's initiative, Jean Monnet's remains were moved to the Panthéon in November 1988. The year 1988, in which he would have been 100 years old, was declared European year of Jean Monnet – no doubt more than as a mere symbolic gesture, as we will see. Jacques Delors, Monnet's congenial disciple, refers to Monnet by name in his programmatic-theoretic writings (see for example his book *La France par l'Europe* (1988) and his foreword to the Monnet biography by Pascal Fontaine). Delors is as much a sober-thinking and hard-calculating 'Eurocrat' as Jean Monnet was. His principle is that the building of Europe is a necessity, that in view of Europe's need to live in a competitive world there is a 'need for Europe'.[7]

The names of Monnet and de Gaulle represent distinct, even mutually exclusive political styles. Monnet never held political office, nor did he aspire to. However, it will be for future historians to decide whether Monnet's influence on politics was not every bit as meaningful and as lasting as that of President de Gaulle, forever in the public eye. One thing is certain: in spite of all their differences, Monnet and de Gaulle were united by a common goal, which each strove to achieve in his own way – namely the greatness of France. They shared the conviction that the protection of national interests was inextricably bound up with European prosperity.

EUROPE IN FRENCH OPINION POLLS

The technical, complicated, opaque mechanisms of the EC and its politics were and are not popular in France. The problem is highlighted by a large-scale survey on the theme 'Being Twenty in Europe', which the *Nouvel Observateur* published in the summer of the first direct elections to the European Parliament.[8] Young Europeans (French, Germans, Britons, Dutch, Belgians and Italians) clearly have a lot in common. They have 'no illusions any more, but still no certainties, even less enthusiasm and more and more disquiet'. On the question of whether they follow European matters 'in newspapers, on the radio or on television', 80 per cent of West Germans, 79 per cent of Britons, and 48 per cent of French said 'no'. Their Europe is different from the 'official' one. It is the Europe of travel, exchanges and friendships. Deep down, 70 per cent of young French people claimed to feel closer to foreigners of the same age than to their older compatriots. Only 17 per cent of them have never left their own country (14 per cent of Germans). For these young Europeans, state boundaries are no longer a necessary reality.

That was in 1979. Opinion polls in the 1980s showed that there was widespread agreement on Europe among the French public.[9] The building of Europe was supported by 85 per cent in a questionnaire in May 1984 (15 per cent more than in 1979). A far-reaching change in attitudes was to be observed, particularly in the parties of the left: among communists, the numbers rose from 46 per cent to 70 per cent, among socialists from 71 per cent to 91 per cent. The supporters of the socialist party (PS) and the liberals (UDF) are the most Europe-friendly. Among blue-collar workers and farmers, acceptance of Europe rose by 21 per cent and 13 per cent respectively. By far the most supportive of Europe are industrialists, wholesalers, self-employed people and executives, at 94 per cent.

The questions in these polls were very general so it is not clear exactly what the interviewees understood by 'the building of Europe'. It became more precise when they were asked about 'the United States of Europe'. Even here, positive attitudes (53 per cent) outnumbered the negative (29 per cent). In the same year (1984), 48 per cent called for an acceleration of the process of European unification (15 per cent more than in 1979). What the 1984 interviewees were hoping for from the building of Europe was the assurance of peace, an end to the economic crisis, and the promotion of Europe to a position of strength equal to that of the two superpowers.

The interviewees attached particular importance to the role of the Franco-German partnership in the integration process. A majority was also willing to abandon the principle of unanimity, and a willingness to transfer national sovereignty to the European institutions is also growing. In the event of the formation of a genuine European government, in 1985 69 per cent of French people would have accepted a West German prime minister and only 19 per cent would have rejected one. Only 26 per cent would have accepted a British premier, which shows that the trust in the Federal Republic is considerably greater than in the British. 'One part of the explanation is that the French associate a close Franco-German cooperation and the building of Europe with the hope of real economic improvement . . . Two thirds of those interviewed in June 1985 were of the view that the Franco-German treaty of friendship is a good thing for the French economy'. Pro-European attitudes on the part of the French appear to have increased continuously throughout the 1980s. A Eurobarometer from the summer of 1988 showed that 61 per cent of the French favoured a federal unification of the Western European states. They were only surpassed by the Italians with 69 per cent, and followed by the Belgians at 58 per cent, the Spanish at 51 per cent and the West Germans, with only 39 per cent.[10]

Like all opinion poll results, these should be interpreted with caution, particularly since, given the complicated subject matter of the questions, the interviewees may not always have been made aware of the range and the implications of their answers. However it is obvious that the willingness of a growing number of French people to overcome national state boundaries in solving political problems both now and in the future, and their trust in a supranational Europe, of whatever shape or form, should not be dismissed. Especially noteworthy about these results are the semantic proximity and positive connotations of the concepts 'Germany' and 'Europe'. The growing pro-European attitudes on the part of the French between 1979 and 1985 cannot be isolated from their increasingly positive perception of the Germans. Indeed, it is as if in the minds of the French the two were inseparably linked. Seen against a background of the horrors of the Nazi regime, still fresh in the memory of the older generation, this is nothing short of revolutionary.

THE POLITICAL PARTIES AND EUROPE

Since the first direct election to the European parliament (1979), European politics has moved progressively into the field of vision of the political parties. Unlike national elections, European elections are traditionally of only moderate interest to the public, and participation is relatively low (around 50 per cent in 1989, in France, Britain, Spain, the Netherlands and Portugal). Six French parties were represented in Strasbourg in 1989: the communists, the socialists, the greens, the centre (CDS), the alliance of liberals and Gaullists (UDF/RPR) and the national front. The French greens entered the European parliament for the first time.

The discourse of all French parties on European politics underlines France's leading role in Europe.[11] 'Nation' and 'state' are two traditionally loaded concepts which are very closely interrelated in discussion. Political elites in France consider themselves heirs to a centralist tradition represented by a strong state, which has been renewed in the Fifth Republic by General de Gaulle. Trust in the nation state's capability of international action is shared by local elites as much as by national ones – of all political shades. It is therefore easy to understand why French politicians can only face the prospect of doing without national sovereignty with great reservation. The political parties' conceptions of Europe can be divided into two pairs of opposites: the dichotomy between left and right overlaps that between Gaullists and anti-Gaullists.

The concept of freedom is at the forefront of the European debate in which French political parties have engaged. It is interpreted differently by the left and by the right. On the right, including the national front, Europe is the stronghold of freedom in opposition to the totalitarianism of the Soviets in particular, and the EC is the instrument for the permanent achievement of liberalism. On the left what is understood by freedom is the possibility of distancing France from majority constraints in the EC, especially in areas of vital national interest. A national sphere of freedom is demanded where goals may be achieved even by interventionist methods, contradicting more traditional interpretations of liberalism. Both ideas of freedom are, of course, controversial in France itself; the theme of Europe gives rise to polemics about concepts such as 'liberty' and 'socialism' which have clearly grown stronger since the change of régime in 1981. The two traditionally right-wing parties, UDF and RPR, find themselves in this case on common ground, which the national front also shares. On the other side, the communists see Europe as being under Atlantic influence and controlled by the interests of big business. This leads them to condemn every step taken towards integration because they see in such an overt supranationality an impediment to the authentic interests of the 'people'. The communist demand for a fundamental reorganisation of social conditions only seems possible if strict national sovereignty is retained. The socialists saw themselves as the defenders of a united Europe, and liked to stress that the Treaty of Rome had been signed during the premiership of Guy Mollet (March 1957). They had in mind a 'socialist Europe', a 'Europe for workers', not held in the grip of multinational companies but rather governed and controlled by democratically elected institutions.

In its early days, the European debate had been polarised into a Gaullist and an anti-Gaullist dichotomy. The 'Europe of States' of de Gaulle and his supporters was denounced by a united opposition front which only the communists did not join. It was branded as 'excessive nationalism', in direct conflict with the ideal of supranationality. In 1974 this polarisation became partially invalid with the recalibration of political forces under Giscard d'Estaing. Gaullism/anti-Gaullism was now joined by the left-right schema already referred to, but with a decisive innovation; the Gaullist presidency had over the years developed a different role for the state and its institutions. From now on the socialists in particular accepted the previously condemned presidential system and with it the constitution of the Fifth Republic. This development encouraged a view of Europe as the sum of its national states, and at the same time every direct reference to supranationality was increasingly frowned upon. Thereafter, the appeal for national independence became part of the permanent repertoire of every political party.[12] This policy of close cooperation between the nation states, with the Franco-German partnership as its driving force, has assumed permanent shape and form, and has been passed on seamlessly from Giscard to Mitterrand. At the same time it seems that the previous demands of all those who had vigorously called for the democratisation of European institutions (UDF and PS) have been silenced, although there are signs that this is again becoming a matter for concern in the 'centre' of French politics.

If the political parties' call for further consolidation of Europe is not to be ignored, then it is not the strengthening of parliamentary democracy, but rather the increased ability of governments to take decisions together that is in question. The political parties in France project on to Europe a way of action which has been shaped by the horizons and experience of their own institutions in France. The same direction is taken when repeated calls are heard in France for the direct election of a European president on the grounds that it is necessary to 'personalise' the European executive in order to give it greater stability.

THE EUROPE OF THE INTELLECTUALS

An important development during the post-war period in France is the shifting attitude of French intellectuals towards Europe. This evolution is difficult to appraise and even harder to measure. Even though the nation as the point of reference for scientific thought and research has kept its validity to a great extent, the European perspective has made considerable progress. There is much to suggest that this will be an important motor in the future.

Among the French intellectuals whom Alison Browning (1984) interviewed on the theme of Europe was Edgar Morin. Morin is a typical 'neo-European', who has undergone a clearly defined development from an anti-European to an interested and committed champion of Europe. His book *Penser l'Europe* (1987) bears witness to this transition. As a Jew he experienced the breakdown of the values of European civilisation (he was born in 1921); during the war he went into the Resistance and joined the communist party. From 1945 to 1975 a form of 'Marxist evangelism' dominated European intellectuals. For Morin in 1945, Europe was a non-concept. For him only internationalism existed. His main interest was in the supremacy of the USSR. He rejected the attempts at European unity through *Realpolitik* by the Christian and social democrats (Schuman, Adenauer, Monnet, Mollet etc.) as insular and reactionary. Later he revised his judgment and thought very differently about the matter.

Today he sees these early attempts at European unity as 'foundations for the construction of Europe in the field of economics'. He believes Europeans live in a 'common destiny' which must be recognised so that a 'new European awareness' can come into being and orientate political actions. Among the peoples of Europe there exists a 'deep need for Europe'. He sees the role of the intellectuals as that of catalysts; their task being to create 'a new European identity'.

For Morin the only common heritage of the Europeans is 'their mutual enmity, disunity and war'. Therefore the common future of Europe cannot be based on historical heritage alone: 'our common destiny does not in any circumstances result from our past, for the latter stands in contradiction to the former'. He describes the national state as 'our original curse'. 'The disappearance of "inherited enemies" among Europeans has fortunately led to a weakening of the inner solidarity of the most strongly centralised states and loosened the national community in favour of a supranational common destiny'. From this Morin comes to the conclusion that national cultures should develop further to become mixed cultures through the full integration of immigrants 'for a half-caste Europe'.[13]

Morin's autobiography epitomises the change of values which the concept of Europe has undergone in the consciousness of many of his contemporaries; from the much reviled to the much loved, as the entry 'Europe' in the *Dictionnaire d'une Epoque* puts it. What coal and steel, the Treaty of Rome, the captains of industry on the Ruhr, the 'two hundred families' or the milk and butter quotas were incapable of doing, human rights and democracy have achieved. Thus, not so much agriculture as culture. How did this occur? In order to understand this inversion which has gained ground in the last decade and which continued to accelerate as 1992 approached, one needs only to pin down developments which have taken place since the war at all points on the compass:

> Northern Europe bespoke Hitler's Germany, and then the economic miracle; the South was draped in the prestige of the Third World; the East identified with the Motherland of communism; the West the representative of American imperialism. What clout was carried by

Europe, then saddled with all the major sins, colonialism, imperialism, nationalism, racism? From Christopher Columbus to the Algerian War, from Verdun to Auschwitz, Europe symbolised the vicious destruction of others, when she was not destroying herself.

In order for a desire for Europe to emerge, it has required the wholesale re-ordering of the planet's basic structures: the dissolution of Third World mythology and its successive stages, the understanding of the totalitarian phenomenon and its absolute specificity, the evaporation of the American curse and of the latent threat of its economic imperialism. Germany has had to distance itself from its Nazi memories and to tone down the bullishness of its economic recovery. French nationalism has needed to lose the grandeur of its Gaullist vision and reveal the hideousness of its Le Penist face. Democracy has had to replace Revolution as the central element, attractive or repulsive, of political philosophy in order for Europe, after ten centuries of sound and fury, to become what she is now rapidly becoming: a conscience, a culture, a history, a thought, a feeling, a hope and even a will.[14]

So what links Europeans, one might conclude, is the awareness of membership of a community of values that has been forged by many negative contacts but has also formed a constructive experience. The peoples of Europe have grown old together; perhaps the certainty of mutual reliance now beginning to crystallise is the result of a wisdom of old age, just as the owl of Minerva first flew away in the evening. Reason, a valuable commodity in individuals' and countries' dealings with each other, should be protected, cared for and made a formal principle of politics, as Raymond Aron described in his *Plaidoyer pour l'Europe décadente* (1976). A number of works are committed to this principle, such as those by Jean-François Deniau and Jacques Huntzinger.

The community of values on the part of Europeans is founded on a common culture: such is the quintessence of numerous works of social scientific and historical research. It is no coincidence that the most convincing explanations of the reality of Europe come from the pens of historians. A culture cannot be conjured up from a retort; to flourish, it needs much more of the humus which generations have gathered from material and spiritual goods. Towards the end of a long and fruitful life of research, Fernand Braudel, one of the greatest historians of all time, published the French-Italian collaborative work *L'Europe* (1982), whose lyrical accents compose a veritable hymn to Europe and whose attractive presentation with numerous illustrations (the work originated from a television programme), appeals to the emotions. It is suitable to stir up a critical awareness but also an identification with Europe. The portrayal of the long history of Europe from the neolithic age to the present day brings out the common ground but also the differences, diversity and contrasts. The history of Europe is one of multiformity, of peculiarities and of the desire, of the dream of unity and uniformity right up to the present, according to Maurice Aymard. This book redeems in an exemplary way the call for 'a Europe with a sensitive heart' as put forward by Pierre Uri, one of the sober companions of Jean Monnet in his old age.[15]

Reflection on the cultural heritage of Europe almost invariably leads to the conclusion that some form of bargaining will prove necessary in order to give the 'content' of European culture the 'form' of adequate political institutions. Culture is understood here as both a factor and a product of Europe at the same time. Consequently a change of view regarding the hierarchy of values and the strategy for action which follows from it seems to have taken place in the last ten years. Monnet's materialistically inspired base, according to which the establishment of economic unity must be begun, so that the political unity of Europe would with a certain inevitability arise from it, has proved to be incapable of carrying much weight. Rather, a voluntary element must be added, without which the political unity of Europe will not happen. That is the conclusion of the book by Alain Minc, *La Grande Illusion* (1989) which caused a sensation in France because it attempted to explode the myth, which many French people took for the truth, that 1992 would open the door to a great Eldorado for them.

So while the intellectuals seek, in their study of the past, dialogue with the politicians, the latter are conversely trying to secure the support both of the scientists and, especially, of the arts scholars. With particular reference to the work of H. Kaelble on the European social history of the twentieth century, at a colloquium of historians on 'National identities and European awareness' in 1988, Jacques Delors formulated the hypothesis that there was 'a European model of society'.[16] Is Delors looking for confirmation in European social history of his own policy of forcing the pace of European integration?

Voices pressing for an acceleration of the process of political integration are increasing in number in France. Alain Minc, a celebrated product of the elite schools Sciences-Po and ENA (Ecole Nationale de l'Administration) who is now a well-known captain of industry, regards the EC commission as the bearer of 'European legitimacy' and at the same time as 'the only envisageable embryo for a European government'.[17] That is naturally grist to the Delors mill. The metaphor of the embryo is well chosen – indeed it signifies an idea of the growth of something which already exists in embryonic form and only needs to be developed.

There is no lack of a strategy to transpose this biological thought. For the supporters of the 'United States of Europe' the USA has long since been rejected as an example, because, as Lacouture notes, in view of its completely different historical prerequisites, it is simply not transferable to Europe. Rather, one should start with the existing institutions of the community, which should be developed further. This is the basic idea behind the observations of Jean-Louis Quermonne on the question: 'Does a European political model exist?' [18]

Transferred to a diagram the developments suggested by Quermonne can be presented thus:

Present	**Future**	
European Parliament	Lower chamber of parliament	*Legislative*
Council of Ministers	Upper chamber of parliament cf. *Bundesrat* in Federal Republic of Germany	*body (two chamber system)*
Commission	Government of the union	
European Council	Collective head of state of the community	

This diagram, based on the 1984 Spinelli report on the development of Europe, aims at the extension of the European parliament as the complete legislative body of the EC, in which the legislative authority will be exercised along with a second chamber originating from the council of ministers (a two chamber system).

The model for this second chamber is the *Bundesrat* in the Federal Republic of Germany. As a legislative organ the second chamber would be put together from representatives of the government of each state, that is the regional executives. The EC Commission will become the government of the European union, that is, the new executive, and the European council will become a sort of collective head of state of the community.

REGIONS IN EUROPE, OR A EUROPE OF REGIONS?

If the Council of Ministers is to be converted into a second chamber, whom will it represent: the governments of the nation states, or, as the West German model suggests, the governments of the *Länder* or regions? This presupposes the existence of regions drawn up politically beneath the level of the nation state and on an equal basis in all member countries of the EC. Is this not the weak point in the model which is so extolled by the French of all people? Is France not, because of its markedly centralist structures and traditions, the country in which (in comparison with the central state's concentration of power), regional relay stations are weak, not to say non-existent? Is it not true that the structural prerequisites for such a model for the United States of Europe are lacking in view of the unevenly developed regional authorities in the different European nation states? Such a conclusion would seem to ignore important recent developments in France.

In France in the last three decades far-reaching processes of socio-economic change have taken place which have led to a new geographical distribution of economic potential and also to the rearrangement of cultural life. The old and comfortable cliché of the contrast between Paris and the provinces, between the all-powerful capital which sets the tone and the powerless, boring, old-fashioned provinces has already become very faded. A substantial contribution to this structural change was made by the state's environmental planning, which was created to carry out a programme of modernisation, especially in designated planning areas, the 'programme regions'. These areas, created in the 1950s and at first purely statistical, have gradually been given representative and administrative bodies. In addition more and more extensive authority for self-administration has been transferred to them, the last instance of which was in the decentralisation reform introduced by Gaston Deferre (1981–86). In this example it is precisely the same organic growth of the institutions which Jean-Louis Quermonne transposes, at a theoretical level, to the EC institutions, an example of how closely his outline for the future follows the horizons of experience in his own country.

The institutional process of growth in the French regions is not only the result of the country's economic modernisation. It is no coincidence that both the regions and the modernisation had the same origins in Jean Monnet's planning commission. This process of growth also expresses a change in France's political culture. During the presidency of Giscard d'Estaing in the 1970s, Gaullists and communists were still sufficiently influential to block, with a joint 'Jacobin front', the decentralisation and regionalisation of France's central administrative system. They prevented the extension of regional authorities on the grounds that they would 'smooth the way for the provinces of a future federal Europe'.[19] With the Gaullists' and the communists' loss of influence as a consequence of social changes in France, opposition to decentralisation at the level of the nation as well as to ideas leading to a federal Europe of regions disappears. Even Jacques Delors seems not to rule out the objective of a European federal state on the basis of its regions, when he declares 'there will be no European unity without a strengthening of the regions'.[20]

To what extent this is vague speculation is an open question. The fact is that the self-awareness of the new regions is clearly expressed, as a gathering of the mandated delegates of all regions recently demonstrated.[21] They can count on widespread approval from the public, as shown in opinion polls in 1988. For more than half of the French (59 per cent), the region is the administrative unit of the future. 'On average 53 per cent (with regional fluctuations from 37 per cent in Nord-Pas-de-Calais to 68 per cent in Alsace) think more optimistically about the future of the regions than of the nation. This optimism has risen since 1985 and is most widespread among 25 to 50 year olds'.[22] The anti-centralist or polycentralist trends expressed in the phenomenon of the modern region is not as new as is widely assumed; as Riemenschneider and von Thadden have suggested, these are constants in French history which have in the past been submerged or blotted out but never quite broken up.

CONCLUSION: IN SEARCH OF A NEW BALANCE

Finally, let us cast a glance at the French government's European policy. President Mitterrand is responsible for negotiating between the various interests and positions regarding Europe in French society and finding a balance. In this role will he give priority to the national or the European interest?

Mitterrand has shown through his emphasis on traditional aspirations for independence and the protection of France's leading international position that he is continuing the policies of his predecessors Pompidou and Giscard d'Estaing. However, he has also developed a much stronger commitment to European politics than his predecessors, which has given the EC an important impetus. Since the final rejection of socialist reform experiments in a national attempt to go it alone, and the decision of March 1983 to remain in the European monetary system, 'the decisive initiatives for the reform of the European Community in the years 1984–85 which finally, in the Single European Act of 1987 and in the single market project, gave the commission substance, were taken after strong endeavours by Jacques Delors and François Mitterrand'.[23] The simultaneous hurrying along of the unity acts and the single market project suggests 'long-term calculations of integration policy' which in the spirit of the Delors strategy comprise, as Krosigk points out, a 'combination of market integration and political integration'. In this context, the 'rediscovery of Jean Monnet' as well as the afore-mentioned transfer of his remains to the Panthéon have their full significance: on the basis of the single market project France has accepted, as Krosigk puts it, 'a European commitment which cannot be supported without grave repercussions for the established Gaullist positions of national independence and a world-wide mission for France'.

This European commitment seems to support the extension of federal structures. Jacques Delors, who is more and more frequently compared with Jean Monnet, declared his belief in federalism at the congress in The Hague on 5 May 1988, and emphasised the necessity for the European states to hasten political integration.[24] Since then, Delors has consistently pursued this line. Influenced by the changes in Eastern Europe, he called in the European Parliament for an acceleration of the conversion of the commission into the European executive and the expansion of the European parliament's authority.[25]

Indeed, the revolutions in Central Europe and especially in the former GDR have generated a dynamism to which the EC states can only react with integrationist measures. In the words of Chancellor Kohl, the events have become 'a driving force for the rapid unity of Europe'.[26] The complexion of European politics has already begun to change, even in the course of the year 1990. Nobody would have believed that circumstances would change in such a landslide way as has been the case since the summer of 1989 when Fitussi could write in a tone of utter conviction that nothing extraordinary was to be expected in Europe until 1 January 1993 when the unity acts and the single market would come into effect: 'The issue of whether European integration should now be pushed forward is not even on the agenda'.[27]

That has all completely changed. The cards have been re-dealt. Together with an economically strong and politically weak Germany, France wanted to form Europe according to *her* ideas and ensure herself a position of prime importance within the new organisation. However, now the relationship with the newly-strengthened Germany must be redefined. The French need some time to adjust themselves to the 'German question', now radically changed by the collapse of the GDR. Their reactions were those of perplexity, then of fear of the 'German demons', and were shaped by indecision. In this phase of very agitated public opinion (early 1990), the commentaries of Jean Daniel and especially of Jacques Julliard in the *Nouvel Observateur* came as agreeable exceptions to the norm: in the conviction that France had no scope for action in European political affairs and therefore no alternative but to grin and bear the facts that were happening before their eyes, they urged the president to show their German partners trust, but also a readiness to negotiate: to hurry along the integration of Europe, to bind the two Germanies firmly into it, in order to prevent the Federal Republic drifting away from the community and the Western alliance.[28]

And Mitterrand did exactly that. He grasped the bull, on which Europe sits, bravely by the horns. He advocated the unification of the two German states to the astonishment of many of his compatriots. Alfred Grosser said: 'Until now I have held the view that France would be for German reunification for as long as it were not possible. However I have been proved fundamentally wrong'.[29] At the same time, in the televised discussion already mentioned (5 May 1990), Mitterrand underlined the necessity of speeding up the 'construction of the community' because he saw this as the only means of solving the problems thrown up by German unification. And finally he declared himself in favour of a 'confederation' to tie the countries of eastern Europe to the EC. [30] That is the new balance which it is necessary for Europe as a whole to seek.[31]

Once again it was the 'German question' around which French foreign policy revolved.'At the heart of the European problem, there is Germany', Josette Alia remarked in a pensive commentary.[32] It looks as if this time once again the worry about 'German uncertainties' lead the French into a more extensive European commitment: binding Germany into the greater context of European structures in order to keep Germany under control, but at the price of sacrificing a certain national independence and sovereign rights. As in 1950 at the time of the foundation of the coal and steel community, the French fear of an over-powerful Germany will make the European federal state more acceptable to them. Control over Germany, keeping their role as a power (not to say a great power) through hegemony in Europe, modernisation of the economy under the pressure of competition from outside, protection of the cultural values of Europe – these are the motives for a stronger commitment to European politics by French men and women in our time.

NOTES

1. The text attributed to the protagonists according to *Le Monde*, 22 May 1990, p. 46: 'Les Douze s'engagent à petits pas sur la voie de l'union politique'.
2. J. Lacouture, *De Gaulle, III: Le Souverain* (Paris: Seuil, 1986), p. 320.
3. There is even a hint from de Gaulle, who was known to think largely in historical categories, of the repayment by England of an historic debt to France, which comes from the following anecdote:

   Among the many voices which publicly expressed their regret about

Great Britain's rejected attempt to join the EEC in 1963 was Paul Reynaud, a former comrade-in-arms of de Gaulle. Reynaud published an article in *Le Monde* on 24 January 1963 condemning de Gaulle. In reaction two weeks later Reynaud received a letter. He recognised the handwriting on the envelope. The envelope was empty. On the back was written: 'If undelivered, please forward to Agincourt (Somme) or Waterloo (Belgium)'. (Lacouture, *De Gaulle III*, p. 338).

4. J. Lacouture, op. cit., p. 315.
5. J. -B. Duroselle, 'Les débuts de la construction européenne', in R. Poidevin (ed.), *Histoire des débuts de la construction européenne 1948-1950* (Brussels: Bruylant, 1986), pp. 11–12.
6. E. Weisenfeld, *Geschichte Frankreichs seit dem Krieg*, 2nd edition, (Munich: Beck, 1982), p. 266.
7. J. Delors, 'Une Europe du possible', *Revue politique et parlementaire*, no. 926 (1986): 3–6.
8. Reported in *Le Nouvel Observateur*, no. 760, 4 June 1979, pp. 62–9.
9. The following remarks are based on the work of H. G. Ehrhart, 1988, pp. 210–14. On the difference between 'public opinion' and 'published opinion', see ibid, pp. 14–18.
10. *Le Monde*, 21 June 1988, quoted from Sukup in *Dokumente (Zeitschrift für den deutsch-französischen Dialog) 45* (1989) 1: 5.
11. This section is based on the work of François Saint-Ouen, who deals with the French-speaking areas – France, Luxembourg, Belgium, Switzerland, Aosta.
12. Virtually classic is Chirac's speech during the debate on Europe in the French National Assembly on 10 April 1990, in which he reiterated all the familiar Gaullist demands: rejection of further federal development of the EC, holding on to national independence, especially in defence and security policy, assertion of France's leading role in Europe (text of the speech in *Dokumente 46* (1990) 3: 253–5).
13. *Le Nouvel Observateur*, no. 1261, 5 January 1989, p. 7.
14. *Le Débat*, no. 50 (1988): 201–2.
15. Quoted by Alison Browning, 1984, p. 335.
16. *Dokumente 45* (1989): 129.
17. *Le Nouvel Observateur*, no. 1261, 5 January 1989, p. 9.
18. J. -L. Quermonne, 'Existe-il un modèle politique européene?', *Revue française de science politique*, no. 46 (1990): 192–210.
19. See J. Daniel, 'La Croisade des Jacobins', *Le Nouvel Observateur*, no. 736, 18 December 1978, p. 38.
20. *Dokumente 45* (1989): 132.
21. *Le Monde*, 23 February 1990, p. 37.
22. L. Albertin in *Frankreich-Jahrbuch 1988*, p. 149.
23. F. v. Krosigk, 'Französische Außenpolitik im Spannungsfeld von Mondialismus und Europäischer Integration', in *Aus Politik und Zeitgeschichte*, Beilage Parlament 39 (1989): 37.
24. Schöndube, *Parlament*, no. 23, 3 June 1988, p. 11.

25. *Le Monde*, 18 January 1990.
26. *Der Spiegel*, 9 July 1990, p. 116.
27. Cited in *Pouvoirs*, 1989, p. 18.
28. *Le Nouvel Observateur*, no. 1320, 22 February 1990; see also issues 1324 and 1325.
29. Grosser in *Brunswick, Brunschweiger Zeitung*, 20 July 1990, p. 5.
30. *Le Monde*, 2 January 1990.
31. Foreign Minister Dumas in the National Assembly on 10 April 1990, reported in *Dokumente 46* (1990) 3: 251.
32. *Le Nouvel Observateur*, 5 January 1989, p. 6.

8 The Euro-Germans: National Identity and European Integration in Germany

Eva Kolinsky

In the first half of the twentieth century, the political history of Europe was written under the impact of German nationalism and the wars it precipitated. In the second half of the twentieth century, the history of Western Europe at least focused on cross-national collaboration and social and economic integration as nationalism seemed to give way to a new collegiate spirit between nations, an era of post-nationalism. In fact, the Federal Republic of Germany has played a key role in the change towards post-nationalism. Since 1950, it has been a member of the European Council, a founder member of the European Coal and Steel Community and of the Common Market and a full member of the military and political alliance of the Western powers, NATO. The Federal Republic has been a strong advocate of the European Monetary System of coordinated European currencies, and under its presidency, the European Commission decided to create a single European market with unrestricted social mobility between member states. The process of German unification, which commenced in the autumn of 1989 and resulted in East Germany joining the West on 3 October 1990, had always been linked to an emphatic commitment to international cooperation and a reaffirmation of the European Community as the economic and political context for the greater Germany of the future. For German governments, as for their West German predecessors, Europe continues to determine their policy agendas, although national themes and notions of a Europe beyond the member states of the European Community have gained ground.

We shall examine later how this commitment to international cooperation and integration has been reflected in orientations and attitudes towards Europe and whether a European identity has emerged alongside that which is specifically German. The specifically German dimension needs to be clarified first. It is not without its own complexities of nationhood and identity.

In 1949, two German states were founded, one in the Eastern and one in the Western political alliance. They displaced the unified nation state, the Reich. In the post-war era, the former German nation was divided into at least two territories with contrasting political systems, and two very different republics. Each differed from the traditional German nationalism which had been discredited, and they differed from one another.

Despite the separate institutional settings in the two German states, a common national consciousness has never fully disappeared. In the German Democratic Republic (1945–90) successive governments insisted that their state was underpinned by a national identity of its own. This East German identity was supposed to have severed all links with German nationalism and to bear no similarities to its equivalent in the West. One could say that an East German identity was decreed from above. The state sought to gain international diplomatic recognition as a separate and distinctive entity; in order to keep a visible distance from the other Germany and the German national past, East German government communications and collaboration with their Western German neighbour were always spiked by *Abgrenzung* and *Abschottung*, distancing oneself and sealing off.

On the informal level of everyday culture, however, a GDR specific national consciousness has been less firmly established as people continued to look towards the West and hope for their share of affluence and freedom as members of the same nation. In their search for a new future at the end of the 1980s and beginning of the 1990s, East Germans could rely on national unity as the lever to transform their economic and political lives. Once the calls for a more democratic socialism gave way to calls for German unity, the movements for political change lost their significance as change began to mean joining the West. While the slogan of the first hour, 'we are the people', challenged the legitimacy of the East German government, institutions and elites, its successor, 'we are one people', accepted the institutional and political answers of the West German polity and used the common nationhood to claim membership and anticipate change. The collapse of Soviet-style communism in East Germany in late 1989, the opening of the borders, the dismantling of the Berlin Wall and the reunification of the two post-war German states have pushed German national identity to the top of the political agenda of the 1990s.

The spotlight on national identity has exposed the uncertainties which have persisted about its scope and political consequences. For some, a German national identity had come to mean a West German identity, based on the Federal Republic and its territory. Others always included the territory of the German Democratic Republic. For others again, Germany still stretches to include territories which were seceded to the Soviet Union or Poland after World War II. The borders of such a reunited Germany would not fit into the present-day map of Europe. Lastly, there are those who aim to rehabilitate the German national past by obfuscating its anti-democratic legacies and the extent to which genocide, persecution and inhumanity were official state policies during National Socialism. For them, a reunited Germany would not only extend beyond the borders of the Eastern and Western partial stakes, it would also claim to develop a special German role, a *Sonderweg* of new national importance as a mediator between East and West in a contemporary grasp for world power.

THE ELUSIVE IDENTITY

At no time in the short history of German nationalism did national identity and political reality coincide. The German nation and national identity always remained something elusive which could not be accomplished. For example, when the first German nation state was established in 1871, it excluded areas which many regarded as part of the German nation since their language and culture were German. The so-called *minor* German solution produced a nation state without Austria. While this facilitated the political dominance of Prussia over the other German regions, the issue of the nation and its boundaries remained unsettled. Imperial Germany, the epitome of the German nation state, did not include the whole of the German nation.

In the Weimar Republic, the territorial settlements after the First World War exacerbated these discrepancies; the state which arose from the Versailles Treaty never gained credence as the political framework for the German nation. State and nation, it was argued by a blend of nationalist and anti-democratic activists, had fallen apart. National Socialism claimed to bring state and nation together. It elevated nationalism into a state doctrine in order to legitimise expanding the state boundaries, asserting the superiority of all things German, exploiting other economies and subjugating other peoples. In the post-war era the division of Germany has crushed the presumed unison of nation and state and resuscitated its unfulfilled dimension: once again nation and state did not match.

Forty years after the two German states commenced their separate development, economic and social pressures forced East Germany to relinquish its adaptation of communist government. East German hopes for an innovative merger of capitalist and socialist traditions, and similar hopes of the West German left that a political alliance with East Germany might serve to recast the institutional structures and political practices in the Federal Republic and render them more democratic, more social, more aligned to the presumed wishes of the people – such hopes were dashed by the reality that East Germans in their majority wanted unification without such preconditions, and that the urgent pace of the unification process itself meant that the East joined the West, rather than influenced or moulded it. The new Germany of the 1990s rests on a kind of *Anschluß* (annexation), an unconditional acceptance of the West German model as the politically and economically more successful system. Given the uneven legitimacy of German unification, it is the political culture of West Germany which dominates the institutions, orientations, attitudes and values in the emergent German-German polity.

In German political history, there had never been a straight match between nation and state. Indeed, the divergence of the two left its own characteristic legacy: the persistence of authoritarian structures and anti-democratic tendencies. At the outset, German nationalism had strong liberal and democratic overtones. Against the proliferation of small states, autocratic rulers, feudal and military elites which dominated Germany in the early nineteenth century, membership of nation did not depend on class, status or power and was seen as a means to ensure equal rights of political and economic participation in German society. One could argue that nationalism brought little more than economic success. After 1834, the Customs Union reduced the factionalism between states and facilitated economic activity. By contrast, the political dimension of equal participation stagnated before it could realise the liberal implications of nationalism in Germany. An attempt at setting up a national parliament and a constitutional monarchy in 1848 failed, although some regions did enjoy a foretaste of democratic government in the last century.

The German unified nation state which eventually emerged in 1871 was an *Obrigkeitsstaat*, an authoritarian state dominated by a blend of aristocratic and military elites, with few powers for parliament and few institutionalised channels of participation for the citizens. A special role for the state in industrial development enabled the latecomer nation to make up economic ground and emerge rapidly as a major industrial power. Dahrendorf aptly speaks of a 'feudal industrial' structure to highlight the discrepancy between economic performance and modernisation on the one hand, and on the other, the backwardness of a political system which excluded the majority of Germans from the political arena.[1] Nationalism became a major device to camouflage the failure of this feudal-industrial construct to respond to social change and increase the rights of social, political and economic participation. By pointing to exterior threats against a newcomer nation, national unity was forged by a rejection of others. This 'negative integration' bred hostility in two directions: externally against powers which seemed to deny Germany her 'place in the sun'; internally, Jews, socialists and foreigners became scapegoats for the unmet social promises of the nation state.

From the late nineteenth century onwards, German nationalism developed strong biological and racist overtones in its defensive stand against social change. In National Socialist ideology, nationalism and racism constituted twin aspects in the claim for German superiority. During the National Socialist dictatorship, the blend of nationalism and racism resulted in an organised system of mass murder. This consisted of an extensive network of concentration camps, death camps and labour camps to separate presumed enemies from presumed members of the German nation. It also meant the ruthless utilisation of foreigners and millions of prisoners from the many camps as labour in inhumane conditions, often leading to their death, and even the utilisation of human remains from the death camps as raw materials for a variety of goods from soap or candles to lampshades or fertilisers.

In May 1945, Allied troops liberated the camps inside Germany and sent first pictures around the world of the horrific conditions, the many victims and the suffering of the few survivors. They prompted Thomas Mann, the famous German writer who had been forced into exile in 1933, to reflect in 1945 on the task – if not the impossibility – of recasting German national identity:

> Everything German, everyone who speaks German, who writes German, who has lived a German way of life is implicated by these revelations. This was not a small number of criminals; hundreds of thousands of a so-called German elite, men, boys and dehumanised women have committed these evil deeds under the impact of mad doctrines and with sickening pleasure. Mankind shudders on seeing this Germany![2]

CREATING A NEW NATIONAL IDENTITY

In accepting the high office to which he had just been elected, the first president of the Federal Republic, Theodor Heuß pointed out that the new state now needed a new national consciousness. This was no easy task. The Federal Republic pursued an ambivalent course in questions of nationhood. On the one hand, it opted for continuity with the past despite the anti-democratic legacies. On the other hand, a clean break was sought with a new, contemporary orientation. The result was an indirect, even hidden identity. West Germans appear to be detached from their nationality and its symbols but they also have a strong sense of German identity, quality and even 'superiority'.

Some examples of post-war readjustments may be useful to clarify how national identity has been hidden before we examine what took its place. Legally, the Federal Republic of Germany considers itself the successor state to the German Reich and the only *bona fide* German state. In the 1950s, it interpreted this legal position as a sole right of representation, while denying the right of representing German affairs to the German Democratic Republic. In the era of détente, *Ostpolitik* found a formula of recognising the political existence of an East German state: post-war realities, it was argued, had created two German states within one German nation.

In the founding decade of the Federal Republic, the East German state served as a negative focal point. Non-recognition was so much part of her political culture that it was not permitted to call the German Democratic Republic by its official name: this would have implied the legitimacy of a state which the West German government regarded as a mere satellite, an imposition, a non-entity. The language of non-recognition highlights the problem. During the 1950s, the German neighbour in the East was referred to as 'Soviet Zone of Occupation', as the 'Eastern Zone', as 'Middle Germany – *Mitteldeutschland*', as the 'so-called GDR', not to mention more expressive names such as state of injustice, of inhumanity, of torture. East of the German-German border, the practices of National Socialism were considered to have continued uninterrupted, albeit under a different name and under Soviet command.

In essence, the GDR served as a negative counter-world of non-democratic practices. The West German identity appeared, above all, as under threat from the East and the presumed imperialism of communist politics. In the political discourse of the day, it was commonplace to counter criticism of West German political life by suggesting that the critic might as well pack his things and live in the East. The negative focus on the GDR provided considerable ideological continuity since anti-communism had, of course, been a major preoccupation of National Socialism and of the German national right. In the post-war era, anti-communist and related pre-democratic attitudes could survive virtually unchanged. Moreover, the obsession with potential dangers emanating from the East made the quality of democratic life in the West seem unimportant. What mattered was stability, the durability of the political system and the visible economic success it could engender.

Overshadowed by the pressures to survive against presumed threats from the East, the Federal Republic pitched its new identity against Cold War realities without relinquishing the broader meanings of Germany. The Basic Law, the constitutional framework for the new post-war state, had been designed for a provisional state, and stresses its own provisional character. The fact that it has now been in operation for over forty years and has gained broad recognition as a democratic and adaptable constitution, never altered its status as a transitional arrangement pending reunification. Other constitutional provisions underpin the continued relevance of German as opposed to West German identity: citizens of the former GDR and also people of German cultural or biological origin from Eastern European countries always enjoyed full citizen's rights within the Federal Republic. On entry they qualified for state support, they held voting rights. They were, in fact, regarded as Germans in exile. This principle had been in operation since the Basic Law was drafted in 1949, and has helped to integrate the various waves of refugees from the East. In the late 1980s, the numbers seeking to return 'Heim ins Reich' (back home to the Reich) soared. From Eastern Europe, people claiming to be of German origin made use of the new rights of mobility to start afresh in the West; from the GDR, a mass exodus commenced in August 1989, as East Germans voted with their feet against the continued economic difficulties and political restrictions in their country and made use of their West German citizen's rights to improve their personal situation. In so doing, they forced the collapse of the East German political system and leadership.

POST-WAR NATIONAL SYMBOLS – CONTINUITIES AND CAUTION

The attempt not to specify whether post-war identity should be West German or German-German or that of the former Reich has also been evident in the search for the symbols of nationhood after 1949. In the interim period of 1945–49, none was used. The question itself was suspended; where symbols were needed, regions and localities remembered their own traditions and revived suitable practices. Once the new democracy had been created, however, national symbols had to be chosen which would express its political intent and provide the public with a focal point for identification. The choice of a day to commemorate post-war changes shows the reluctance to focus on the meaning of West German developments: as the symbolic day to define its purpose and history, the Federal Republic instituted 17 June, the day on which East German workers had staged an uprising in 1953. For the new consciousness which Theodor Heuß had envisaged one might, for instance, have chosen 23 May, when the Basic Law was passed, or the day of the first federal elections, the first parliamentary session, the election of the first democratic government. If Thomas Mann's warnings had been heeded, a day to commemorate the National Socialist crimes against humanity might have been instituted as an occasion to face up to the past and as a symbol of a new beginning. On unification, 3 October was designated as the new national holiday, replacing the defunct Day of German Unity, and replacing the anti-communist by a national, German focus.

The conventional symbols of national identity, flag and anthem also reveal the complexities of choice in a national tradition where little has remained untainted by injustices; they also show the determination to seek continuity with the better segments of the past rather than create a new flag, compose a new anthem and start from scratch. For a flag, the Federal Republic chose black, red and gold, the colours of the national-liberal opposition of the nineteenth century and the flag which should have replaced the black, white and red of Imperial Germany and World War I in the Weimar Republic, but which was never fully accepted in the anti-democratic political culture of the period. Through this flag the Federal Republic declared herself heir to German democratic traditions; the same national flag, with an additional emblem, was later adopted by the GDR. Although the *Bundesflagge* has not been rejected as in the Weimar Republic, it has been accepted reluctantly. In the early 1950s, one in five West Germans declared they liked seeing the flag; the remainder were indifferent or stated their dislike. In the eighties, the split was about half and half. The united Germany – the Federal Republic of Germany to use its official name – will continue to use the flag which had been adopted for West Germany.

The choice of national anthem shows the uncertain nature of the post-war German identity even more clearly. Initially, the new state had no anthem. When official occasions required official music, an excerpt from Beethoven's Ninth Symphony could be heard. Without waiting for a formal decision, the Federal Chancellor at the time, Konrad Adenauer resolved the matter in 1950 by giving a public rendering of the third verse of the *Deutschlandlied*. With its emphasis on unity, liberty and the rule of law this verse could not be faulted easily and was subsequently endorsed by the Bundestag. The music has been taken from a Haydn quartet, written in support of the Austrian emperor against Napoleon. With a text to celebrate the emperor, the tune became the national anthem of the Austro-Hungarian monarchy; after 1945, Austria changed her anthem. In Germany, the *Deutschlandlied* was sung to the words of Hoffman von Fallersleben, a liberal nationalist of the early nineteenth century. It was adopted as a national anthem in 1922 on the recommendation of the Social Democratic President, Friedrich Ebert. During the National Socialist period, it remained the national anthem, but had to be sung in conjunction with the so-called Horst Wessel song, the theme song of the SA and SS. Although tainted by its affiliation with National Socialism, the *Deutschlandlied* could also be regarded as a symbol of the democratic element in the Weimar Republic or the liberal traditions in German nationalism. It has led a shadowy existence. Eight out of ten West Germans confess that they do not know the text, and most schoolbooks do not include it. In the new climate of national unity, the anthem also gained new prominence. It could be heard during demonstrations in East Germany in the early stages of the unification process; and it could be heard in the Bundestag, when the House accepted the formal agreement – the *Staatsvertrag* – for the political and economic inclusion of East Germany into the West. Prior to the new national emphasis, the anthem was more readily sung by activists of the extreme or national right. They, however, regard singing it as a statement against the contemporary democratic state and the division of Germany (which persists in their eyes until German territory extends to the border of 1937). For their protest gesture they tend to select those verses which had been dropped as expansionist. As a symbol of a post-war German identity, the revived anthem failed.

NATION AND NATIONAL CHARACTER

Generally speaking, Germans have been reluctant to admit to a national identity; among Americans or Britons, 80–90 per cent take pride in their national identity; among West Germans, less than half do so, the remainder hold reservations or do not voice an opinion. Compared with other European countries, openly articulated national pride has been rare in West Germany. Older people express more positive views about their national identity; younger people are more reluctant. Overall, however, the Federal Republic of Germany seems to lack a clear identity. Indifference instead of pride, detachment instead of emotional ties, characterise today's fatherland.

One of the reasons for the apparent non-national stance is to be found in the relationship with the past. Not in the manner Thomas Mann had in mind, that Germans should face up to their guilt; on the contrary, the majority is against probing into the past and favour putting it behind them, obliterated by the new beginning. In 1979, the television serial *Holocaust* brought a short-lived surge of concern; in general, however, most West Germans object to being reminded of the concentration camps and the National Socialist horrors; even today, nearly 40 per cent are convinced that National Socialism was basically a good idea although bad leadership steered it into war and what Germans commonly call the 'catastrophe of total collapse'. Successive West German governments, and public opinion, have tried to relate to the acceptable aspect of German national history and exclude others as untypical of German national and cultural traditions. Central for the hidden German identity is the assumption that the German people were victims, not perpetrators of criminal policies. Bad government, it seems, had dazzled, manipulated and ultimately betrayed a well-intentioned people.

The development of democratic government in the post-war era and an emphatic condemnation of the government and leadership of National Socialism and of Hitler go hand in hand. Less evident has been the implication that the German national character has survived untainted. A study of political behaviour in the late 1950s, for instance, found that Germans at the time were hesitant to express pride in their national identity, symbols or institutions, but did express pride in their national character. A recent example of the hidden assumption that a good nation had endured bad leadership stems from 1988: at a memorial session to remember the victims of the 1938 pogroms, the president of the German Bundestag at the time, Philip Jenninger, devoted much of his speech to reminding his audience of parliamentarians, survivors of the Holocaust, West German political dignitaries and international diplomats how trusting, easily-led and essentially innocent the German people had been in following National Socialism. Jenninger's speech caused a storm of indignation and forced his resignation. Inside the Federal Republic, the critics felt that he had not tackled a complex issue intelligently enough; outside the Federal Republic, the use of National Socialist categories to describe the victims and also to excuse the German people stirred concerns that not enough had changed between then and now. More to the point would have been to indicate the way in which past and present are compartmentalised: West Germans have solved their twofold problem of a national identity and its links with the past by separating them out as if the past had no links with the present. From schoolbooks to public discourse, it has become common practice to 'explain' National Socialism in its own language as if it had been a logical system of laws and regulations and as if it had applied acceptable categories of thought.

ACHIEVEMENT AND 'SUPERIORITY': THE GERMAN MODEL

In 1977, the weekly magazine *Der Spiegel* published a survey on cross-national perceptions between France and West Germany, at a time when West German responses to left-wing terrorism were seen by many as a resurgence of authoritarian and antidemocratic practices. In our context, the German self-perceptions are of particular interest. When asked to name typical German characteristics, the French regarded their neighbours as more hard working, braver, and as cultivated as themselves – in other respects, Germans seemed less well endowed than the French. When asked to comment on French characteristics, West Germans conceded that the French may be a little more imaginative than they; on all other accounts, the French were perceived as inferior. A similar picture emerged with regard to the social environment. The French felt that living standards in West Germany were higher than their own and that the political system was more stable. In France, however, civil liberties seemed more developed and criminality lower. For West Germans, their own country appeared vastly superior on all accounts; none of the institutions or characteristics France or the French had to offer were regarded as better than their German equivalents.[3]

In view of the attempt to distance the nation from its past, West German identity has not been articulated in terms of national themes or orientations. Conventional landmarks of national identity have been substituted by a strong sense of institutional identity. Pride in German institutions can be regarded as the contemporary equivalent of nationalism. In the founding years of the Federal Republic, the majority of the population remained indifferent to the democratic remodelling of their country which went on around them. Distrustful of politics and politicians after their experience with National Socialism, they focused on the private sphere and a normalisation of their personal living conditions. Democracy and the new political opportunities of the post-war era seemed less relevant than living standards, housing, employment and a general sense of economic security. At the economic level, of course, the recast Germany of the post-war years was a success. Internally, the economic miracle improved the circumstances of all social strata and generations beyond living memory; externally, the new state became a fledgling economic power. The acceptance of the political processes and institutions of democracy followed the economic lead. To this day, concerns about economic stability have remained at the top of the political agenda when surveys probe into popular preferences at election times. More than eight in ten Germans regard their economic system with pride, and as a model for their own and other countries. East Germans tend to be even more convinced of the superiority of German economic achievement. The economic hardship and unemployment following the transformation from a planned to a market economy are not blamed on the West German model or the West German government, but are explained as the fruits of socialist mismanagement and the fault of the deposed system and its elite. On the eve of the 1990 all-German elections, confidence in the German economic model and confidence in the administration of Chancellor Kohl to ensure economic stability and cope with the adjustment processes in people's lives, were even higher among former GDR citizens than among their Western brethren.[4] As we shall see later, this high profile of the economy and the high degree of acceptance of economic performance, have played a major role in the Federal Republic's move towards Europe.

German identity in the Federal Republic today is, above all, an achievement-based post-war identity. In 1976, more than 90 per cent thought of the successes of German industry when they were asked what they thought of as typically German; 87 per cent thought of *Heimat* – homeland – and 86 per cent of *Leistung* – achievement. The political system which had stirred so few positive feelings in the late 1940s has been accepted as the best political system on offer – better, that is, than a one-party state or other non-democratic format, and German democratic processes are widely regarded as a model which other democracies should follow. There is none of the modesty of the late-comer. The identification with the political and economic system, which began to take shape in the 1950s, complemented the positive views about national characteristics such as diligence, cleanliness, reliability to forge a conviction that the new German way of doing things was best.

Broadly speaking, conditions were favourable for the development of such a system-based identity paired with the belief in a positive German national character. In their concern to contain the Cold War and transform their occupied part of Germany into a stronghold and ally, the Western powers soon ceased to treat their zones as enemy territory and began building up their economic potential and political infrastructures. The foundation of the West German state in 1949 followed the decision at the London conference of foreign ministers that a political framework for the Western integration of occupied Germany was needed. The currency reform of 1948 and the Marshall plan had already prepared economic integration into the West, and the consolidation in West Germany of a capitalist market economy despite pressures from the left to establish a socialist economy as a safeguard against any fascist tendencies in the future. The 1949 elections resulted in a near stalemate between the two major parties, the Christian Democratic Union and the Christian Socialist Union (CDU/CSU) and the Socialist Democratic Party (SPD) and their juxtaposed policy priorities: under the leadership of Konrad Adenauer, the CDU/CSU had opted for rejoining the powers by becoming a partner of the West in economic, political and ultimately military terms, the SPD, by contrast, rejected West integration as an obstacle to reunification and as contrary to the German national interest. While Adenauer's position accepted semi-sovereignty and restricted recognition as a tactical step towards full equality, the SPD under Kurt Schumacher insisted that those political forces which suffered at the hands of the National Socialists deserved full and immediate equality and political sovereignty. Success was on the side of the government and its policy of equal status through an alliance with the West. Against the rehabilitation of West Germany on the international political arena and against the persuasive realities of the economic miracle, the opposition fought a losing battle. In the 1953 elections, the governing CDU/CSU – heading a coalition government as has been normal practice in the Federal Republic – increased their share of the vote by 14 per cent; four years later they won an absolute majority, the first and only time a political party has done so at national level. By the end of the 1950s, the SPD passed the Godesberg Programme and adjusted its political priorities to fit more closely with the priorities which had become firmly established as preferences in the West German public: a capitalist social market economy, a stable alliance with the democratic powers of the West, and a place as a partner in the newly emerging European Community. The personal popularity of the first chancellor, and his acceptance as an equal partner among world leaders during the 1950s, laid the foundations for an acceptance of the political system. In 1952, opinions were still divided: most West Germans who named a best leader opted for Bismarck, followed by Hitler and Frederick the Great – the eighteenth century king of Prussia who had created the basis of the economic, military and political dominance of his region but who had also refused to speak German, claiming that it was a language fit only for grooms and not suited for sophisticated discourse. By the mid-1950s, Adenauer had overtaken Bismarck and has since held the top rank among the model German leaders. His acceptance and the political acceptance of West Germany were perceived as political and personal rehabilitation after difficult times.

THE GERMAN EUROPEANS

The Federal Republic of Germany became one of the founder members of the European Community in 1957. At that time the democratic political framework had already proved more cohesive than that of Weimar. Anti-system extremisms had either been banned or had been absorbed by the centre. The Christian democrats in particular had developed sufficient integrative force to dominate the party spectrum and to create a new forum for consensus-based politics across social classes and groups: the German equivalent of the catch-all party, the *Volkspartei*. West Germans began to enjoy a lifestyle which had not been accessible to previous generations. The onset of mass tourism facilitated contacts with non-German people and widened the range of experiences of other cultures. After a decade of catching up with war and post-war devastations of their living environment and culture, West Germans began to feel pride in the reconstruction of their country, and in the physical, economic and political evidence of a new beginning.

Internationally, memories of a previous Germany were more persistent. In the 1950s, visitors to Britain could still see notices ('Destroyed by German bombs') explaining the gaps and ruins in many cities. In countries which had been occupied by German troops, a sense of fear that Germany might again become a danger to democracy and peace has never fully subsided. From West Germany's perspective, the Cold War, the potential threat emanating from the Soviet Union, and her key role in Europe and the West should have obliterated these memories and given credence to the Federal Republic as an ally and partner in a democratic and peaceful world. That other countries and populations have been more hesitant to change their views and trust in the transformation of post-war Germany has remained a source of irritation to this day.

For the Federal Republic of Germany, membership in the European Community signified a further step towards full recognition and political equality. Official interpretations of the uses of Europe stress that European cooperation occurred at a time when the East/West polarisation could only be moderated by a third, independent force. In this perspective, the European Community helped to secure peace. The German involvement in Europe has been presented as a commitment to peaceful cooperation and a break with those political aims which led to wars in the past. Even in Europe, West Germany remained an outpost of the Western world on the Iron Curtain. The architect of the doctrine of non-recognition of the GDR, Walter Hallstein, chaired the European Commission from 1958 to 1967. European Community membership has been regarded as closely linked to security issues, and as one dimension of West German membership in the Western Alliance.

A second and no less important focus on Europe has been economical. West Germany joined as one of the dominant economic powers in Europe, and she has retained and consolidated that position. Although the possibility of political integration has always been implied as a long-term goal, the initial process of integration and cooperation concentrated on economic matters. From the German point of view, the primacy of economic affairs facilitated her recognition in Europe as a fully fledged and equal partner. Indeed from the very outset, public opinion held that the Federal Republic was economically stronger than her European partners and that the economic gains which did arise from European cooperation tended to benefit the weaker member states. In our context of Euro-German identity, it is worth noting that West Germans have regarded the economic dimension as the key dimension in Europe, their economic performance as the best in the European context, but their gains as doubtful overall. Germans tend to see themselves as everybody's paymaster, in Europe and beyond.

German views on the uses of Europe have been varied: in matters of military security, environmentalism or a more independent foreign policy towards the United States and the Soviet Union, European approaches seem preferable to national ones. The European options have been less attractive in those areas which, like economic achievement, emerged as substitutes for a national identity. This applies especially to the economy. Here, West Germans have preferred national solutions. To secure economic growth, price stability and investment, they tended to look towards their own government rather than the European partnership.

Despite such economic reservations, West Germans have been ardent Europeans. Public support for the European Community has never fallen below 60 per cent and has at times topped 80 per cent.[5] Only the Dutch have been more enthusiastic in their support for Europe. If system support denotes model citizens, West Germans have been model Europeans. Some have even argued that something like a European consciousness has been emerging in the Federal Republic, notably among the post-war generations who looked with new hope towards international cooperation as a guarantee for peaceful change and equal opportunities. Yes-answers to Europe, however, do not amount to a European consciousness. What seems to be lacking is an affective attachment to Europe. West Germans tend to support European goals but their orientation towards Europe has been instrumental. Europe is accepted but not liked. In 1988, for example, 70 per cent of West Germans thought the European dimension was important. However, far fewer (45 per cent) expressed an interest in it.[6] The difference between finding European affairs important and finding them interesting points to a difference in the pragmatic and affective acceptance. Affective orientations have not tallied with the manner in which European politics have been organised and perceived. In the founding decades, the attachment of citizens to their polity was, above all, pragmatic. West Germans favoured stability. They tended to regard their political role as following the regulations set down in the constitution and the relevant legislation. In turn, the state had to satisfy policy expectations in order to retain their support. This kind of political support has been called 'performance orientated' since citizens tend to base their regard for the political process on the policy successes it can deliver. It has been suggested that performance-based support is too conditional to underpin a political democracy: citizens' support might be withdrawn and switched to non-democratic forms of government in case of discontent or dissatisfaction. Instead, political support should be diffuse, not linked to performance but aimed in a less specific way at the democratic process itself. In the Federal Republic, a change from an institution and performance-based political culture to a democratic political culture with diffuse support has been evident since the mid-1960s. The post-war generations of West Germans had grown up in a democratic polity and most expected to participate rather than just fit into an established institutional setting.

This change in the political culture in the Federal Republic has changed the agenda for Europe. At the time when the European Community was founded, West Germans regarded democratic politics as a system which they would follow 'by the book': a set of regulations, legislation, institutions and practices which constituted the political arena. From the West German perspective, its existence was essential; opportunities for citizens to make their voice heard did not become a political issue. Even within the Federal Republic, West Germans in the 1950s and 1960s had little confidence that they could influence politics and politicians other than by doing their duty and turning out to vote. This personal dimension of politics changed significantly as the new generations entered political adulthood: the generations of post-war democrats were more confident that they could influence political processes. Since citizens' initiative and new social movements created a variety of organisational channels for political participation, expectations have hardened in West German political culture that policy processes and politicians should respond to expectations voiced from below. With the emergence of issue politics in the 1970s and 1980s, jostling the established catch-all parties into new approaches and a new flexibility towards political movements, political expectations have become a significant dimension of political behaviour.

Here, Europe has been an awkward target. The central position of the European Commission in the policy process, which had not troubled early generations of West Germans in their approval of Europe, is now seen by many as too removed from their own political environment and not responsive enough to their needs. The institution which aims at representing the citizens of Europe, the European Parliament, has hardly met the participatory expectations of today's West German voters. Although the Federal Republic has sent delegates to the European Parliament from the very beginning, the parliament itself is regarded as an institution of little significance, less important in fact than local assemblies. Direct elections may have increased the visibility of the parliament, at least at election times; in Germany, they have not increased its credibility. Electoral turnout has been low by German standards, and the elections are openly dismissed as of secondary importance. Clearly the composition and the political role of the national parliament, the *Bundestag*, are deemed to be more significant than those of its European equivalent. One reason for the lukewarm reaction to the European Parliament may be found in its relative lack of political muscle. One further reason is worth noting. Given the new political relevance of expectations, the organisational practice at the European parliamentary level makes it difficult for citizens to determine whether their support would or would not have an impact. Political parties have tended to organise in supranational groupings and, more importantly, they have tended to work in cross-party alliances in order to strengthen their position vis-à-vis the Commission. This grand coalition stance has made it impossible to single out party successes and measure the policy impact of any one party or position. In a climate where people monitor issue success and where they are in principle prepared to change their preferences to a party which appears more competent, the blurred, institutionalised and non-partisan practice of the European parliament has generated scepticism rather than support.

In today's Federal Republic, and commencing prior to the preoccupation with German unity, the positive predisposition towards Europe has somewhat faded. Although at government level, the emphasis on Europe has remained strong – not least to pacify critics who feared the massed economic force and political dominance of a united Germany as a destabilising factor in Europe – public opinion seems more ambivalent as the model Europeans of yesteryear have become more doubtful. In the past, Germans were the strongest advocates of a politically unified Europe. Today, German support for the political unification of Europe has slipped to the second lowest in Europe; in addition, one in three declare that they have no opinion in the matter.[7] Not expressing an opinion may suggest indifference and a view that European developments are not relevant from the national perspective. It may also point to a negative view which is not expressed openly in order not to conflict with general political assumptions. This camouflaged negativism was a strong feature of the German political culture in the 1940s and 1950s, when members of the pre-democratic generations in particular were reluctant to voice their misgivings about democratic processes.

Today, a similar mechanism may be in force: accepting Europe has become an unspoken assumption of German politics which not everyone may wish to challenge openly. Comparative European surveys since the mid-eighties leave no doubt that Germans have reservations about a European future which had not been in evidence earlier: only the Danes and the British tend to be more sceptical about political realisations of European unity, such as a European constitution, government, or the predominance of European over national concerns.

EUROPEAN INTEGRATION AND 'ACHIEVEMENT IDENTITY'

For the German population, a common European future has been less attractive since it became more imminent. The prospect of a Single European Market has been greeted with misgivings rather than hope. Within the Federal Republic, opinions have been equally divided about 1992;[8] within the European Community, Germans are more fearful of 1992 than most. In 1989, 49 per cent of West Germans and 67 per cent across Europe welcomed 1992; 42 per cent of West Germans and 19 per cent across Europe held reservations.[9]

These reservations about 1992 are closely linked to the nature of the contemporary German identity; the pride in the economic achievements of the country and her people since World War II. 1992 may undermine West German standards of industrial production, of vocational training, of educational qualifications, of environmental protection. At the time of the European elections in 1989, about half the population felt that opening the borders and creating European mobility would undermine established West German practices and systems.

On the personal level of employment prospects, however, fears that unemployment would rise after 1992 were twice as frequent as hopes that employment opportunities would widen.[10] Economic stability and secure employment have long been priority issues of the West German public which could make or break party majorities at election times. Now, confidence that the European dimension would consolidate German economic growth and benefit employment has collapsed. The effects of Europe have become less predictable in the very sector on which West Germans had based their Euro-orientation: the economy and its two anchor points, secure growth and secure employment.

The unease about employment prospects is paired with more widespread concerns about the durability of living standards. Since the world-wide recession in the early 1970s the post-war economic 'miracle' was clearly at an end and no measure of crisis management could succeed in holding unemployment much below two million. Moreover, West Germans have been concerned about social provisions and the future of the welfare state. On the one hand, the demographic changes in the wake of the falling birth rate and extended life expectancy have been discussed in terms of generational burdens; in order to secure a minimum standard of pensions, health care and social services, those in employment have to bear an ever increasing burden. Public alarm about a possible bankruptcy of the welfare systems for health, unemployment benefit or social security payments has been endemic for years. In addition, cut-backs on housing and on welfare provisions in general have created real hardship and exacerbated the sense of crisis looming over public welfare in a state with too many non-working people, too few working people and too much competition for welfare support. At the threshold of the 1990s, Germans are not as confident about the economic and social superiority of their society as they seemed to be in the 1950s and 1960s. It is also worth noting that economic and social conditions which compare favourably with those in other European countries, are regarded as deficient by Germans, and a cause for concern by many.

POLITICAL DIVIDES AND PERCEPTIONS OF EUROPE

Two political groups stand out in their perceptions of a unified Europe: the Republican Party and its supporters, who are the most hostile, and the Green Party and its supporters, who appear most strongly in favour of European unity. The extreme right in West Germany has always been more interested in German nationalism and reunification than in the existence or future shape of Europe. If Europe came into view it was Central Europe, not Western Europe. Its boundaries were those drawn in the build-up towards the World War I and Germany's craving for an economic hegemony, or they were borrowed from the SS and their schemes of uniting the forces of Central Europe to oppose the Soviet Union. Western Europe not only seemed to perpetuate the division of Europe; its close affiliation with democratic institutions and government also made it unpalatable to the extreme right who continue to search for a modern adaptation of the *Führer* state.

The Republicans are building on these anti-European orientations and also on contemporary grievances about the European Community and its impact. They have mobilised support among farmers, who feel short-changed by the EC; they have also mobilised support among a clientele threatened by or fearful of unemployment. The latter are the least educated, the craftsmen, semi-skilled or unskilled, from different regional and party backgrounds, who distrust European integration and its effects. The Republicans have been the only political party with an openly anti-European political stance: in the 1989 European elections in particular, they won the anti-European vote. With 7.1 per cent of the vote, they gained 6 seats in the European Parliament: the first political party of the extreme right to win parliamentary seats above the regional level since 1949. The first party, also, to win seats in a parliament and an institutional setting – Europe – in which it had no trust.

The social and political mobility which a unified Europe after 1992 holds in store has been a further issue to mobilise anti-European sentiments. The Republican Party and its voters are anti-integrationist; they are hostile to all newcomers, even those from Eastern Europe who claim to be of German origin but do not speak the language or know the culture, and they are resentful about the rivalry for housing and employment. Given that 1989 alone saw the arrival in the Federal Republic of over 350 000 East Germans, some 200 000 so-called resettlers from Eastern Europe and about the same number of people seeking political asylum, the challenge of integration does not commence with 1992 but seems rather to have already commenced. The potential Republican voters may subscribe to the nationalist purpose of reintegrating Germans into Germany, but fear a deterioration in their own social and economic prospects. In its new course towards integration, the European Community is perceived as a threat rather than a promise.

The very opposite is true for the Green Party and its supporters. In the early 1980s, traditional arguments of the political left against the European Community as an agent of capitalism or big business were still audible. Since the Greens entered the European Parliament in 1984, they developed a different perspective and now perceive Europe as a forum for international collaboration. In the 1989 European elections, the Greens enthusiastically looked towards a united Europe and the promise it seemed to hold for environmental protection and for creating an international, fairer and more prosperous society. The programmatic stance of the party articulates the view held by its supporters, the *milieu* of well-educated, urban middle-class people between the ages of 25 and 50. These seem to be the most ardent Europeans today – but their perception of Europe neither matches the intricate structure of European bureaucracy nor the tendency of the European Parliament to blur the political intent of policies in a common stance of opposition against the commission. These new Europeans do not share the priorities of their government: Western integration, economic stability and growth, and a moderate internationalisation of political processes. For them, the promise lies in a transformation of national to international policies. They are not interested in economic growth but in halting growth by international consensus and creating a new quality of life. Their understanding of political processes is that of a direct democracy, based on participation, and responsive to its citizens. As we have seen earlier, existing European processes are far removed from this. In fact, the enthusiasm for Europe which has emanated from the Greens since the late 1980s is not an enthusiasm for the existing Europe or even for the Europe after 1992. It is for a utopian Europe where the parameters of politics would be different and the limitations of national political traditions a thing of the past.

EUROPE BEYOND THE COMMUNITY

In the immediate post-war period and throughout the Cold War, Europe meant Western Europe and, more specifically, the member states of the European Community. Although Europe had a geographical and territorial identity, the focus on Europe implied a more political cohesion: an endorsement of democratic government and of a free market economy. The enlargements of the community in 1972 and in 1986 made these very aspects preconditions of membership and excluded applicants which had not yet reached the required democratic and liberal practices. Within her place in Europe as one of the democratic polities, the Federal Republic has concluded special friendship treaties with France. They intensified cultural contacts between the two countries and their peoples. Their real significance, however, was a symbolic one: to testify to the world that the assumptions of German nationalism no longer applied. France, the French and French democracy in particular had been vilified as Germany's principal enemy since the time of the French Revolution, while the French sorely remembered the destructions and injustices suffered during war-time occupations in the twentieth century.

Since the mid-1960s, Eastern Europe, which had been cut off by the Iron Curtain during the Cold War, came into political view in the era of détente and *Ostpolitik.* In the early 1970s the Federal Republic concluded treaties with the Soviet Union, the German Democratic Republic and other Eastern European countries. They were framed to recognise officially the territorial outcomes of the World War II, and pave the way to increased economic and cultural cooperation. For the Federal Republic, an Eastern dimension of Europe began to emerge. As mentioned above, the practice of communicative politics with East Germany sustained a Western orientation in the population of that country beneath the official credo of a socialist identity. In the Federal Republic, the 1970s brought a new dual orientation. Alongside the established orientation towards Western Europe and the broad commitment to European integration, the special liaison, which had been stalemated during the Cold War, developed a momentum of its own. Contacts with East Germans intensified as people began to visit each other's countries; more importantly, the Federal Republic supported the East German economy with favourable trading terms and indirect access to the European Community. Some claimed that even before the collapse of the socialist system, and the call for membership of the EC as part of the reunification agenda for the people of East Germany, the GDR had actually enjoyed a clandestine membership of the EC for some time.

During the chancellorship of Helmut Schmidt, the Federal Republic finally seemed to leave behind the legacy of semi-sovereignty, and take a leading part among the big powers. Schmidt tried to carve out a special German role as foreign policy mediator, as the link between the two power blocs, and the facilitator of international policy innovation. Although his successes as the super-leader of Europe fell short of his aspirations, the policy direction has remained important as the Federal Republic consolidated her leadership position – economically and politically – in Western Europe, as she became strong enough to carve out an independent policy stance *vis-à-vis* the United States and the Soviet Union, she based her expectations of political influence on her special geo-political position. In the past this had been as an outpost of the West at the Iron Curtain; now there were overtones of a special German role as a mediator between West and East, and a gateway from Western Europe to a wider Europe. Europe, which West Germans had understood to mean Western Europe, began to be perceived as Western and Eastern Europe together. In the early 1980s, one in three West Germans favoured a Europe of West and East. Among young people under the age of 25 a majority preferred a wider Europe while older generations opted for a Europe of the West. Supporters of the conservative CDU/CSU parties thought of Europe as located in the West;

supporters of the Greens tended to include the East. Broadly speaking, the notion of Europe as a political entity beyond Western Europe, a Central Europe – *Mitteleuropa* – is gaining ground. As with all issues of nation, German motivations are contradictory: some would hope for more democracy in the East, others for a more central political and economic role for Germany towards the West and the East; others still might remember older concepts of *Mitteleuropa* and wish for their restoration.

Regardless of their specific political vantage point, Germans and the German government no longer equate Europe with Western Europe but are looking towards the East. At a time of uncertainty about the role of Germany after 1992, this new European dimension seems to promise a leading role with few of the drawbacks envisaged for the single European market. Economic dominance, at least, would be guaranteed. The new Europe of Eastern and Western countries would include both former post-war German states; its place would be central and powerful. Before unification estimates of its effects on the European Community suggested that such a Germany would dominate on all accounts. Economically, it would be one and a half times as strong as its nearest rival, France; its workforce would amount to 37 million people, followed by Britain with 26 million; its combined armies would include close to 700 000 soldiers compared with 500 000 in France. In sport, the FRG and GDR hold 142 Olympic medals, about three times as many as France, Britain and Italy together. After unification, estimates of the long-term legacies of East German mismanagement and economic backwardness seemed to imply that a German economic giant might be slow in coming. Yet revelations of the economic morass of the former model state of the socialist bloc had been timed to hasten the pace of unification and to ensure an electoral bonus for the Kohl administration, restoring the aura of the CDU/CSU as the guarantor of a social market economy and economic recovery. Fact and fiction of economic development are impossible to separate neatly enough to determine whether and when a second economic miracle might be in the making. Even without the prospect of a miracle, the status of Germany as a European and world power has already been enhanced through unification.

The Europe beyond the European Community holds attractions for the Federal Republic and the chance of a new leadership role over and above Western integration. The post-war era of semi-sovereignty and reduced legitimacy seems truly at an end as the borders open to fashion new alliances and recast political Europe. However, the competing nationalisms which have been levers of change and the dismantling of socialist control in the East, have yet to reach an equilibrium of co-existence, and a commitment to political organisational structures which would generate and sustain democratic government. In their disenchantment with Western Europe which appears to threaten their economic predominance, and in their search for uncontested leadership status as a model economy and polity, Germans seem to be looking to the East with fewer concerns about the future of democracy in this remodelled Europe and central European Germany than her Western European neighbours would wish. In this drive towards central Europe, the hidden nationalism in the German identity surges back.

NOTES

1. Cited in R. Dahrendorf, *Society and Democracy in Germany* (London: Weidenfeld & Nicolson, 1967).
2. T Mann, 'Über deutsche Schuld. Botschaft zum 8. Mai 1945', *Bayrische Landeszeitung*, 18 May 1945.
3. See *Der Spiegel*, no. 48, 1977, pp. 146–8.
4. *Der Spiegel*, no. 38, 17 September 1990, p. 32.
5. Data from the annual EC surveys *Eurobarometer*.
6. *Eurobarometer*, 1988, p. 6
7. *Eurobarometer*, 1989, p. 39.
8. *Trends im Vorfeld der Europawahl*, Konrad Adenauer Foundation, 1989.
9. *Eurobarometer*, 1989, p. 28.
10. *Trends, op. cit.*, p. 16.

9 Westminster versus Brussels – the Last Crusade?

Alan Butt Philip

The attitude of successive governments, Labour and Conservative, towards European integration since 1945 has combined a mixture of caution, suspicion, arrogance and disdain, with only few exceptions. Indeed, even as late as 1990 British government ministers rarely permit themselves or their spokesmen to allow the words 'European integration' to pass their lips in public. Their preferred formula has been to talk of European cooperation, an altogether looser and less threatening concept, which even keener advocates of Britain's membership of the European Community (such as Michael Heseltine) seem to prefer as much as sceptics, such as Mrs Thatcher. The language of the discussion about Britain's place in the European Community, as used by the British, tells us a great deal about the problems Britain continues to have in adjusting to the new framework of European integration that has been in the making since 1945.[1] British people and the British mass media (the BBC included) still think of themselves as being separate from the rest of Europe. They refer in conversation, as much as in news broadcasts, to 'Britain and Europe', to 'going across to Europe', to 'the continent of Europe'. Our EC partners see Britain as an integral part of Europe and the EC, but most UK people and politicians see Britain as 'semi-detached' from the rest of Europe.

British people think of other Europeans as continentals, but other Europeans do not easily understand this distinction when they are confronted with it, nor the reason for it.

The main line of argument in this essay is that British obstructiveness in the development of European integration, and especially its institutional supports, are the product of Britain's unique political experience and of attitudes that lie deep in Britain's political, economic and social culture. The tragedy for Britain is that those political and economic actors that have tried to change these attitudes and the whole thrust of British culture, have lacked the power to do so. Meanwhile other political actors (such as

Edward Heath) who have used the power they had to strengthen British ties with the community preferred to play down the implications of EC membership and to avoid confronting the prejudices and suspicions of the wider public and their elected representatives. The result has been to leave the British political class and the wider public very poorly prepared for the consequences of the acceleration of the process of European integration which began in 1984 and 1985.

WALKING BACKWARDS TOWARDS AN INTEGRATED EUROPE

Almost as soon as the World War II was over the differences between Britain and other West European states in regard to the future direction of their inter-state relations became manifest. The British emerged from war with their national pride enhanced, the durability of their national political institutions reinforced, their self-esteem and their super-power ranking apparently confirmed by the events of history. For recently occupied continental European states, the paramount concern was to create a new political order which would bind the emerging democracies and prevent a recurrence of intense political and economic rivalries which had led to war three times in the previous century. Britain's post-war Labour government saw the maintenance of the 'special relationship' with the United States as its first priority, Commonwealth links as the next most important concern, with European cooperation in third position. Winston Churchill's professed interest in a sort of United States of Europe, in the much quoted Fulton and Zurich speeches of 1946, was exposed at the Hague Congress of Europe's parliamentarians in 1948 as lacking in substance. Britain in the 1940s was not looking for a blueprint for post-war Europe, outside the realms of defence, but other countries were. Comforted by support from Scandinavian countries, British leaders may have thought that their objections to too close-knit a system of economic cooperation between states would be enough to kill off ambitious French plans. Not for the first time, the British deceived themselves and were left behind as the European Coal and Steel Community was put together in 1950–51. Those who foresaw the unwisdom of standing aside – mainly liberals, committed federalists and the editorial staff of *The Economist* – represented a tiny fragment of public opinion. British reluctance to accept any political constraints on key economic policy decision-making was common to government and opposition alike, and succeeded in shaping the intergovernmental character of the Organisation for European Economic Cooperation (OEEC) set up in 1948 to guide the rise of Marshall aid funds from the United States.

This was to be the exception to the post-war norm. Subsequently British concerns to retain sovereignty over economic decisions were to split Western European states into two camps by the end of the 1950s, and later still to divide both Conservative and Labour parliamentary parties even in the early 1990s. Edward Heath, who took charge of Britain's negotiations to join the EC between 1961 and 1963, was proud to recall that his first speech as a newly-elected MP in 1950 was to support British membership of the ECSC. But Harold Macmillan, Conservative prime minister at the time of Britain's first application to join in 1961, had been among the most outspoken critics of the ECSC plan in the early 1950s, refusing to accept government by 'technocrats and experts' from the continent.

When the next steps along the road to European integration were planned the British government adopted once more a position of reticence and suspicion. The proposal to set up a common European Defence Community (EDC), facilitating German rearmament by putting Western Europe's military forces under a unified command structure, was finally sabotaged by the French National Assembly in 1954. The only outcome of the EDC, and one that Britain was keen to assist, was the formation of the West European Union in 1955 – a singularly low-profile intergovernmental institution whose function remains to coordinate its member governments' views on defence policy and international security issues. The EDC episode may have revealed that Britain might not be alone in its instinctive resistance to the pooling of sovereignty, but the 'reassuring' failure of the plan left British political circles even less prepared to take seriously the conference at Messina, called in 1955, to lay plans for the formation of a European economic community. A middle-ranking official was sent from the Board of Trade to observe the proceedings, but despite his reporting that a major development might be afoot, the official Whitehall view was that nothing would come of all this continental rhetoric and over-ambition. When the EEC plan began to look like a serious threat to British economic interests in the run-up to the signature of the Treaty of Rome on 25 March 1957 the British authorities did all they could to derail the EEC train as it prepared to leave the station. They pressed for a looser confederal free trade area to be set up which would embrace a much larger number of countries, but they failed to find a response from the original six EC member states who had already decided to move at a faster and more ambitious rate towards integration. Britain then set about setting up an alternative regional trade grouping in western Europe based on a free trade area rather than the EEC's customs unions. And so the split between the EEC six (pop. 170 million) and the European Free Trade Association (EFTA) seven (pop. 85 million) emerged formally in 1960, although the significance of this was to be only of a short duration. For in 1961, four of the EFTA seven, led by Britain its dominant member, applied to the EEC for membership. This was to herald some bridge-building between the two groups, which was quite independent of individual country transfers of allegiance to the EC. The experience of the 1950s and 1960s amply confirmed Dean Acheson's early diagnosis that 'Britain had lost an empire but failed to find a role'. It was not to be until January 1973 before Britain was to become a full member of the European Community, by which time (it is now clear) Britain had run out of options if she wanted to benefit from the effects of economic integration and to wield some influence over the political stance of western Europe. The major factor behind British willingness to join the EC was the fear that British goods risked being shut out of the all too successful emerging common market and the realisation that British exports would have to be sold strongly in the community if the British economy was not to continue its decline. It was the economic rewards that persuaded the establishment by 1960–61 that British entry to the EC was a necessity, not any commitment to political integration as a means of resolving longstanding national rivalries in Europe.

HOLDING ON TO SOVEREIGNTY FOR FEAR OF SOMETHING WORSE

The rehearsal of the British approach to European integration after 1945 is extremely pertinent to understanding the difficulties British politics and society continue to have in accommodating the obligations of EC membership in the 1990s. The economic benefits of EC membership have continuously been played up, while the political costs have been ignored or played down deliberately. Indeed the very process of integration appears to have been studiously written out of the script of many British political commentaries which refer instead to the process of strengthening 'cooperation with our EC partners'. At heart this is a barely concealed code for saying that the British priority is to strengthen intergovernmental relations with other EC member states, but to avoid if at all possible any concessions of power to the EC's supranational institutions. It is a code that both Mrs Thatcher and her supposedly more pro-European leadership challenger Michael Heseltine were still using late in 1990. The result has been that from the mid-1970s Britain has pushed for more decision-making, affecting foreign policy, internal security, immigration and judicial cooperation to be shared at an intergovernmental level. It was a British initiative that led to the creation of the Trevi Group in 1976 which still handled these issues among the Twelve. At the same time, Britain has resisted where it can the extension of the legal competence of the European Community. In 1989, for example, this was manifested in the UK government's refusal to allow the EC institutions to extend their influence into the field of secondary education under the Lingua programme which encourages foreign language learning; or to agree to the EC stipulating rules about the characteristics of health warnings to be displayed on cigarette packets; or to agree to a common card for pensioners entitling them to reduced travel fares and other concessions all over the community. It also underpins the government's refusal to abolish border controls and its rejection of the social charter adopted by the other eleven member states at the Strasbourg summit in December 1989. These contrasting stances – encouraging intergovernmentalism and restraining supranationalism – have been justified on the grounds of protecting national sovereignty. Certainly the intergovernmental approach leaves control of the process of shared decision-making firmly in the hands of each state's government and avoids the need for governments to tangle with the European Commission and the European Parliament. However this has led to the decisions agreed using intergovernmental structures being reached in complete secrecy between the executive branches of different governments, without prior parliamentary scrutiny at any level, and with none of the certainty of application that the legally binding quality of EC directives, decisions and regulations affords. The sovereignty of the state may be protected in this way but not the sovereignty of parliament. Until the mid-1980s the Labour party's remedy for the loss of parliamentary sovereignty was the repeal of section 2 of the European Communities Act 1972: which gave Parliament's assent to the supremacy of EC law over national British laws in cases of conflict. But this position has since been abandoned as Britain's membership of the EC came to be seen by Labour as irreversible and as Labour politicians acquired a better understanding of the rules of the EC political game.

A HOSTILE POLITICAL CULTURE

The hesitations about Britain's accession to the community, the politically contested fact of Britain's EC membership, the widely-believed assertion that the EC was an economic community and little else, the wrangling that has accompanied so many EC decisions where British interests are involved, and the absence of many tangible benefits arising from EC membership, have all combined to reinforce suspicion among the British political class and mass media about the European Community. A sizeable bloc of both conservative and labour MPs voted against their leaderships' instructions when the House of Commons came to consider the terms of British membership of the EC in 1971–72. With the exception of the Liberals, a high-profile stance on European integration has always risked being divisive for British political parties, and so it has not been pressed. The civil service has meanwhile been faithfully transcribing EC law into national legislation or administrative practice, with a degree of success only surpassed by their Danish counterparts. But the full extent of the community's role in prompting changes of national policy and practice has more often than not been concealed from parliament by being mediated through national political institutions. The British have in the main been treated to nearly twenty years of integration by stealth, oblivious of the range of EC-led policy changes, their instinctive suspicion of all things continental unchallenged by facts or by their political leaders. Indeed until the late 1980s few positive actions or developments emanating from the European Community were ever reported to the mass of British people. Britain's relations with her EC partners were dominated at least until the Fontainebleau settlement in 1984 by disputes about the costs and consequences of the common agricultural policy (CAP), and by concern about the size of Britain's net contribution to the EC budget. It was only in the peripheral areas of the country that EC grants and loans for economic development, training and job creation were much in evidence and reached public consciousness. Public opinion, in the absence of good news from Brussels or a firm lead from the two largest political parties, remained volatile (but generally hostile) on the main issue of Britain's EC membership, and was rather bored by any details. MPs and ministers, whether in favour of EC membership or not, banged the drum to defend national interests at every opportunity, surrounding themselves with a comforting smokescreen of national pride and prejudice which obscured the real nature of Britain's commitment to the European Community. This only became clear when the winds of change on the continent of Europe in the late 1980s blew the smoke away and as the pace of economic integration, triggered by the single market's 1992 deadline, gathered speed. Public opinion had long been confused by the failure of tangible economic rewards from EC membership to materialise, and by horror stories (many of them true) about mountains of food going to waste and the excesses of Brussels bureaucrats. It was not prepared for the change of gear in the community's development and was still adjusting to the prospect of the single market by 1993 while most other EC countries were looking beyond this to economic and monetary union (EMU). It is scarcely surprising then that in all the direct elections to the European Parliament Britain has the worst record for electoral turn-out among EC countries, struggling to rise to 36 per cent in 1989.

Two events in the late 1980s were to start the process of change in public perceptions of the community. First came the mass advertising campaign starting in the spring of 1988 to promote the single market. Although launched by the Secretary of State for Trade and Industry, Lord Young, to persuade the business community to pay attention to the creation of the single market, under the slogan 'Europe Open for Business', this campaign in fact spread awareness of the new development of the EC across the whole of British society in a refreshingly upbeat fashion. Secondly, the Labour party reversed its previous hostility to the European Community after its 1987 election defeat and began to compete with the conservatives for better 'European' credentials – a tactic effectively deployed during the European election campaign in the summer of 1989. This change succeeded in moving discussion of the community in political circles on to new ground. The issue was no longer whether the UK should remain in the EC or on what terms, but what sort of community should be developed and whether the British were well positioned to shape this development. Nevertheless much of the by now traditional knee-jerk antipathy to the aspirations of the community remained undisturbed. Mrs Thatcher and her ministers rubbished the rather anodyne European social charter as 'socialism by the back-Delors' and popular newspapers, such as *The Sun* and *The Star*, were happy to print horror stories of what the EC might in future do to British traditions and institutions. *The Sun's* incitement to its readers in November 1990 to go to the cliffs of Dover and hurl abuse at the President of the European Commission was a manifestation of frustration, incomprehension and real aversion to what was implied by high-speed European integration.[2]

MEMBERSHIP OF THE EUROPEAN COMMUNITY

Britain did not finally become a member of the European Community until 1 January 1973, fifteen years after it had been established and over eleven years after the first application for membership had been made. In the end, Britain had to wait until General de Gaulle resigned the Presidency of France before membership could successfully be arranged. Labour ministers laid the groundwork for entry in 1969 and 1970, under George Thomson and Michael Stewart. But the premiership of Edward Heath after June 1970, with Geoffrey Rippon in charge of the negotiations, saw the process through, with a five-year transition period, some budgetary concessions, trade concessions to ex-Commonwealth countries and the promise of a regional development fund, all forming part of the package deal.

Yet the internal party agony that approval of the entry terms caused the political actors in Britain should have made it clear to the other EC states just how riven and ambivalent were the leading political parties on the subject of European integration. They presaged the continuance of a very awkward relationship which was set to continue for the rest of the century.

The process of joining the European Community was achieved with great difficulty. The House of Lords was enthusiastic, the House of Commons was not. On the first reading of the legislation ratifying the accession agreement, sixty-seven Labour MPs defied their party whip to vote with the government while thirty-nine Tory MPs voted with Labour against the terms of entry. Twenty other Labour MPs abstained. Thereafter the government was forced to impose a guillotine on the acrimonious debate and emerged undefeated only thanks to the votes of the Liberals and some strategic Labour abstentions. This was less than the 'full-hearted consent' of the British people that Edward Heath had promised at the previous general election.

Labour was only able to overcome its own divisions while in opposition by promising to hold a referendum on EC membership if returned to power and to seek renegotiation of the entry terms. Public opinion was briefly favourable to entry but quickly reverted to its customary antagonism. When Labour took office in the spring of 1974 it had therefore to reopen formally the issue of UK membership with our EC partners and, after agreeing some largely cosmetic changes in Brussels, to organise a referendum on continued British membership. The government itself was unable to give a unanimous recommendation to the voters, with six Cabinet ministers campaigning against the pro-EC line of their political colleagues, using a rare suspension of the convention of collective responsibility which had been agreed to avoid a more fundamental Labour party split. The dissident minority was, however, heavily outgunned, with all the main party leaders and the business community lining up behind the pro-EC campaign. The result in June 1975 was a two to one vote in favour of Britain staying in the community on the revised terms, with two-thirds of the country taking part in the vote. Even so, the referendum result was less than it seemed. For the most powerful influence on the vote was the feeling that, having only just joined the EC, it would be rash to withdraw quickly: the British voter preferred to wait and see. The voters had been promised substantial economic benefits as a result of EC entry, but these had not had time to show through. The political costs were said to be minimal as Britain retained a national veto on all EC matters of importance, a 'veto' that had first been claimed in 1965 by General de Gaulle.

Edward Heath had himself said that no national sovereignty would be lost as a result of EC membership and had dismissed the promise of direct elections to the European Parliament as not a serious immediate prospect. There was therefore a real sense that the favourable referendum result was obtained both by deceit and by playing on the inertia factor. A referendum held prior to EC entry could well have given a negative response. Indeed, many independent observers at the time concluded that the referendum had been held more to get the Labour government out of its difficulties than to obtain the consent of the British electorate to the process of European integration. That is why the 1975 referendum did not settle the question of EC membership at the level of party political debate.

Nowhere was this more evident than within the Labour party. The gyrations of Labour's views on the community have been numerous. Under Gaitskell's leadership, they had opposed Britain's application to join in 1961. Under Wilson's leadership, they applied to join in 1967. Under Wilson, they opposed British membership in 1973. Under Wilson, they endorsed British membership in 1975. Under Michael Foot, they called for British withdrawal from the EC. After 1987, with Neil Kinnock as leader, Labour appeared to be reconciled to the permanence of UK membership.

Before the 1975 referendum was held, Labour indeed refused to accept the decision of Parliament and did not send representatives to the European Parliament. Anti-EC Labour ministers, such as John Silkin and Tony Benn, exercised high-profile responsibilities as part of the EC Council of Ministers after 1974. Back in opposition after 1979, Labour swung fully against Britain's EC membership and this in turn was one of the triggers in 1981 for the formation of a new Social Democratic Party, led by Roy Jenkins, Shirley Williams, William Rodgers and David Owen – all former Labour ministers. Only the passage of time and the succession of three general election defeats persuaded Labour to look again at its EC position – outright hostility appearing to be increasingly futile and unrealistic.

After the 1987 election Labour's accommodation with Brussels proved surprisingly rapid, in part encouraged by the view that some of the most regrettable actions of the Thatcher administration could successfully be challenged or even overturned in the EC institutions. The new model Labour party was thus able to espouse the single European market as long as it was tempered by a social dimension. In this approach they were encouraged by the intervention of the President of the European

Commission, Jacques Delors, at the TUC annual congress in September 1988 and by the prospect that some of the workers' rights lost in the 1980s could be clawed back via EC legislation emanating from Brussels. The most telling illustration of Labour's new approach came in the campaign for the elections to the European Parliament in May 1989 when Labour adopted a 'more European than thou' stance for the first time in regard to the Conservatives and gained some electoral advantage thereby. However the speed of events in Europe still caused Labour difficulty. The federalist stance of many Labour MEPs was firmly stamped on by the Labour leadership in late 1990 in the run-up to the intergovernmental conferences in December, but economic and monetary union has not been excluded at some point in the future if a number of tough conditions are met.

The most critical position in managing Britain's relations with the European Community has been occupied by the civil service which has had to navigate carefully between the claims of the Commission and the rhetoric of Downing Street. In many respects the civil service has succeeded in building a constructive relationship with Brussels and in internalising the norms of the European Community.[3] EC legislation and the rulings of the European Court of Justice in Luxembourg have been applied with exemplary faithfulness, on a par with nationally derived law. A system of coordinating government positions on individual issues has been evolved which has attracted fulsome praise outside Britain.[4] The European secretariat of the Cabinet Office acts as navigator for the UK government in this respect and as a broker between government departments when there is a clash of policy interests.

Some government departments have only recently been drawn into EC business, while others such as the Foreign and Commonwealth Office (FCO), Ministry of Agriculture, Fisheries and Food (MAFF) and the DTI have always had a high level of interaction with the community's institutions, and have developed specific internal structures for handling the large volume of EC business. Other departments such as the Home Office and the Department of Social Security have a more recent involvement. A recent internal study by the Department of Health concluded that the main framework of future health policy is now also being settled in Brussels. If this suggests that the civil service has been supple in its evolution *vis-à-vis* the EC, this approach has not been successful on all fronts and has revealed dangers. The UK has had great difficulty in finding civil servants to go to work in the European Commission, and only launched the 'fast track' scheme to overcome this problem in 1990 – some fifteen years late. Senior civil servants are very short of EC experience: with only a quarter of the top management in the DTI – the key government department in relation to the

EC single market and trade policy fields – having had any EC exposure as recently as 1990. At the same time, government departments and officials that adopt European colours too enthusiastically risk being accused of 'going native' and may be regarded as being 'unreliable', a sentiment which certainly harmed the FCO in its relationship with Downing Street throughout the 1980s.

The accession of the UK to the community has of course changed the level and content of the workload of the prime minister, as the agenda of the EC has become part of the agenda of each member state's government. This has meant that Downing Street has had to prepare for at least two summit meetings a year with all the EC heads of state or of government. The specially constituted European secretariat of the Cabinet Office keeps the prime minister informed of all significant EC developments, coordinates UK government policy positions, and has to manage – alongside the FCO – the six-month tenure of the EC presidency which Britain has occupied in 1977, 1981, 1986 and will again take on in the second half of 1992. The prime minister has also had to nominate the two UK members of the college of Commissioners, the most senior executives of the European Commission.

Of the nine nominees only two have made an outstanding contribution – Roy Jenkins as President of the Commission in 1977–80 and progenitor of the European Monetary System, and Lord Cockfield who launched the single market programme during his term of office from 1985 to 1988. Generally it is middle-ranking political figures who have been sent to work in Brussels, many of whom have done their respective jobs well but at the risk of being seen to be too pro-integrationist and of having a serious career re-entry problem back home once their term of office has expired.

Nevertheless all those who have been despatched by Downing Street to the European Commission have adopted a highly *communautaire* stance. Indeed it would be difficult for a Commissioner not to do so and to carry weight with his or her colleagues. So the result has been that the prime minister has not been able to count on having allies within the college of Commissioners, even if Mrs Thatcher did seek to influence the portfolios some of them have been given.

THE BRITISH RECORD ON EC ISSUES

There appear to have been so many crises affecting Britain's relations with the EC that one might be forgiven for thinking that the history is one of continuous bad feeling. Yet this would be a wholly unjustified conclusion to reach.

At the outset of the UK's accession to the EC, the obvious foci of British policy were the reduction in the British contribution to underwriting the cost of the common agricultural policy, the launch of the European Regional Development Fund (ERDF) with the UK a major beneficiary, the successful development of foreign policy cooperation at an intergovernmental level, and the enlargement of the Franco-German leadership circle within the EC to include Britain. In the event, Britain continues to underwrite to a significant degree the CAP, even in the 1990s. An ERDF was set up but initially with very small-scale resources. Since 1988, much larger sums have been devoted to the EC's structural funds (of which the ERDF is the largest), but Britain's share has been much reduced. Foreign and security policy cooperation has progressed well, most notably at the time of the Falklands war, despite embarrassing demonstrations of disarray occurring at the time of the 1973–74 Arab oil embargo threat and the USSR's invasion of Afghanistan in 1979–80. Although there have been occasions when the UK and France or the UK and the Federal Republic of Germany have made common cause within the Council of Ministers, in no sense can the British be said to have joined or come near to joining the Franco-German leadership of the community. Britain's political vision of the community has always been too limited, and often its economic weakness has forced its government into a position of asking for favours, especially from Germany. Britain has therefore allowed itself to be led on most issues within the EC framework, has not adopted the language of the community and has not been content for the most part to play to the rules of the game.

The reality of economic integration was somewhat different. British overseas trade patterns experienced a marked shift towards trade with the EC/EFTA block and away from the Commonwealth and North America. By 1990 some 60 per cent of UK trade was with the EC/EFTA countries, compared with 40 per cent in the early 1970s. Trade policy has been determined in Brussels since British entry except in a few products (e.g. bananas, textiles and cars) where the EC permits national import quotas to continue. In trade matters, the UK has often found itself in alliance with the Commission against other EC countries which are more protectionist. And on the single European market initiative from the mid-1980s, the British can rightly claim to have played a major part in the conception and launch of the 1992 programme. In this instance, French, German and British economic and political interests coincided to considerable effect! The programme was agreed and arrangements made to alter the legal base of the EC all within a period of fourteen months – a rare feat which speaks eloquently of the impact of divisions among EC member states on other critical issues.

Another area of success for Britain can be found in the intergovernmental links formed between EC member states to cooperate on policies in regard to countering terrorism, protecting internal security, and a whole variety of police, customs, judicial and immigration matters. The Trevi Group of ministers and officials formed in 1976 to discuss such matters of mutual concern was set up at the behest of the UK, but outside the treaty-based structure of the community, and has worked well.

While few commentators have even noticed the successful development of these linkages in such politically sensitive areas, many were tempted to suggest that after 1984 Britain had finally secured a settlement of its financial demands in regard to the EC budget. Certainly the switch of British policy concern at that time away from the size of its budgetary contribution towards future EC policy development was as dramatic as it was welcome. Yet the size of Britain's net contributions to the EC budget shows every sign of being larger in the 1990s than it was in the early 1980s, and the main cause of this high contribution – the cost of storage and disposal of the EC's agricultural surpluses – may have been addressed at the behest of the UK, but has not been fully resolved.

Another area where Britain has with some justice claimed to be a 'good European' is in the field of implementing EC legislation and the rulings of the European Court of Justice. Only Denmark can claim a better record during the 1980s, while some very integrationist countries such as Italy and Belgium have rather a poor record in this regard.

Yet British spokesmen have a poor memory about some examples where Britain has been in the dock for breaking the rules – for example, the refusal to make the use of tachographs in commercial road vehicles mandatory after 1978, or the attempt to legislate away for at least a decade commitments made in the Council of Ministers to improve water quality by 1985.

Three areas where conspicuous failures of will or nerve were manifest were the social dimension of 1992, the eleven-year delay in joining the exchange rate mechanism of the European Monetary System, and the inability to contemplate an eventual economic and monetary union. Perhaps irritation on the part of the Conservative government was largely responsible for the British attacks on the social charter – irritation that the labour movement might thereby be able to claw back some employee rights *vis-à-vis* employers in a move that countered the thrust of Thatcherite deregulation. This resistance did not show Conservatives in a particularly good light as it suggested that they neither understood the politics of the social dimension of 1992, in terms of winning popular consent for the single market programme, nor did they recognise the long tradition of EC involvement in social policy issues dating as far back as the Treaty of Paris. However the advent of John Major as prime minister did lead to a final admission that some form of social dimension to EC policies is appropriate even if its scope is still contested.

The UK government spent almost twelve years between the end of 1978 and the end of 1990 supporting the idea of an exchange rate mechanism within the newly established European Monetary System, while refusing to submit the pound to its disciplines. This was ostensibly because of the relatively high rate of inflation in the UK and the special features of managing a reserve currency like sterling. A formula developed by the Thatcher government that Britain would take part in the ERM 'when the time was right' began to look very thin after ten years of procrastination. At the June 1989 EC summit in Madrid, Mrs Thatcher was cornered by her own senior advisers and persuaded to amend the formula to a series of conditions, upon the fulfilment of which the UK would join the ERM. Although the essence of these conditions was not met, Britain nevertheless joined the ERM in early October 1990 because the downturn of the British economy made this both possible and advantageous in terms of a reduction of interest rates. Two former Chancellors, Nigel Lawson and Sir Geoffrey Howe, quickly made it clear that they felt a decision not to join the ERM in 1985 or earlier had been a 'tragic' policy error. The misgivings of Mrs Thatcher, and her personal economic adviser, Sir Alan Walters, seem to have been crucial in denying the United Kingdom a period of currency stability and low inflation – subject to strict monetary discipline – which greatly benefited the other participant ERM member economies in the mid- and late 1980s. As the recession of the early 1990s took a grip of the UK economy, many thousands of failed businesses and of the unemployed could point to the Thatcher approach on joining the ERM as the main cause of their misfortunes.

The key reason for Britain's participation in the ERM was tactical and political. This was the drive to set up an economic and monetary union among the EC member states, a drive which gained great momentum with the publication of the Delors Report in May 1989 and then from the rapid unification of the two Germanies. With an intergovernmental conference beginning in mid-December 1990 the British were afraid that by staying outside the ERM they would be denied any effective influence over the discussions or outcomes of this landmark conference. Once again Britain was going along with an EC policy development not out of ideological commitment but for reasons of state.

The strong emergence of the EMU dimension caught Whitehall with its trousers down. The community had attempted to set up an economic and monetary union in the early 1970s but this had to be postponed indefinitely because of the economic divergences attributed to the sudden rise in oil prices in 1973–74. Technically Britain was committed to EMU from the day it joined the EEC in 1973: most government ministers and opposition frontbenchers conveniently forgot this fact in the 1980s. The issue did not, however, go away. For some, the creation of the European Monetary System in 1979 was a step along the road to EMU. For others, the whole notion of a single European market appeared to be of limited value unless it was supported by a single currency managed by a European Central Bank under the conditions of EMU. These possibilities were discussed at the 1985 intergovernmental conference which led to the adoption of the Single European Act. Economic union or EMU were only given isolated and oblique mentions in the SEA, mainly because of British objections. However, while in British government circles the subject was apparently 'undiscussable' because of the prime minister's implacable opposition, in other west European capitals, EMU was given extra attention and priority because of the rush towards German unification and the implications this might have for the future economic and political balance between the member states. This led to the issue of EMU dominating the Madrid, Strasbourg and Rome summits of 1989 and 1990 and drew Britain into making a commitment to join the first stage of the EMU process provided for in the Delors plan to start on 1 July 1990. By now the Treasury had to move rapidly to try to find alternative proposals which would enhance economic and monetary integration in the community.

First, it hit upon a scheme for competing currencies without any central economic or monetary policy-making institution, but this was laughed out of court by EC finance ministers meeting in Antibes in November 1989. Then a new Chancellor, John Major, put forward plans, in June 1990, for a parallel currency (or hard ECU) to be backed by a new European Monetary Fund and to compete against the individual national currencies within the EC as a thirteenth currency. Although this proposal has won some grudging acknowledgment in EC financial circles, the general view was that it had surfaced at least a year too late to have a major influence on the policy debate, and that its provenance from the British was a distinct handicap. President Mitterrand of France was quoted at the Rome summit as saying that it ill behoves the slowest country in the EC (i.e., Britain) to dictate the speed of economic and monetary union.

Of course, the real concern of the British government in the EMU debate centred on the political implications of becoming a part of such a union – the transfer of critical economic decision-making powers to a central European institution, the means of political control of this body, and the loss of national sovereignty that would follow.

The British approach to EMU was predictably negative while trying hard not to be unhelpful. The case for EMU itself was not attacked on technical grounds or on matters of substance, only its timing in the absence of greater economic convergence and its federalist overtones. Little weight seems to have been given to the possibility through EMU of subjecting the dominant position of German economic and monetary policies to EC-wide control. Despite Nicholas Ridley's protestations in the summer of 1990, the government clearly preferred German economic hegemony to continue rather than back a new quasi-federal EC economic institution in which sovereignty was pooled. Britain's commissioner, Sir Leon Brittan, tersely commented that this would preserve Britain's national sovereignty nominally intact for all of about thirty minutes – the time it would take the British financial markets to get into line with any changes in German interest rates.

The example of the official British position on EMU brings out several continuing aspects of British policy towards the EC. A deep reluctance to accept changes in the community institutions which might strengthen Brussels as against Whitehall and Westminster, however lacking in accountability the present arrangements. There has also been a marked scepticism about the effectiveness of existing EC institutions, especially the European Parliament, without any desire to reform them. The impression given by the UK government is, therefore, that it suits Britain if the EC's political institutions are weak, and that the latter provide a convenient whipping-boy when things go wrong. This is as true in regard to the high level of fraud associated with the administration of the common agricultural policy (where the main culprits are the member states, as well as the Commission) as for the failure of the EC to take a united and consistent stance on issues such as the Uruguay round trade talks or the Gulf crisis.

In effect Britain continues to demand a unity of purpose from the community without allowing it the institutional means best fitted for securing this. That is because Britain does not want to run the risk of being an outvoted minority on issues of vital national interest. In other words, European unity must only be on terms that suit the British.

This false position leads on logically to another pair of contrasting attitudes regularly struck by the British government. Britain has been hostile to most of the initiatives which have been advanced to further develop the community – the calling of the intergovernmental conferences in 1985 and 1990, the commitment to economic and monetary union and to the social charter, the demand for political union and a strengthening of the powers of the European Parliament. Yet Britain has made few proposals herself that would significantly enhance the role of the European Community, other than on a purely intergovernmental basis (e.g. enhanced foreign policy, defence, security, and police cooperation). The suggestions Britain has made have reflected a desire rather to consolidate the positions already agreed by the community and to make existing policies more effective. Britain is thus cast in the role of a 'finisher', but not a 'shaper'.

This approach has left the UK government free to tilt at the windmills of Brussels in defence of her national sovereignty. Others have argued that the willingness of Britain to share with other governments the development of its foreign, defence and security policies represents the most significant sacrifice of state sovereignty. Britain has had no qualms about pushing in such directions under the banner of 'cooperation' at an intergovernmental level.

What has infuriated the British government are encroachments by Brussels into much of the domestic arena of policy. Britain has therefore fought tooth and claw to keep the EC out of secondary education, or sponsoring concessions for pensioners, or setting the rules for health warnings on cigarette packets. These are of course issues that traditionally the British Parliament has dealt with – everyday detailed domestic issues that MPs feel at home with. That is why the interest of Brussels in such issues is resented, a resentment that is compounded when it is remembered just how much the sacrifice of 'sovereignty' has been obfuscated by ministers ever since British accession to the community. In fact, ministers are well aware of the tilting balance of power between Westminster and Brussels: it is just not cricket to spell this out to backbenchers. When ministers claim to be defending national sovereignty they are trying to wrap the Union Jack around a rather different purpose. They have been trying to protect the sovereignty of Parliament in those areas of policy in which MPs and peers have traditionally had exclusive competence.

Mrs Thatcher herself exemplified the point in 1989 when she claimed that taxation was an area of policy that should continue to remain wholly in the national domain, a comment which indicated just how little understood by top politicians has been the EC's direct involvement in the structure of indirect taxes (such as VAT and excise duties) since British accession in 1973.

Thus much of the protest, from sympathisers of the Bruges group and others, about the need to draw a line between what is properly the concern of the EC and what must always remain to be decided at Westminster, turns out to be based on some fundamental misconceptions as to where such a dividing line has already been drawn – misconceptions so great on the part of otherwise well-informed and street-wise politicians that it is not unreasonable to presume that much of this concern is in reality either posturing, or evidence of self-deception or, worse still, a mere pretence designed to reassure public opinion and the press that the distribution of power between Brussels and Westminster has not changed much and is still heavily weighted in favour of the latter.

Indeed, one plausible explanation of Mrs Thatcher's attitudes of reserve and scepticism in regard to the political development of the European Community is that her initial support for British entry into the EC in the early 1970s was based upon a static view of the EC's potential, and a belief in assurances given at that time that British accession involved no sacrifice of sovereignty. Imagine her irritation therefore, on taking office, on discovering that she had been deceived about the implications of EC membership, that, despite the erroneously portrayed 'right' of national veto, it was still possible for Britain to be outvoted in the Council of Ministers (e.g. the vote on agricultural prices for 1982–83). This irritation may have developed into intense suspicion once her agreement to the single market programme and a change in the voting rules from 1987 to speed its progress was shown to have opened a Pandora's box of demands for extending the EC's competence, in the face of which the UK appeared to have few means of escape. The rush towards economic and monetary union in response to the unification of Germany and the relative success of the single market programme must have seemed like the last straw. Mrs Thatcher blew a fuse at the Rome summit in October 1990, and unwittingly triggered the leadership contest in the Conservative party which ended in her removal from office. By then the EC issue had provoked the resignation or removal of the Prime Minister, the Chancellor of the Exchequer, the former Foreign Secretary and the Secretary of State for Trade and Industry – all within the space of eighteen months.

PARLIAMENT AND THE EC

This account of the British record on EC issues does not throw an especially favourable light upon the attitudes of senior politicians who should have known better. Nor, given Mrs Thatcher's repeated claims that Parliament would not stand for a single European currency, an independent European central bank, or any transfer of its powers to the community, does the position of the House of Commons as a whole look much better in this regard.

Under the European Communities Act of 1972, Parliament essentially delegated some of its sovereign powers to be exercised in EC institutions. The House of Commons has ever since failed to require effective accountability for EC actions. It is now recognised, even by the House of Commons' own select committee on procedure, that MPs completely misjudged the significance of the EEC Treaty and the Single European Act.[5] The House of Commons failed to adapt its scrutiny and debating procedures to accommodate adequately the wave of new legislation and administrative measures that flowed from the community – up to 800 legislative measures per annum in the 1980s, for example. EC affairs were treated as a side-show – not worthy of much time or effort, and the regular debates on EC affairs were staged late at night, attracting only a handful of MPs, usually very committed anti-EC or integrationist MPs, and earning a reputation for being rather desultory affairs in which all the old arguments about whether the UK ought to be a member of the EC seemed regularly to be rehearsed. Most MPs were, until the late 1980s, not interested in community business. They shared a disdain for or suspicion of EC institutions, even denying MEPs any special rights of entry to the precincts of Parliament until 1989. The Single European Act which was debated in 1986 was dealt with, under the guillotine procedure, in a few hours and was presented as a technical amendment to the EEC Treaty.

Protests to the contrary from the integrationist liberals and the anti-EC right and left were swept aside. MPs were content to be hoodwinked, out of apathy or ignorance; it was only in 1989 that they began to realise just how much they had missed by not having their eye on the ball, and how badly they had fallen down on their duty to the electorate.

The evidence was there, plain for all to see. MPs need only have walked a few yards down a corridor to the House of Lords to have found a wholly different approach, and a vastly better understanding of the issues at stake. In the House of Lords the Select Committee on the European Communities is the largest permanent House committee, engaging the time and interest of 80 peers working in six sub-committees. The structure was put into place in the mid-1970s in order to scrutinise in depth the more significant proposals emanating from Brussels. Given the near unanimity of peers in favour of Britain's membership of the EC, this reform was not difficult to achieve. A large part of the Lords timetable is devoted to EC business, and up to twenty reports a year are produced by the Select Committee. Their reports command attention all over Europe, especially in Brussels, Strasbourg and in Whitehall. MPs have let slip to the unelected Lords the responsibility for watching effectively over the EC, and in the process have ensured that the debate between and within the parties on the details of EC measures has usually been minimal and low-key. One exception, which surfaced at the time of the 1987 general election, was the possible extension of VAT – at Brussels' behest – to bring children's clothes, books and newspapers within its scope.

A few MPs have been frustrated by this situation, but most MPs collaborated in a mass dereliction of duty. They combined their own ignorance of EC affairs with a public disdain for other national parliaments and the European Parliament. It would seem that MPs' failure to debate many major EC proposals before they had been agreed by ministers, or their relegation of prime ministerial accounts of summit meetings to the usual parliamentary 'yah-boo' ritual, were expected to be treated as mere peccadilloes. In reality the House of Commons has shown itself to have acted wholly incompetently.

A clear example is provided in the Commons' reaction to the ruling of the European Court of Justice on Spanish fishing boats' ability to tap into the British quota for fish catches by virtue of being British-registered vessels.

In 1990, the ECJ decided, in the case of Factortame, that the British courts had the right to suspend the operation of parts of the Merchant Shipping Act 1988 (designed in part to prevent Spanish-owned vessels from taking some of the British quota) while its compatibility with EC law was examined. The British courts duly took advantage of this right, but the House of Commons was outraged. The ECJ has shown that there were circumstances in which a national law could be set aside by the higher European jurisdiction. Parliament was thus subordinate to EC rules, and the illusion of sovereignty was gravely punctured. What was so shocking about the reaction of MPs was that the supremacy of EC law over national law had been underscored and written into UK legislation by means of the European Communities Act 1972 which paved the way for UK accession to the community. Yet MPs seemed to have been ignorant of this fact and of the consequences that could follow. They had evidently been lulled by their own ignorance, and by ministerial assurances, into believing that the sovereignty of Parliament was intact. The quota-hopping case showed how wrong this impression was in reality.

Earlier in 1989 another failure of the House of Commons to do its job properly was highlighted by the Select Committee on Procedure, during its investigation of how the Commons exercised its scrutiny of EC business. At the notorious Madrid summit of EC heads of state and government in June 1989, Mrs Thatcher had been persuaded to alter the

British position in regard to the conditions which should be met before the UK would join the EMS exchange rate mechanism, and to commit the UK to joining the process of economic and monetary union at least as far as the first stage – to take effect from 1 July 1990. Senior MPs were appalled that this very critical decision in regard to the management of the economy had been taken by the UK government without any consultation of Parliament. But the deed was done and almost no protest was made publicly. The Select Committee's report does however take the British government severely to task for preventing the House of Commons from exercising its scrutiny function – but then this was by no means the first time this had happened. The Madrid incident was indeed crucial in persuading the Select Committee, and later the government itself, to initiate a wholesale reform of the Commons arrangements for dealing with EC business. Since the autumn of 1990 three new standing committees dealing with EC documents have been created, albeit with a rather small number of MPs involved.

FUTURE PROSPECTS

Despite the difficulties that have continued to mar the UK's relations with the EC and her EC partners, there have been some tangible changes in the quality of those relationships since the mid-1980s and in the British attitude, at a political level, to the changing community. The espousal by Labour of a watered-down form of integrationism, whatever the real motives behind it, has succeeded in changing radically the grounds of debate about the EC in the House of Commons. The campaign to promote awareness of the single market programme also paved the way for a much more positive assessment of the EC among the British public, and in the mass media, which the crumbling of Soviet power in central and eastern Europe has confirmed. The replacement of Mrs Thatcher by John Major as prime minister has also heralded the substitution of a new pragmatism for raw ideology in the determination of the UK government's attitudes towards the EC.

Yet events in the EC and in Europe generally are moving other European countries and governments further and faster down the road towards European integration and eventual union, just as Britain is starting to want to catch up. The gulf between Britain and her other EC partners remains therefore a wide one. There may indeed be new opportunities for Britain to play a more influential role in the shaping of the community in the wake of German unification and the predicted erosion of the Franco-German axis on which development of the EC has so far been built, but there is little evidence to suggest that a common vision of the EC's future exists which could bring the UK and Germany together to exercise joint leadership over the EC. The formidable Hans-Dietrich Genscher's vision of a 'European Germany' rather than a 'German Europe' still chimes much more easily with French objectives than the British position, even if there are some critical issues, such as the details of economic and monetary union, when the reverse appears to be the case. Moreover, a much greater change in attitude by Britain will be needed than has so far taken place if Britain is ever to join the Franco-German leadership grouping. There is no sign yet of the quantum leap in political perspective among those in or near to control of the political process in the UK which might make this achievable. Britain thus appears destined to miss a critical chance to enter the mainstream of EC development. Instead she will remain a marginalised, disoriented and disconsolate member state. There is indeed a pile of unfinished political business in regard to the UK's relations with the EC, with which British political and social institutions have yet to deal, and which are essential if Britain is to become reconciled swiftly to the EC in which she finds herself. For a start, the perception among much of the political and journalistic class that the EC is a branch of foreign policy-making, of low news value and real significance, a handy Aunt Sally to be rubbished at whim, requires radical revision. British attitudes as reflected in the wider popular culture will not change if current British prejudices about the EC and European integration are daily reinforced by political leaders and the mass media. British political culture is still not attuned to the newly emerging Europe. The debate in the UK about the future of the EC, economic and monetary union, and political union has assumed a very different tone, style and order of magnitude from all other EC countries. Public opinion is becoming more well-disposed towards the EC and European integration, and is probably ahead of the political class in its support for them. Yet the public's reservations about loss of sovereignty and national identity run deep. The British remain a nationalistic people even if they hesitate to say so, and politicians and the press continue to pander to this sentiment rather than confront it, for understandable reasons. At the same time there is little evidence to suggest that EC issues are a very high priority for most voters.

Although there have been perceptible changes in the political structure of the UK to accommodate the EC dimension, the overriding impression remains that British institutions and society remain trapped in a cultural time-warp. They are ill at ease with the European dimension. Indeed most British people would deny they have any European identity at all. Britain's experience of the two world wars was qualitatively very different from that of its continental neighbours, and the British still cling to the myth of being a first-rank world power, despite a century of relative economic decline. The British state remains an increasingly unitary state while all around are decentralising their administrations. The British polarised and confrontational style of politics and its party system do not conform to the more consensual and pluralistic systems and approaches to be found on mainland Europe.

The British remain embarrassingly ignorant of other European languages, societies and institutions: the backwardness of Britain's educational system in this respect will take at least twenty years to reverse. All this accounts for the minimal harmonisation of Britain's political culture with those of other West European states. The foundations for a successful accommodation of British society to European integration have not been laid.

Internal cultural and political pressures are likely to severely restrain any enthusiasm for European integration that mainstream British political leaders may share, despite the external pressures that indicate a radically different stance is called for.

The main government and opposition parties in Britain clearly hope that the demands to enlarge the European Community after 1992, introducing new members from western, central and eastern Europe, will lead to a widening but not a deepening of the EC. A loose confederation of EC states could then develop from the present, more tightly structured institutional arrangement. This vision is wholly unrealistic. Almost all the existing EC member states want the present EC institutions to be strengthened because they see political and economic advantages arising from this, and because they recognise that much of the effectiveness and dynamism of the EC to date has depended upon states accepting legally enforceable community obligations and a gradual pooling of sovereignty in rising numbers of policy fields as and when this seemed appropriate. The EC institutions may need reform as well as development but they have proved their worth. The existing EC member states, other than Britain, would not countenance throwing the baby out with the bathwater as part of the process of adjustment to a major new influx of members. As for the applicant countries, they are interested in joining the EC because it has shown itself to be an effective political instrument for promoting economic and political integration within Europe, and increasingly for defending EC states' interests on the world stage. Despite the reservations of some EFTA countries, the applicant states are not likely to demand, and the existing member states are most unlikely to agree to any revised institutional structure which does not permit further EC institutional and policy development along federal lines. Any other alternative will cause the community to atrophy and to lose its coherence.

The British preference for widening but not deepening the European Community is but the most recent example of the UK's desire to have its cake and eat it. The British have always wanted to take the benefits of European economic integration without incurring a political cost.

Throughout the 1970s and 1980s they pretended to themselves that they had succeeded in doing just this, despite the crucial concession of replacing the unanimity rule by weighted majority voting in EC decision-making on all single market business, a change which the UK accepted when signing the Single European Act. Traditional British approaches to economic integration and political integration of EC states remain incompatible. The benefits of economic integration cannot be achieved without a large measure of political integration. That lesson Britain learned from the EC's failure to deliver a genuine common market, when EEC decision-making processes set up in the 1950s and 1960s allowed one member state to block progress indefinitely. Now the argument has moved on, and most governments and most observers agree that economic and monetary integration is essential both to support the creation of a single market and to build upon its success. Britain supports the objective but does not will the means of achieving it. The other member states are likely to insist that Britain resolves its ambivalent attitudes and toes the general EC line.

Even if British caution does succeed in watering down the strength of the central EC institutions that will be set up as a result of the intergovernmental conferences of 1990–91, another factor is likely to push Britain along the integrationist path – the market itself. Not only will the business community and others demand more and more concerted EC action to rectify anomalies in the legal, tax, regulatory and social security systems of member states – which are important obstacles to the creation of an integrated single market after 1992 – but other social institutions not formally or immediately part of the 1992 programme have had to react to its progress and its impact.

Thus the mass media have begun to adjust their content to match the new importance of the EC and European politics, and to organise themselves in terms of resources, cross-border alliances and technology to fit in with the emerging reality of a single audio-visual market in western Europe, albeit one strongly fragmented by cultural differences. Similarly in each member state, the education system, from primary schools through to universities, polytechnics and business schools, is having to prepare its students for an integrated Europe, and to restructure its research and teaching priorities, its organisation and its institutional links accordingly. Britain is no exception in this regard. Little of this was predicted or programmed in the original 1985 Commission White Paper on completing the single market: it has happened nevertheless in response to market pressures. The lesson to be drawn from this experience is that attempts to draw a political line around areas of sovereignty loss at the political level are quite likely to prove futile. The dynamic of integrationist pressures unleashed since the signing of the Single European Act is now so strong that its logic cannot for long be denied.

If politicians refuse to facilitate the process, the market will often find a way around the political obstacle or just ignore it.

British caution in regard to the further integration of policies, societies and markets within the EC is distinctive in one further feature. A new fear has gripped the British political class in the early 1990s – the fear of being left out by other EC states. This fear was fuelled both by a largely unspoken recognition amongst opinion-formers that Britain's refusal to join the EC in its early stages of development had inflicted severe damage to Britain's interests for a whole generation, and also by pressure from industry and City lobbyists. The 'we can't afford to be left out' school of European integration exercised a dominant role in both Labour and Conservative thinking in regard to the EMU debate in 1990 and 1991. It obviously weakened the UK's negotiating position in the intergovernmental conferences and at the same time provided no principled ideological basis upon which to win popular consent for the major political changes about to be ushered in after further amendment of the Treaty of Rome to pave the way for EMU. This school may offer the only strategem for neutralising the strongly held anxieties about loss of sovereignty which can expect to surface when MPs are asked to ratify any new treaty providing for EMU that the inter-governmental conferences have agreed. The deception that underscored the ratification of the Single European Act has been recognised and MPs have signalled that they will not allow a repeat performance to occur over EMU. Once again their real worry is likely to be about the formal and implied losses of sovereignty if economic and monetary policy is dictated by decisions to be taken at the EC level.

Despite appearances, the sovereignty argument will not really be about the protection of national independence, since this has already been very heavily circumscribed by the previous EC treaties and by the rapid internationalisation of business and the financial markets. Any new treaty on EMU will present a direct challenge to the House of Commons to publicly accept this loss of autonomy to date, as well as the prospect of further loss in the future. It is the power of the House of Commons to control future economic decisions, crucial to the UK's interests and to the political prospects of the political parties, that is on the line. Hitherto many MPs have turned a blind eye to the erosion of Britain's political independence arising from the interdependence of trading nations and membership of the EC and NATO. Indeed the emergence of summitry engaging senior ministers has provided superficial grounds for thinking that MPs still retain some control over major economic, foreign and defence policy positions, even if only vestigially and at one remove. The new EMU treaty and the political union treaty are likely to be bitter pills for British parliamentarians to swallow, for they will mark an end to their illusions about sovereignty and may well provoke a radical review of the whole UK government structure.

It is curious that the sacrifice or pooling of so much sovereignty since the 1950s – in the areas of defence, trade and foreign policy – should have given rise to so little adverse comment. Settling the details of economic policies is evidently viewed as part of the MPs' core curriculum which ought not to be interfered with or hived off. Such a response is not simply professional protectionism on the part of MPs who want to keep hold of some interesting work. It also reflects a concern that national governments are judged by electors firstly on their record of economic policy management and that they are thus genuinely accountable to the voters on this point, if on little else. If the key economic decisions are removed to Brussels, what influence will MPs have and how credible an institution will Westminster be in the eyes of the voter? The parliamentary agenda may still be a long one after EMU, but clearly many MPs are worried that its subject matter will lack significance, the most important decisions having been taken elsewhere.

Another element in the lack of enthusiasm in the House of Commons for EMU, and the moves towards a federal Europe that it implies, is the shared perception among MPs, and many politically-interested outsiders, that the Westminster system of government is a quintessential part of Britain's national identity. Any sacrifice of the powers of the Westminster parliament to Brussels is thus represented as an attack on Britain's national identity. The symbolism of Big Ben, and the parliamentary tradition is undoubtedly an important part of British political culture and gives meaning to the British identity. But little of this would in fact be altered by further integration, and other parts of the British political tradition (the high value it places on tolerance and fair play, not to mention the monarchy) would remain intact. MPs exaggerate the importance of the legislature when the executive branch of government is able to bypass the Commons, withhold information from MPs and discipline them if they rebel. Legislatures in democracies all around the world are in decline, and lines of accountability have already become more tenuous as responsibility for government decisions has become blurred by international pressures. Westminster is no exception, despite its long hours of work.

The UK government's reaction to the discussions on political union between the member states has been characteristically downbeat and unenthusiastic, while other states have called for a strengthening of the Council of Ministers and the European Parliament, in the wake of EMU, or called for the development of EC citizenship rights, Britain has proposed an extension of the powers of the EC Court of Justice to impose fines on member states which do not implement EC laws, and an amendment to the powers of the European Parliament to enable it to scrutinise EC spending more effectively. It is a manifesto designed to stir up apathy and not to frighten the horses. It is already clear that a proposal much more ambitious than the British suggestions will be adopted by the other EC member states, and the UK is likely to have to accept it.

In one area of the discussions on economic and political union, a striking example of Britain's capacity to apply double standards has already been revealed. One of the main British objections to EMU is the loss of accountability of the executive to parliamentarians for their stewardship of economic policy. The UK is not however prepared to compensate for this loss by strengthening the powers of the European Parliament to achieve such accountability at an EC level. Indeed the whole argument raised by the British government supposes that Westminster currently enjoys extensive powers of scrutiny over monetary and economic policy and the actions of the central bank, when in fact it does not. The UK is thus demanding higher standards of accountability at the EC level than it is prepared to adopt in its own parliamentary system.

In other moves, however, taken outside the framework of the intergovernmental conferences on economic and political union, the UK is pressing ahead with practical proposals to increase police, customs, immigration service and judicial cooperation. These often involve legal and administrative changes which also demand a sharing or pooling of sovereignty, the exercise of which is the prerogative of the state, and largely outside parliamentary control. Intergovernmentalism of this kind – which operates behind closed doors, outside but in parallel with developments within the EC institutions, is apparently to be commended.

The intergovernmental road leads not to integration but to cooperation between executives with common concerns, whether these be foreign and security policy interests or dealing with international crime. Democratic process and accountability do not feature on this agenda, and so the sovereignty of parliament is not protected by intergovernmentalism, only the sovereignty of the state apparatus which handles most such issues away from public scrutiny. Intergovernmentalism, as a substitute for deciding political issues through supranational EC institutions, simply obscures further the line of policy and the responsibility for actions adopted by national governments. It is the most anti-democratic formula on offer for harmonising European policy-making. Yet it is the preferred option of the UK government which is at the same time protesting at the inadequate forms of democratic control provided within the EC's institutions and refusing to support suggestions from other states which could rectify this.

The angst of MPs about the loss of Westminster sovereignty is but a symptom of their longstanding inconsistencies in regard to the development of the community and Britain's role within it. Still ignorant about the EC, still flushed with national pride despite the evidence of Britain's many failures since 1945, still convinced that British political traditions and institutions are superior to all others, the British political elite – with few exceptions – has yet to come to terms with the fact that the UK is a second-class European power, and standing eleventh in the European economic league table, if income per head is taken as the yardstick.

Clearly there must be real doubt about whether the House of Commons will ratify any treaties on EMU or political union that any foreseeable government will present to MPs. Two factors may help to achieve a favourable result, provided that the more integrationist EC member states take on board some of Britain's worries. The first factor which may help is if the decision to be taken can be presented as one which MPs are free to take or not to take, rather than just a 'fait accompli'. Parliamentary sovereignty will thus be seen to be paramount – for a day, and no 'imposed' solution will be forced on MPs. Secondly, there is the impact of the 'we can't afford to be left out' syndrome which is already common political currency and which has already been discussed.

In fact, the UK will have little choice but to accept what the intergovernmental conferences agree and British negotiators will clearly have used all their negotiating skills to mitigate the scope of the new draft treaties.

The impact of what is agreed will be considerably greater than it seems on paper, just as happened with the Treaty of Rome, the Single European Act and the 1992 single market programme. The tide of European integration is too strong for the UK to resist. British society and its people will have to adjust to its speed and direction, even if most will do so reluctantly, without conviction and late in the day.

NOTES

1. For a full discussion of the UK's approach to European integration after World War II see M. Camps, *Britain and the European Community 1955–63* (Oxford: Oxford University Press, 1964) and U. Kitzinger, *The Politics and Economics of European Integration* (New York: Praeger, 1963).
2. *The Sun*, 1 November 1990.
3. See the discussion by A. Butt Philip and C. Baron in the UK national reports included in H. Siedentopf and J. Ziller (eds), *Making European Policies Work* (London: Sage, 1988), pp. 639–713.
4. See the comments by the former secretary-general of the Commission, Emile Noel, in an interview with *The Financial Times*, 19 October 1987.
5. House of Commons Select Committee on Procedure, The Secretary of European Legislation, Session 1988–89, HC Paper no. 622, vol. 1, pp. xviii-xxi.

Bibliography

L. Albertin, 'Frankreichs Regionalisierung – Abschied vom Zentralismus?', *Frankreich-Jahrbuch 1988* (Opladen, 1988), pp. 135–56.

R. Aron, *Mémoires* (Paris: Julliard, 1983).

R. Aron, *Plaidoyer pour l'Europe décadente* (Paris: Laffont, 1976).

M. Aymard, 'Les Minorités' in F. Braudel *et al.*, *L'Europe* (Paris: Arts et Métiers Graphiques, 1982).

J. -L. Barsoux and P. Lawrence, *Management in France* (London: Cassell, 1990).

R. A. Becker, 'International Competition, Income Distribution and Economic Growth', *Cambridge Journal of Economics*, no. 3 (1989): 395–412.

S. Berger,'Lame Ducks and National Champions: industrial policy in the Fifth Republic', in W. G. Andrews and S. Hoffmann (eds), *The Fifth Republic at Twenty* (New York: State University of New York Press, 1981).

D. Berg-Schlosser and J. Schissler, *Politische Kultur in Deutschland*, *Politische Vierteljahresschrift*, no. 18 (1987; special issue).

C. Bluth, *New Thinking in Soviet Military Policy* (London: Pinter, 1990).

C. Bluth, 'SDI: the Challenge to West Germany', *International Affairs*, vol. 62 (Spring 1986) 2: 247–64.

F. Braudel *et al.*, *L'Europe* (Paris: Arts et Métiers Graphiques, 1982).

A. Browning, *L'Europe et les intellectuels* (Paris: Gallimard, 1984).

W. H. Buiter and M. H. Miller, 'Changing the Rules: economic consequences of the Thatcher regime', *Brookings Papers on Economic Activity* (1983).

S. Bulmer and W. E. Paterson, *The Federal Republic and the European Community* (London: Allen & Unwin, 1987).

Bundeszentrale für politische Bildung, *Bundesrepublik Deutschland, Geschichte, Bewusstsein* (Bonn: Bundeszentrale für politische Bildung, 1988).

M. Camps, *Britain and the European Community 1955–63* (Oxford: Oxford University Press, 1964).

H. Carrère d'Encausse, *L'Empire éclaté* (Paris: Flammarion, 1978).

H. Carrère d'Encausse, *La Gloire des nations ou la fin de l'Empire soviétique*, (Paris: Fayard, 1990).

A. Cawson *et al.*, *Hostile Brothers; competition and closure in the European Electronics Industry* (Oxford: Clarendon Press, 1990).

P. Cecchini, *The European Challenge, 1992: the benefits of a single market (Hounslow: Wildwood House, 1988).*

P. G. Cerny, 'From *Dirigisme* to Deregulation? The case of financial markets', in P. Godt (ed.), *Policy-Making in France* (London: Pinter, 1989).

I. Clark and N. J. Wheeler, *The British Origins of Nuclear Strategy 1945–1955*, (Oxford: Oxford University Press, 1989).

I. Commichau, W. Cremer and G. Dallinger (eds), *Westeuropa und die USA* (Bonn: Bundeszentrale für politische Bildung, 1988).

P. Conradt, 'Changing German Political Culture', in G. Almond and E. Verba (eds), *The Civic Culture Revisited* (Boston: Little Brown & Co., 1980).

R. Dahrendorf, *Society and Democracy in Germany* (London: Weidenfeld and Nicolson, 1967).

D. David, 'La France, l'Europe et les enjeux stratégiques des années 90', paper presented to annual meeting of Association for the Study of Modern and Contemporary France, Wolverhampton, 1990.

D. David, *La Politique de Défense de la France: Textes et Documents* (Paris: FEDN, 1989).

R. Debray, *A demain de Gaulle* (Paris: Gallimard, 1990).

J. Delors and Clisthène, *La France par l'Europe* (Paris: Grasset, 1988).

J. -F. Deniau, *L'Europe interdite* (Paris: Seuil, 1977).

C. Deubner, 'Change and Internationalisation in Industry: toward a sectoral interpretation of German politics', *International Organisation*, vol. 38, (1984) 3: 501–35.

S. Dowrick and D. Thoniguyen, 'OECD Comparative Growth 1950–85: catch up and convergence, *The American Economic Review*, 1988.

A. Dunnet, 'The Role of the Exchange Rate in the Decline of UK Manufacturing', *Royal Bank of Scotland Review*, March 1989.

D. Easton, 'A Reassessment of Political Support', *British Journal for Political Science*, 1975.

L. J. Edinger, *Germany*, 2nd edn (Boston: Little Brown & Co., 1986) .

H.-G. Ehrhart, *Die 'deutsche Frage' aus französischer Sicht 1981–87*, (Munich: Tuduv, 1988).

European Commission (ed.), *Eurobarometer* (annually).

W. Feld, *West Germany and the European Community* (New York: Praeger, 1981).

J. Fenske, 'France and the Strategic Defence Inititiative: speeding up or putting on the brakes?', *International Affairs*, vol. 62 (1986) 2: 231–46.

F. Fillon, *Sécurité européenne et défense nationale* (Paris: RPR, 1990).

P. Fontaine, 'Jean Monnet, l'inspirateur', preface to J. Delors, *La France par l'Europe, op. cit.*.

G. Fuchs, 'Quel système de Sécurité et de Défense pour l'Europe de l'Ouest?', PS working paper.

J. Gaffney and E. Kolinsky (eds), *Political Culture in France and Germany*, (London: Routledge, 1990).

I. Gambles, 'Prospects for West European Security Cooperation', *Adelphi Papers*, no. 244 (London: IISS, 1989), pp. 28–33.

P. Godt (ed.), *Policy Making in France* (London: Pinter, 1989).

M. and S. Greiffenhagen, *Ein schwieriges Vaterland: zur politischen Kultur Deutschlands* (Munich: List, 1979).

D. Grimm *et al.*, 'EC 1992: Strategien, Hindernisse, Erfolgsaussichten', *Kiel Discussion Papers*, 151 (Kiel: Institut für Weltwirtschaft, 1989).

A. J. R. Groom, *British Thinking About Nuclear Weapons* (London:

Pinter, 1974).

A. Grosser, *Les Occidentaux* (Paris: Fayard, 1978).

D. Haack *et al.* (eds), *Das Wiedervereinigungsbot des Grundgesetzes*, (Cologne: Wissenschaft und Politik, 1989).

H. Haftendorf, 'Transatlantische Dissonanzen. Der Bericht über "Selektive Abschreckung" und die Strategiediskussion in den USA', *Europa-Archiv*, no. 8, pp. 213–22.

P. Hall, *Governing the Economy: the politics of state intervention in Britain and France* (Cambridge: Polity Press, 1986).

W. F. Hanreider, *Germany, America and Europe* (New Haven: Yale University Press, 1989).

J. Hayward, *The State and the Market Economy: industrial patriotism and economic intervention in France* (Brighton: Wheatsheaf Books, 1986).

D. Healey 'NATO, Britain and Soviet Military Policy', *Orbis*, vol. 13 (1969) 1: 48–58 .

D. Healey, *The Time of my Life* (London: Michael Joseph, 1989).

P. Herzog and Y. Dimicoli, *Europe 92: construire autrement et autre chose*, (Paris: Messidor/Editions Sociales, 1989).

W. N. Hitchens and J. E. Birnie, 'Productivity Levels in Northern Ireland Manufacturung Industry: a Comparison with Great Britain', *Regional Studies*, no. 23 (1989).

S. Hoffmann, 'France and Europe: the dichotomy of autonomy and cooperation', in J. Howorth and G. Ross (eds), *Contemporary France: a review of interdisciplinary studies*, vol. I (London: Pinter, 1987).

G. Hofstede, 'The cultural perspective' in A. Brakel (ed.), *People and Organisations Interacting* (New York: John Wiley, 1985).

Horizon 1993: *La France dans la perspective du grand marché, Economie et Statistique*, no. 217–18 (Paris: Institut National de la Statistique et des Etudes Economiques, January-February 1989).

A. Horne, *Macmillan* 1957–1986 (London: Macmillan, 1989).

J. Howorth, *Defence and Dissent in Contemporary France* (London: Croom Helm, 1984).

J. Howorth, *France: the Politics of Peace* (London: Merlin, 1984).

J. Howorth, 'France since the Berlin Wall: diplomacy and defence', *The World Today*, July 1990, pp. 126–31.

S. Hübner-Funk, 'Nationale Identität', in Deutsches Jugendinstitut (ed.), *Immer diese Jugend* (Munich: Kösel, 1985).

J. Huntzinger, *Europes* (Paris: Ramsay, 1977).

K. Kaiser and P. Lellouche (eds), *Le Couple franco-allemand et la défense de l'Europe* (Paris: IFRI, 1986).

N. Kaldor, *The Economic Consequences of Mrs Thatcher* (London: Duckworth, 1983).

K. -H. Kamp, 'Die Modernisierung der nuklearen Kurzstreckenwaffen in Europa', *Europa-Archiv*, vol. 83 (1988) 10: 269–76.

P. J. Katzenstein (ed.) *Industry and Politics in West Germany* (Ithaca and London: Cornell University Press, 1989).

U. Kitzinger, *The Politics and Economics of European Integration* (New York: Praeger, 1963).
H. Kohl, *L'Europe est notre destin* (Paris: Editions de Fallois, 1990).
W. L. Kohl and G. Basevi (eds), *West Germany: a European and Global Power* (Lexington and Toronto: Lexington Books, 1980).
E. Kolinsky, 'Generations and Gender', in G. Smith, W. E. Paterson and P. Merkl (eds), *Developments in West German Politics* (London: Macmillan, 1989).
E. Kolinsky, 'Voting for Europe?', in J. Lodge (ed.), *The 1989 European Elections* (Brighton: Wheatsheaf, 1990).
K. -R. Korte, 'Deutschlandbilder – Akzentverlagerungen der deutschen Frage seit den siebzigen Jahren', *Aus Politik und Zeitgeschichte*, 1988.
M. Kreile, 'West Germany: the dynamics of expansion' in P. J. Katzenstein (ed.) *Between Power and Plenty* (Madison: The University of Wisconsin Press, 1978), pp. 191–224.
F. von Krosigk, 'Französische Außenpolitik im Spannungsfeld von Mondialismus und Europäischer Integration', in *Aus Politik und Zeitgeschichte*, Beilage Parlament, 39 (1989), pp. 35–45.
J. Lacouture, *De Gaulle*, vol. III, *Le Souverain* (Paris: Seuil, 1986).
La France et l'Europe, *Cahiers français*, no. 244 (Paris: Documentation française, 1990).
T. Läufer, *Europäischer Gemeinschaft, Europäisches Parlament, Europe Wahl* (Bonn: Bundeszentrale für politische Bildung, 1989).
A. -M. Le Gloannec, *La Nation orpheline* (Paris: Calmann-Lévy, 1989).
Lettre de l'OFCE (Paris) no. 56 (1988).
J. Lodge (ed.), *The European Community and the Challenge of the Future*, (London: Pinter, 1989).
P. M. Lützeler, *Western Europe in Transition: West Germany's Role in the European Community* (Baden-Baden: Nomos Verlagsgesellschaft, 1986).
H. Machin and V. Wright (eds), *Economic Policy and Policy-Making under the Mitterrand Presidency 1981–84* (London: Pinter, 1985).
T. Mann, 'Über deutsche Schuld. Botschaft zum 8. Mai 1945', *Bayrische Landeszeitung*, 18 May 1945.
K. Matthews and P. Minford, 'Mrs Thatcher's Economic Policies, 1979–1987', *Economic Policy*, October 1987.
H. Ménudier (ed.), *La République Fédérale d'Allemagne dans les relations internationales* (Brussels: Editions Complexe, 1990).
A. and J. Merritt, *Public Opinion in Semi-Sovereign Germany* (Urbana: University of Illinois Press, 1980).
A. Minc, *La Grande Illusion* (Paris: Grasset, 1989).
F. Mitterrand, *Réflexions sur la politique extérieure de la France*, (Paris: Fayard, 1986).
J. Monnet, *Mémoires* (Paris: Fayard, 1976).
E. Morin, *Penser l'Europe* (Paris: UGE, 1987).
H. G. Mosley 'The Social Dimension of European Unity: national standards of social protection in a common market', paper presented at the

1989 Annual Meeting of the American Political Science Association, Mimeo.

K. J. Müller, 'Les deux tentations de la politique extérieure allemande de Bismarck à nos jours', *Revue de l'IHTP*, Autumn 1990.

M. S. Navias, *The Sandys White Paper of 1957 and the Move to the British New Look: an analysis of nuclear weapons, conventional forces and strategic planning 1955–57*, unpublished PhD Thesis, London, King's College, 1989.

A. Pierre, *Nuclear Politics* (Oxford: Oxford University Press, 1972).

K. O. Pöhl, 'The Path to European Monetary Union', *IFO-Digest*, no. 12 (1989): 1–5.

R. Poidevin (ed.), *Histoire des débuts de la construction européenne 1948-1950* (Brussels: Bruylant, 1986).

L. Poirier, *Des Stratégies nucléaires* (Paris: Hachette, 1977).

L. Poirier, *Essais de stratégie théorique* (Paris: FEDN, 1983).

J. -L. Quermonne, 'Existe-t-il un modèle politique européen?, *Revue française de science politique*, no. 40 (1990): 192–210.

K. -H. Reif, 'Einstellung zur Europäischen Einigung in den Mitgliedstaaten der Europäischen Gemeinschaft', in J. Commichau *et al.* (eds), *op. cit.*.

R. Riemenschneider, *Dezentralisation und Regionalismus in Frankreich um die Mitte des 19. Jahrhunderts* (Bonn: Rörsheid, 1985).

R. Riemenschneider, 'Forschungsprojekt: vom Planungsraum zur Gebietkörperschaft. Regionenbildung als Element einer sich wandelnden politischen Kultur in Frankreich' in E. Hinrichs (ed.), *Regionalität. Der 'kleine Raum' als Problem der internationalen Schulbuchforschung* (Frankfurt am Main: Diesterweg, 1990), pp. 69–73.

W. Röhrich, *Die verspätete Demokratie. Zur politischen Kultur der Bundesrepublik Deutschland* (Cologne: Diedrichs).

F. Saint-Ouen, *Les partis politiques et L'Europe. Une approche comparative*, (Paris: PUF, 1990).

F. Scharpf, 'The Joint Decision Trap: Lessons From German Federalism and European Integration', *Public Administration* 66 (1988 Autumn): 239–78.

D. N. Schwartz, *NATO's Nuclear Dilemmas* (Washington: Brookings Institution, 1983).

G. L. Schweigler, *National Consciousness in Divided Germany* (London: Sage, 1975).

G. L. Schweigler, *Grundlagen der außenpolitischen Orientierungen der Bundesrepublik Deutschland* (Baden-Baden: Nomos, 1985).

G. L. Schweigler, 'Normalität in Deutschland', *Europa-Archiv*, no. 44 (1989).

M. Sharp and P. Holmes (eds), *Strategies for New Technology: case studies from Britain and France* (New York: Phillip Allan, 1990).

M. Sharp and C. Shearman, *European Technological Collaboration* (London: Routledge & Kegan Paul, 1987).

R. J. Shepherd, *Public Opinion and European Integration* (Westmead: Saxon House, 1975).

H. Siedentopf and J. Ziller (eds), *Making European Policies Work* (London: Sage, 1988).

G. Smith, *Politics in Western Europe*, 4th edn (Aldershot: Gower, 1988).

F. Steinkhler (ed.), *Europa '92* (Hamburg: VSA Verlag, 1989).

C. Stoffaës, 'Industrial Policy and the State; from industry to enterprise' in P. Godt (ed.), *op. cit.*.

Tableaux de l'économie française 1989: la France et l'Europe dans le monde (Paris: Institut National de la Statistique et des Etudes Economiques, 1989).

T. Taylor, 'Britain's response to the Strategic Defence Initiative', *International Affairs*, vol. 62 (1986) 2: 217–30.

R. von Thadden, *Restauration und napoleonisches Erbe. Der Verwaltungszentralismus als politisches Problem in Frankreich 1814-1830* (Wiesbaden: Steiner, 1972).

E. Todd, La Nouvelle France (Paris: Seuil, 1988).

Trends im Vorfeld der Europawahl, Konrad Adenauer Foundation Interne Studien 12, Sankt Augustin, 1989.

R. H. Ullman, 'The Covert French Connection', *Foreign Policy*, no. 75, (Summer 1989).

G. Valance, *France, Allemagne, le retour de Bismarck* (Paris: Flammarion, 1990).

A. A. Walters, *Britain's Economic Renaissance – Margaret Thatcher's Reform 1979–1984* (Oxford: Oxford University Press, 1985).

H. -U. Wehler, *Das deutsche Kaiserreich 1871–1918* (Göttingen: Vandenhoeck & Rupprecht, 1973).

W. Weidenfeld and W. Wessels (eds), *Jahrbuch der Europäischen Integration* (Bonn: Europa Union).

W. Weidenfeld (ed.), *Nachdenken über Deutschland; Materialien zur politischen Kultur der deutschen Frage* (Cologne: Wissenschaft und Politik, 1985).

W. Weidenfeld (ed.), *Die Identität der Deutschen* (Munich: Hanser, 1983).

W. Weidenfeld and H. Zimmermann (eds), *Deutsche Handbuch. Eine doppelte Bilanz 1949–1989* (Munich: Hanser, 1989).

K. Weigelt (ed.), *Heimat und Nation zur Geschichte und Identität der Deutschen* (Mainz: Hase & Köhler, 1984).

E. Weisenfeld, *Quelle Allemagne pour la France?* (Paris: Armand Colin, 1989).

E. Weisenfeld, *Welches Deutschland soll es sein? Frankreich und die deutsche Einheit seit 1945* (Munich: Beck, 1986).

E. Weisenfeld, *Geschichte Frankreichs seit dem Krieg*, 2nd edn (Munich: Beck 1982).

Western European Union, *The Reactivation of WEU: Statements and Communiques 1984 to 1987* (London: WEU, 1988).

H. Wittmann (ed.), 'Nationale Identitäten und europäisches Bewußtsein, Deutsch-französisches Historikerkolloquium 1988 in Paris', *Dokumente* (1989) 45: 93–132.

Index